T0393829

INDIA AND MYANMAR BORDERLANDS

This book explores the India–Myanmar relationship in terms of ethnicity, security and connectivity. With the process of democratic transition in Myanmar since 2011 and the ongoing Rohingya crisis, issues related to cross-border insurgency are one of the most important factors that determine bilateral ties between the two neighboring countries. The volume discusses a diverse range of themes – historical dimensions of cooperation; contested territories, resistance and violence in India–Myanmar borderlands; ethnic linkages; political economy of India–Myanmar cooperation; and Act East Policy – to examine the prospects and challenges of the strategic partnership between India and Myanmar, and analyzes further possibilities to move forward. The chapters further look at cross-border informal commercial exchanges, public health, population movements, and problems of connectivity and infrastructure projects.

Comprehensive, topical and with its rich empirical data, the volume will be useful to scholars and researchers of political studies, international relations, security studies, foreign policy, contemporary history, and South Asian studies as well as government bodies and think tanks.

Pahi Saikia is Associate Professor of Political Science at the Indian Institute of Technology Guwahati, Assam, India. She is the author of *Ethnic Mobilisation and Violence in Northeast India* (2011). Her areas of specialization are international relations; foreign policy between India and neighboring countries; ethnic identity politics, tribes and indigenous people in Northeast India; governance and political development in developing areas; security issues in borderlands Asia; social movements; and conflict prevention. She has published articles in books and in peer-reviewed journals such as *India Review* on security concerns and risks of conflict in the South Asian sub-region, subnationalist insurgency, ethnofederalism and marginalized tribal ethnic minorities in India's northeast.

Anasua Basu Ray Chaudhury is Senior Fellow with the Observer Research Foundation's Neighbourhood Initiative, Kolkata chapter, India. She specializes in South Asia, forced migration and women in conflict zones. Among her published work are the books *Connecting Nations: India and Southeast Asia* (co-edited, 2019); *State of Being Stateless* (co-edited, 2015); *Women in Indian Borderlands* (co-edited, 2011) and *SAARC at Crossroads: The Fate of Regional Cooperation in South Asia* (2006). She is a regular contributor to peer-reviewed journals, newspapers and magazines on energy crisis and subregional cooperation in South Asia, religious violence, connectivity and refugee issues in South Asia.

INDIA AND MYANMAR BORDERLANDS

Ethnicity, Security and Connectivity

Edited by Pahi Saikia and Anasua Basu Ray Chaudhury

Routledge
Taylor & Francis Group

LONDON AND NEW YORK

First published 2020
by Routledge
2 Park Square, Milton Park, Abingdon, Oxon OX14 4RN

and by Routledge
52 Vanderbilt Avenue, New York, NY 10017

Routledge is an imprint of the Taylor & Francis Group, an informa business

British Library Cataloguing-in-Publication Data
A catalogue record for this book is available from the British Library

Library of Congress Cataloging-in-Publication Data
A catalog record for this book has been requested

ISBN: 978-1-138-32846-4 (hbk)
ISBN: 978-0-367-36483-0 (pbk)
ISBN: 978-0-429-34636-1 (ebk)

Typeset in Bembo
by Apex CoVantage, LLC

CONTENTS

ILLUSTRATIONS

Figures

Tables

CONTRIBUTORS

Sreeparna Banerjee is a research assistant at the Observer Research Foundation (ORF), Kolkata chapter, India. Her interest areas are gender studies and identity politics.

Apurba K. Baruah is former Professor of Political Science and former National Fellow Indian Council of Social Science Research (ICSSR), New Delhi, India. He is currently the Academic Adviser and Managing Trustee, Assam School of Journalism, and the Academic Adviser, Assam School of Mass Communication and Media Research. He has published a number of books and articles on ethnic identities and democracy, student movements and elections.

Pratnashree Basu is Associate Fellow with ORF's Neighbourhood Regional Studies Initiative and Maritime Initiative, Kolkata chapter, India. Her recent publications include a Special Report titled *India's Maritime Connectivity: Importance of the Bay of Bengal* (2018, co-authored) and a Special Report titled *India's connectivity with its Himalayan Neighbours: Possibilities and Challenges* (2017, co-authored).

Rakhee Bhattacharya is Associate Professor in the Centre for the Study of North East India, School of Social Sciences, Jawaharlal Nehru University, New Delhi, India. Her current areas of interest include political economy, development economics, regional economy, transnational economy and geo-economics, poverty and inequality, geopolitics, India's Northeast and its neighborhood. She is the author of *Northeastern India and its Neighbours: Negotiating Security and Development* (2014) and *Development Disparities in Northeast India* (2011).

Rajeev Bhattacharyya is a senior journalist and author based in Guwahati, Assam, India. He has worked for *The Times of India, The Telegraph, The Indian Express, Times Now, Bengal Post* and was the Managing Editor of *Seven Sisters Post*. He has authored two books – *Rendezvous with Rebels: Journey to Meet India's Most Wanted Men* (2014) and *Lens and the Guerrilla: Insurgency in India's Northeast* (2013).

Mihir Bhonsale is Junior Fellow with ORF's Neighbourhood and Regional Studies Initiative, Kolkata chapter, India. He is the coordinator of ORF's South Asia Weekly monitor and a regular contributor on Bhutan and Myanmar for the Weekly, Kolkata chapter, India. His research areas include India's Look East/Act East Policy, Sino-Indian border, ethnicity, tourism and culture.

Alana Golmei is Director of Burma Centre Delhi, India, which was founded in 2008 to work for restoration of peace, justice, democracy and human rights in Burma and to strengthen relationships between the people of India and Burma. Golmei is also a social activist and the General Secretary of Northeast Support Centre & Helpline based in New Delhi which was launched in 2007 with the aim to prevent harassment, discrimination, molestation and abuses meted out to people from Northeast India living in Delhi and NCR, particularly women.

Nehginpao Kipgen is Associate Professor, Assistant Dean (International Collaboration) and Executive Director of the Center for Southeast Asian Studies, Jindal School of International Affairs, O.P. Jindal Global University, India. He is the author of *Myanmar: A Political History* (2016) and *Democracy Movement in Myanmar: Problems and Challenges* (2015). With specialization in comparative politics and international relations, he has published several peer-reviewed academic articles and over 190 articles in various leading international newspapers and magazines in Asia, Africa, Australia, Europe and North America.

Ngamjahao Kipgen is Assistant Professor of Sociology at the Indian Institute of Technology Guwahati, Assam, India. His major research interests are environmental sociology, political sociology, religion and cultural politics. He has published several book chapters and articles in journals such as *Asian Ethnicity and SAGE Research Methods Cases*.

Ingudam Yaipharemba Singh is a guest faculty in the Department of National Security Studies, Manipur University. Yaipha completed his doctoral research from the Department of Defence and National Security Studies, Panjab University, India. His research interests include international relations, conflict resolutions and border crisis.

K. Yhome is Senior Fellow at Observer Research Foundation (ORF), New Delhi, India. His research interests include India's regional diplomacy, regionalism in South and Southeast Asia and subregionalism in the Bay of Bengal and the Himalayas. Before joining ORF, Yhome worked with the *Indian Foreign Affairs Journal*. He is the author of *Myanmar: Can the Generals Resist Change?* (2008) and has coauthored *Looking Beyond the Conflict: Changing Dynamics of India-Sri Lanka Ties* (2013) and coedited *Emerging Trans-Regional Corridors: South and Southeast Asia* (2017).

FOREWORD

In ancient times, Aristotle had defined the state as the highest form of human community aiming at the highest good; but a modern definition of state, such as by James Wilford Garner, would necessarily refer to territory as an essential component of state. If the state has to have a territory it must be marked by a border to distinguish one state from another. This is simple common knowledge today. Yet the implication of this idea of a border when transformed into a palpable reality through force, diplomacy or law is quite complex.

Border is a line that divides one country from another or a line that separates two countries, so defines OED or CED. When border is marked by sea or barren land it constitutes less of a human problem than when it runs through human habitat. In the latter case it is supposed to divide two distinct communities with distinct identities but more often than not it does not do so. It divides human groups or communities having much commonality. The border idea was perhaps pushed to its extremes in the case of division between India and East Pakistan where it often ran through the same village or even the same family home. But even in less extreme cases there are likely to be people on both sides of a border sharing common rituals, languages, family relations, similar culinary practices and eating habits, trading practices etc. which are not quite like the mainstream practices in either country. Thus, border people would likely have only thin commonalities with the mainstream population. In this sense, a border truly means 'margin.' The mainstream identity tends to evanesce as it moves toward the margin on both sides of the border leaving the border peoples to 'enjoy' a semi-autonomous identity of their own across the border. Border, then, becomes a space where the 'self' merges with the 'other.'

While this view of the border is more sensitive to the felt needs of the marginal populations (or in cases such as the Indo–Myanmar borders, *ethnies* residing in borderlands), this militates against the norm of the nation-state with its politico-legal identity. One of the most prime features of the model nation-state, as it developed in western Europe, is that 'it controlled a well-defined continuous territory' which was also 'relatively centralized.' And it wants to achieve this through 'blending coercion, co-optation, and legitimation as means of guaranteeing the acquiescence of different segments of the population.'[1]

Thus, it is possible to conceptualize border in multiple ways. If the first view advances the concept of border as a mental construct, the second view wants to make the border concrete and palpable representing the limits of a state's politico-legal jurisdiction. If one view can be called liberal/constructivist, the other view conforms to political realism. If one view tends to promote closer people-to-people connectivity, substantial border trade and a relaxed approach to the border, the other view emphasizes neat demarcation of the border, intensive border security and omnipresence of the arm of the state. The beauty of this volume is that it delineates and elaborates through different chapters these different conceptualizations of border in the context of the concrete case of Indo–Myanmar border at the junction of South and Southeast Asia.

The relaxed view of the border that I have just mentioned could be a product of globalization which prophesied much closer than hitherto existing economic, commercial and people-to-people interaction across international borders as the process of globalization would proceed on the wheels of fast changing technology and World Wide Web. As Gillette's chairman was credited to have said, he finds no country foreign (as his product had supposedly conquered the world).[2] Books like George Ritzer's *The McDonaldization of Society* (1993) or Benjamin Barber's *Jihad vs Mcworld* (1995), while drawing attention to the process of melting sovereign boundaries of states under globalization regime, also highlighted the dangers implicit in it. While Ritzer talked about the impending sameness that could engulf societies across the globe, Barber posited that the struggle to retain ethnic identity (*jihad*) could be at loggerheads with the forces of globalizing sameness. Such assessments have largely been proved right as we find state's backlash has come in the form of a more rigid stance on border maintenance and securitization. The editors rightly point out in the Introduction, territoriality became more noticeable post-September 11 in the form of creation of 'biometric borders, regulation on immigration, tariffs and quotas.' The creation of the Department of Homeland Security by the US government was symbolic in this sense. The state's approach to border maintenance hardened in the face of unchecked immigration, human trafficking and above all, the threat of terrorism.

In the Introduction, the editors have discussed numerous instances across the globe where states have sealed their borders, erected fencing, constructed walls and enhanced border vigilance, and they have pointed out how the circumstance for doing these has proved to be fertile ground for the emergence of hard states and authoritarian rulers. As borders have been securitized, surveillance states have emerged.

South and Southeast Asia is going through this process as much as the US and even Europe. Ultra-nationalism has emerged as globalization's unwanted child. How, under these very adverse circumstances, people living in the borderlands where

India and Myanmar meet are trying to negotiate their existential needs, retain their traditional rights, make use of contemporary technology and preserve their moral universe is the subject matter of the different chapters in this edited volume.

The volume, in fact, goes even beyond that. The contributors examine the multifaceted nature of the Indo–Myanmar borderlands not only in the light of alternative conceptual constructs; in its different chapters they examine the complex interplay of the forces of domestic and international politics as represented by India, Myanmar and China and highlight the prospects of closer Indo–Myanmar relations. This, I suppose, makes the subtitle of the book, 'ethnicity, security and connectivity' very apt indeed. I believe the volume will be a major contribution to a better understanding of the nature and possibilities of Indo–Myanmar borderlands.

Rakhahari Chatterji
Advisor, Observer Research Foundation (ORF), Kolkata and former
Professor of Political Science, Calcutta University, India

Notes

1 Charles Tilly (1975). "Reflections on the History of European State-Making," in *The Formation of National States in Western Europe*, Charles Tilly, ed. (Princeton: Princeton University Press), 24–27. See also, Eugene Weber (1976). *Peasants into Frenchmen* (Stanford: Stanford University Press).
2 Benjamin R. Barber (1995). *Jihad vs. Mcworld* (New York: Ballantine Books), 29.

ACKNOWLEDGMENTS

This volume is an outcome of a national seminar on "India–Myanmar Bilateral Ties: Ethnicity, Security and Connectivity" jointly organized by the Department of Humanities and Social Sciences, Indian Institute of Technology Guwahati; Observer Research Foundation (ORF), Kolkata; and the Indian Council of Social Science Research (ICSSR), New Delhi held during September 25–26, 2016 at IIT Guwahati.

We are grateful to Professor Manorama Sharma; Ambassador (Retd.) Rajiv Bhatia; Dr Binayak Dutta, Department of History, NEHU; Professor Bipul Bhuyan, Department of Physics, IIT Guwahati; Professor Akhil Ranjan Dutta, Department of Political Science, Gauhati University; Dr Dilip Gogoi, Cotton University; Dr Rupakjyoti Borah; and Pradip Phanjoubam, an eminent journalist, for helping us conceptualize the theme and framework of the conference in a way that could give opportunity to scholars, journalists and policy makers to discuss relevant aspects in relation to India–Myanmar borderlands. The sub-themes covered in the conference and subsequently in the volume received immense historical importance and international recognition in contemporary times.

We wish to thank the India Council of Social Science Research (ICSSR), New Delhi for the financial support to organize the seminar; Indian Institute of Technology Guwahati; and Observer Research Foundation, Kolkata for extending the support in this endeavor. We offer our heartfelt thanks to all the participating scholars and contributors who have shared their ideas on India–Myanmar borderlands with their learned contributions and extended their cooperation throughout the process of making this volume possible. We are especially indebted to the volunteers Aniruddha, Jimmy, Konkumoni, Pankaj and Bhasker for their hard work during the conference. Our sincere thanks to Rubul Gogoi for helping us with the editing of the photographs.

Our friends and fellow colleagues in ORF, Kolkata deserve special thanks for their moral and mental support in making our drive successful. We are especially thankful to Professor Rakhahari Chatterji, Advisor, ORF, Kolkata for his academic involvement and constant support in this project.

Finally, we wish to thank Rimina Mohapatra, Antara Raychaudhury, Shashank Shekhar Sinha, Anandan Bommen and Anvita Bajaj for helping us with the preparation, copy-editing and the final completion of the manuscript.

We hope that the present volume will generate further interest amongst scholars and researchers working in this field and the study would be useful to the teachers, students, journalists and policy makers to understand the dynamics of the borders and borderlands against the backdrop of India–Myanmar relations.

1

CONCEPTUALIZING INDIA AND MYANMAR BORDERLANDS

Ethnicity, security and connectivity

Pahi Saikia and Anasua Basu Ray Chaudhury

Borders and boundaries are important frames and narratives used in the discourses of nation, citizenship, sovereignty, state and territoriality. In the recent decades, border studies have mushroomed and taken a scholarly turn to include debates on personal and group identity, gender discourses and ethnic minorities. This scholarly transition is not simply a

> reflection of ivory tower thinking but is fomented by real world phenomena in the 1990s such as the fall of the Berlin wall, expansion of regional engagements, enlargement of EU, spread of neoliberal political economy and the upsurge in ethnonational politics.
>
> *(Wilson and Donnan 2016, 2)*

These events demonstrate the interface of local and global forces and have made borders and borderlands 'new sites of empirical investigation' (Wilson and Donnan 2016, 2).

A large part of the borderland studies in political geography or the field of geopolitics is concentrated on the nature of borders from a military point of view. National borders were understood from realist perspectives along static territorial lines as policed and are considered as 'empirical manifestations of a state's territorial power, located in specific contexts known as borderlands' (Passi 2009). In the recent decades, there has been a search for newer approaches to understand the dynamics of borders and borderlands from diverse perspectives. From a liberal perspective, borders have been re-imagined and deconstructed. Using this approach, some argue that there has been a 'new regionalist response' and retreat of the state (Passi 2009). There is a consistent move beyond the notion of borders as 'bounded spaces' toward a borderless and post-national global system (Ohmae 1995; Strange 1996). From similar perspectives, borders have become more porous and constitute points of contact between peoples and cultures as well as socioeconomic linkages. Transnational economic and political linkages across borders, cross-border mobility of population and creation of cultural networks are constitutive of these transformations and therefore redefine power, norms and collective identity in the interconnected global system. Borders are highly 'mobile, diffused and proliferating' (Mountz and Hiemstra, 2016, 455).

From a constructivist approach, mobility and migration of people deconstruct the notion of borders as 'discrete, fixed and dichotomous' (Houtum 2016, 406). The focus has shifted from borders as 'two-dimensional lines that delineate territorially differentiated sovereignties to borders as transnational links' (Houtum 2016, 406). Borders are conceptualized as 'socio-spatially constructed mindscapes, meanings and identities' (Houtum 2016, 406). These studies have linked the study of international borders and boundaries to larger approaches on 'territory, identity, sovereignty and citizenship' (Megoran 2016, 475). They emphasize international boundaries 'are not fixed but evolving entities that permeate the fabric of nation-states' (Megoran 2016, 475). Examples may be drawn from various borderland areas in North America, Europe and Asia. The European Neighborhood Policy (ENP) launched in 2004 offers multifaceted goals to create spaces of engagement between the European partners through effective economic, security and cultural cooperation (Brunett-Jailly 2016, 106). The aim is to 'establish an area of prosperity and good neighborliness founded on the values of the Union and characterized by close and peaceful relations based on cooperation' (Brunett-Jailly 2016, 106). The EU experience reveals permeability of borders. Similarly, the Canada–US border deconstructed the notion of fixity of borders by creating transnational linkages and a trade-friendly border between the US and Canada.

On the contrary there are debates that point out that despite the 'erosion of borders and shifting identities,' state-territoriality has gained immense significance in recent decades (Mountz and Hiemstra 2016, 456). Governments still exercise their authority over the territorial borderlands. Scholars argue that nation-states impose their border enforcement strategies and make territorial borders 'impenetrable' (Mountz and Hiemstra 2016, 456). Post-September 11, territoriality became more noticeable in the form of creation of 'biometric borders, regulation on immigration, tariffs and quotas' (Passi 2009, 4). Twenty-first-century 'border security,' as studies suggest, is grounded in 'the deployment of resources, manpower and technology, (Chalfin 2016, 284). The constitution of the US Department of Homeland Security (DHS) and its associated division, the US Customs and Border Protection (CBS) which exercises control at the borders, add to the border security regime of the twenty-first century. Labor migration policies to regulate the flow of mobility in the US–Mexico border are another aspect that is added to the perspective of securitization of borders. Similarly, the policy responses within the border security framework of the Trafficking Protocol and the Migrant Smuggling Protocol within the UN Convention against Organized Crime to check human trafficking and illegal sale of arms and drugs across borders add to the existing border security regimes (Ford and Lyons 2016, 442). Such regimes became necessary to regulate the flow of undocumented people and human trafficking in the context of globalization. To take an example, the government of Indonesia passed the Local Regulation No. 12 in 2007 on the "Elimination of Trafficking in Women and Children" from places like the Riau Islands in Indonesia. Riau Islands form a part of 'Indonesia's border with Singapore and Malaysia' (Ford and Lyons 2016, 442). The Islands gained importance in the 1980s and 90s due to the trilateral subregional cooperation between Indonesia-Malaysia and Singapore. In the 1990s, a free trade zone and the cross-border growth triangle (IMS-GT) were established between these three countries. As a result, Riau Islands became attractive for international investments for tourism. These investments heavily depended on the "recruitment of low skilled labor force" from different parts of Indonesia (Ford and Lyons 2016, 442). Over time, the Riau Islands became 'identified as a trafficking hotspot, primarily of women and girls from other parts of Indonesia' (Ford and Lyons 2016, 442). The counter-trafficking measures taken by the government of Indonesia, Malaysia and Singapore are aimed to securitize and regulate the mobility of the 'illegals, smuggled persons and migrants' in the borderlands (Ford and Lyons 2016, 442).

In the recent decades, there have been attempts to enforce border controls at sea in Europe, North America and Southeast Asia. Florida in the US, Lampedusa Island in Italy, Canary Island in Spain and the islands north of Australia are some of the most attractive destinations for undocumented migrants and asylum seekers through sea routes from politically unstable states in North Africa and Asia. It was estimated that between 2005 and 2007, nearly 50,000 migrants arrived in Lampedusa due to political unrest in countries like Tunisia and Libya (Mountz and Hiemstra 2016, 465). In the early 2000s, the European Union adopted strategies of 'joint policing and interception operations in the Mediterranean' to regulate the flow of asylum seekers. The FRONTEX, the EU agency was created to 'coordinate the control and surveillance of border security between the border states of EU.' The task of FRONTEX is to 'deploy boats, helicopters and planes in the Mediterranean Sea and along the coasts of North and West Africa to prevent boats with migrants from entering the territorial waters of the EU' (Houtum 2016, 410). Similarly, the US adopted various immigration enforcement policies to prohibit undocumented immigration through the US–Mexico border. The border is dotted with 'various technologies like electronic fencing, ground sensors, and digital surveillance towers' to enforce immigration controls (Coleman 2016, 430).

In Central Asia, new borders were created and materialized between Uzbekistan and Kyrgyzstan after international boundaries were redrawn in the 1990s. The borderlands in the region are marked by complex administrative boundaries and geographies that were inherited from the earlier Soviet period (Megoran 2016, 475). The boundaries between these former Soviet republics, prior to 1990s, hardly manifested in the 'practices and imaginations of borderland dwellers' (Megoran 2016, 475). Ethnic minorities crossed the borderlands to acquire education in their mother tongue. Similarly, agricultural and industrial workers and pilgrims moved across the borders on an everyday basis ferried by the Soviet-era bus services.

These networks, however, discontinued and were severely affected in 1993 when the government of Uzbekistan 'formally sealed its border with Kyrgyzstan to prevent the movement of people and Russian rubles flooding the border economy of Uzbekistan' (Megoran 2016, 475). In continuation with Uzbekistan's border control policies, in February 1999, the bus services were discontinued between the two states, particularly in the Osh and Jalal-Abad provinces in the remote border areas. These measures manifested 'the official nationalism and a discursive tool promoted by the politics of authoritarianism' in the presidential regime in Uzbekistan (Megoran 2016, 475).

In postcolonial South Asia, borders and borderlands are sites where contest over inclusion and exclusion is a constant phenomenon. They make a division between the 'inside' and the 'outside,' 'sovereignty' and 'anarchy' and also the 'singular' and 'pluralistic space' (Banerjee and Ray Chaudhury 2012, 27–29). Michel Agier (2016) in his book Borderlands argues "we are living the whole time with borders and thresholds, as soon as we move around to a minimum extent, we never stop crossing these." The border is a 'place, a situation or a moment that ritualizes the relationship to the other. . . ' (Agier 2016, 7) and South Asia is no exception to it.

Therefore, borders are not merely cartographic lines on maps (Banerjee and Ray Chaudhury 2012, 27–29). Rather, they are zones where the jurisdiction of one state ends and the other begins. While borderlands are the common ground of two or more states that share them, they also interpret their meanings in very different ways to their citizens in their national narratives, history writing and collective spatialized memories (Banerjee and Ray Chaudhury 2012, 27–29). In this context it is noteworthy that in the South Asian scenario security concerns always loom large over all other equally legitimate concerns and values and precisely, it is the notion of military security that dominates over human security in the border region.

Enforcing barriers along the borders raises the fundamental question of political citizenship ascribed to people living within the territorial limits of modern nation-states. Scholars argue that citizenship and borders provide the institutional framework of inclusion and exclusion of people and mark the contours of political membership and socioeconomic justice (Gastelum 2005). Citizenship, as scholars argue, serves as 'instruments of social closure' embodied in institutions and practices of suffrage, benefits, protection and territory in the national and global contexts (Brubaker 2009, x). The term has been extended to incorporate legal, social and cultural dimensions of membership and occupies a crucial position in the 'administrative and political culture of modern nation-states' (Brubaker 2009, 23). Citizenship in the context of borderlands is to be understood in relation to transitional social practices across borders. Despite the presence of rigid state structures, citizenship in the borderlands is manifested in various transnational sociopolitical forms constructed through a process of continuous interaction of inhabitants along the international borders. Cross-border exchanges of trade, access to schools, everyday employment and other resources determine these interactions and the dynamics of political membership of borderland communities. Borderlands are therefore important sites of examining how the inhabitants in the remote borderlands relate to the state conceptions of territoriality and citizenship. It is important to examine how these inhabitants negotiate with state conceptions of political membership and redefine their sense of belongingness to citizenship defined by modern nation states. It is also important to examine how the borderlanders negotiate with a continuous process of exclusion from national structures of citizenship, the security and entitlements tied to citizenship structures. Exclusionary policies of political membership and practices adopted by authoritarian states often resulted in involuntary migration of marginal communities such as borderland inhabitants in search of asylum and security across international borders. How do these groups of individuals negotiate with citizenship claims and the framework of ethnic nationalities defined by host states? How do border crossings of the borderland inhabitants in search of physical protection in the wake of repression and human security threats impact inter-state relations and the discourse of citizenship and nationality in modern nation-states? These are pertinent questions that need to be addressed with reference to mobility across the India–Myanmar borderlands.

India–Myanmar borderlands in perspective

Borders and borderland studies as the preceding analysis reveals have proliferated over the years. These studies have generated a number of intellectual traditions across disciplines and therefore reflect the convergence of ideas on national security, nation-state building, power, political economy, identity and citizenship, articulated from realist, non-realist and social constructivist perspectives. This edited volume intends to contribute to these debates on borders and borderlands and examines three important dynamics: ethnicity, connectivity and security. The metaphor of borders and borderlands are used to examine the convergence of debates on power, inter-state relations and territory with issues of identity, culture and everyday politics using ethnographic case studies from interdisciplinary perspectives, a common thread that runs through the chapters in this volume. The authors in this volume demonstrate through case studies the multifaceted ways in which borderlands between India and Myanmar respond to the processes of postcolonial bordering, control and militarization of inter-state borders and at the same time, negotiate with political, economic and social transformations generated by interdependent, deterritorialized relations in the new order of subregional political economy between the two states.

In this volume we move beyond the classical geopolitical and international relations approaches where border is conceptualized as a geographical reality and take cues from post-structuralist and critical debates in international politics (Passi 2009, 213–234). While drawing lessons from existing approaches, our aim is to understand the creation of borders and borderlands as physical realities in India–Myanmar borderlands through historically informed analysis. As borders in South and Southeast Asia have been redefined constantly in decolonized political order, the states in these regions seem to be more connected and are no longer considered to be territorially bounded entities. Yet, they are vigorously assertive (Rosenau 2006). How do borderlands in India and Myanmar negotiate with these transformations and changing narratives on the geopolitical borders? Our main concern is to address this question with the help of bottom-up, locally grounded perspectives. Our aim is to explore the continuous colonial and postcolonial challenges and prospects of security and connectivity in the borderlands of India and Myanmar. We also examine the prospects and challenges of integrating ethnicities and the local polities into transnational networks of economic and sociopolitical ties in the securitized borderlands of the two countries.

The borderlands of Myanmar, as we argue in this volume, are inhabited by multiethnic non-Burman ethnic nationalities like the Chins inhabiting the western part of Myanmar along the borders of India and Bangladesh, the Mons inhabiting the eastern and southern fringes of Myanmar along the borders of Myanmar and Thailand and various other sub-groups such as the Naga, Lahu, Lisu among others. Myanmar's borderlands as scholars describe are "marked by unique ethnic cultures and diversity that ranges from the Kayan (Padaung) on the Shan/Karenni borders, where the 'long-necked' women wear extraordinary brass necklaces, to the Salum sea-gypsies of sub-tropical Tenasserim and the once headhunting Naga along the India frontier" (Smith and Allsebrook 1994, 17). Ethnic separatism and political instability however marred the ethnopolitical landscape of the ethnic minority borderlands. The political situation in these borderlands has been described by scholars in these words, "In the deep mountains and forests of the borderland periphery, over 20 armed opposition groups controlled, under their own administrations, vast swathes of territory and continued to reflect an often changing alignment of different political or nationality causes" (Smith and Allsebrook 1994, 17). Ethnic minorities feared political domination and marginalization. The situation is complicated in Myanmar where armed ethnic ceasefire groups are in control of the border economic activities through special regions controlled by the ceasefire groups. Despite declining fatalities, there have been only a handful of cases where ceasefires have sustained or peace talks have been possible between the governments and the insurgent leadership. Most ceasefires have practically resulted in internal discord within the insurgent group, or renewed existence of 'quasi-independent armed groups' or opportunistic alliances between different insurgent groups (Cline 2015).

Evidence drawn from India's eastern frontiers illustrates similar complexities. India's Northeast borderlands represent multiethnic composition and cross-border ethnic ties with the border regions of Upper Myanmar. With the formation of postcolonial borders and change of regimes, the region suffered from continuous stirrings of violent insurgencies in varying degrees, produced by ethnocultural differences among the inhabitants. To draw some recent examples of insurgent violence, on June 4, 2015 armed militants attacked a state security personnel convoy in Manipur's Chandel district bordering Myanmar. At least 18 soldiers from the Indian army were reportedly killed, while 11 were injured. National Socialist Council of Nagaland (NSCN-K), the Kanglei Yawol Kanna Lup (KYKL) and a faction of the Kangleipak Communist Party (KCP) claimed responsibility for the attack (Sharma 2015). In May 2015 the NSCN-K killed and injured security personnel of the Assam Rifles paramilitary unit in Mon district of Nagaland. These attacks were coordinated by a coalition of several active insurgent groups, including the NSCN-K, the Kamtapur Liberation Organization (KLO), the United Liberation Front of Asom (ULFA) and the National Democratic Front of Bodoland (NDFB-Songhbhijit) (*The Indian Express*, June, 2015). These groups have been opposed to negotiation, unlike their counterparts including the NSCN (IM) and NDFB (R) ceasefire groups and pro-negotiation United Liberation Front of Assam. The Indian army avenged by using preemptive strikes along two different locations in Nagaland in Nokklak, Tuensang district and Manipur in Ukhrul district along the India–Myanmar border (Pandey 2015).

Ethnic insurgencies in the region led to forcible displacement of population, underdevelopment, complex inter-state relations, affected majority-minority relations and further contributed to illegal border crossings in the region. Moreover, these insurgencies pose a serious challenge to the national modernizing projects, human and regional security as well as the global political economy. Many of these insurgencies thrived not only because of civilian support but also because of external links and support of neighboring countries.

The recent democratic transition in Myanmar, however, opened up the scope to capture the country's experiences with colonialism, a ravaged political history, ethnic conflicts and possible outcomes through political and economic reforms. With the rapid changes in the political conditions, followed by the electoral gains of the National League for Democracy (NLD) in November 2015, changing media landscape, suspension of construction work on Myitsone dam since September 2011, strengthening of economic ties with ASEAN countries, and the ongoing peace talks with the Panglong Peace Conference comprising different ethnic minorities, Myanmar raised the expectations for regional integration and strategic changes in the subregion. At this juncture the Indian government vehemently pursued the Look East Policy, recently refurbished as the 'Act East' policy to engage with Myanmar. India's policy is aimed at bridging the discontinuities of commercial links with the Asia–Pacific including Myanmar, by breaking the notion of 'spatial boundedness' and transforming the peripherally located conflict-ridden borderlands as flourishing zones of growth and economic development of an integrated economy.

Practical challenges of implementing the policy however occurred on account of lack of physical infrastructure, endemic security concerns or underdeveloped markets and lack of adequate industrial base in the border zones of these countries. The ASEAN-India summit held in Myanmar in November 2014 provided an important platform for the Indian government to reiterate its commitment to maintain regional peace and security and to combat international terrorism by joining hands with its regional partners. Concerted moves recently undertaken by India and Myanmar are designed to translate these challenges into opportunities.

At this point, it is also important to highlight the role of China in the entire gamut of multilateral ties in the Southeast Asian region vis-à-vis India's bilateral ties with Myanmar. India and China's competing interests on Myanmar is driven by the process of democratization and the strategic location of Myanmar at the 'tri-junction of East Asia, Southeast Asia and South Asia.' According to historical writings, Myanmar was at the crossroads between India and China. Scholars argue that 'for Chinese traders and explorers, the dream was to make Myanmar, the southwest access route to India.' By the end of the twentieth century, China tried to get closer to the borders of Burma and establish 'a direct passage to India' (Myint-U 2011, 3). The British and the French had similar aspirations and wanted to 'connect India and China through a passage across Burma' (Myint-U 2011, 15). Accordingly, 'soldiers, surveyors and scientists were sent by the imperial administrators to map the unknown borderlands of Burma' (Myint-U 2011, 15). A British intelligence officer H.R. Davies in his account written in 1890s suggested ways to connect India and China in these words, 'In an age when railways are penetrating to the most out-of-the-way places on the earth, it is impossible to suppose that India and China, the two most populous countries in the world, would remain without being connected by railway' (Myint-U 2011, 15). Strategic ties and interest between India, China and Myanmar therefore dates back to history. The interests and competition became stronger with modern state formation in the Asian subregion. China's growing interest in Myanmar was articulated through the communist party that established important links with the insurgent organizations like the Communist Party of Burma (CPB) through military and financial aid since the 1940s. In an article entitled 'Opening to the Southwest: An Expert Opinion,' published in the *Beijing Review* on September 2, 1985, the former Chinese Vice Minister of Communications expressed the possibilities of finding 'an outlet for trade from China's land-locked provinces of Yunnan, Sichuan and Guizhou, through Burma to the Indian Ocean' (Lintner 2012, 223). By the late 1980s, China had already signed bilateral agreements on border trade with Myanmar. Chinese economic investments and mega infrastructural projects are manifestations of increasing bilateral ties. Booming markets in the border towns like Panghsang, located in the borderlands between Myanmar and China, are other examples of the ties between Chinese officials and the local governments located in the peripheries of Myanmar. It needs to be noted that Panghsang, dotted with small shops with toys and trinkets made in China, paved roads and casinos, flooded with Chinese goods and currency is controlled by the United Wa State Army. The process of democratic however created difficulties for further Chinese investments in various parts of Myanmar. China-Myanmar relations entered into a phase of uncertainty after 2011 when the military junta opened up the political structure for reforms. Suspension of projects like the Myitsone dam in 2011 and Letpedaung coppermine in 2013 are just a few examples of the strained relations (Yhome 2018). Despite uncertainty, China's long-term interests to build up bridges between the Indian Ocean and China through Myanmar's territory will remain. At the same time, Myanmar's domestic conflict in the peripheral regions is advantageous for China. What would be the implications of China's interests on India's projections of future economic and infrastructural ties with Myanmar? How does this impact the bilateral ties between India and Myanmar?

It is within this framework that this book explores the implications that contemporary changes in Myanmar have on India–Myanmar borderlands in terms of ethnicity, security and connectivity. Documentary evidence, interview narratives and field experiences collected in the borderlands of India and Myanmar inform the understanding of the issues related to ethnicity, security and connectivity discussed in the book. From a political economy perspective, we argue that the borderlands located in the geographical margins of India and Myanmar is of immense importance to determine the bilateral ties and the geopolitical security dynamics of the two countries. We use the perspective of borders and borderlands to understand a range of transborder connections. We argue that the security landscape in the borderlands has been changing with response to transborder flow of people, goods and information. Borderlands in India and Myanmar have become important for closer scrutiny by the national governments because of untapped minerals and energy resources, fluid territorial boundaries, continuing multidirectional exchanges, cross-border ethnic ties and most critically, due to persisting challenges of nontraditional security (NTS) issues such as transborder criminal networks, human trafficking, public health and disaster relief, among others. Our focus is to deepen the analytical framework of understanding security by incorporating nonmilitary security dimensions such as society and economy (Buzan 1998).

We argue that security concerns, especially issues related to cross-border insurgency and undocumented migration, is one of the most important factors that determine bilateral ties between these two neighbors. For years, the northeast of India has faced its own set of unique challenges and insurgency has crippled the development of the region. Although the face of insurgency has been gradually changing, many such groups take shelter across the border in Myanmar and continue to plan and execute their will. Additionally, the recent Rohingya crisis raises issues of cross-border migration, border management and security between the two countries. Mutual cooperation between the two countries in this regard therefore needs to be strengthened. Additionally, people residing in India's northeast and those across the border in Myanmar often share common ethnic origins and the porous nature of the border between these two countries allows free cross-border movement to an extent. While people-to-people exchanges across the border is welcome and also needs encouragement, it at times gives rise to law and order problems. Some mechanisms that would allow people-to-people interactions while enforcing a check on smuggling, informal trade and law and order have recently been agreed upon. For instance, India and Myanmar signed seven agreements including the land border agreement on May 10 and 11, 2018, to facilitate the movement of people across the land border with valid documents. The agreements are aimed at providing assistance to Myanmar for the restoration of religious sites damaged by earthquakes in Bagan, enhancing tourism, pilgrimage, access to health and education services between the two countries, providing training of Myanmar Foreign Service Officers and setting up an Industrial Training Centre (ITC), as well as providing assistance to Myanmar on the Joint Ceasefire Monitoring Committee (MEA, Press Release, May 11, 2018). In December 2017, India also signed a MoU with Myanmar to assist Myanmar on the Rakhine State Development Programme. The challenge would be to see how these agreements are worked out at the ground level in the two countries.

Connectivity in the region holds the key to economic ties and people-to-people interactions. To this end, many infrastructural projects linking the two countries and the region as a whole are in various stages of planning and implementation. The book takes the position that connectivity has a lot of scope for fostering self-sufficiency of the frontier minorities by enabling cross-border exchanges, for instance through tourism and agro-based industry. The northeastern states of India, which have huge potential for health and ecotourism and businesses in food grain and indigenous products, have a vital role to play in this regard. Therefore, the approach toward increasing and strengthening established modes of connectivity need careful examination.

We also argue that the issue of ethnicity poses certain complex and unique challenges in the bilateral relations between India and Myanmar. Behind the positive developments for reform undertaken since 2011 lay the real challenges of democratic governance and problems of integrating Myanmar's ethnic minorities. Myanmar is known for its multiethnic composition. During the Tatmadaw regime the separatist movements of the Karens, Shans and many other groups intensified and led to political instability in the border regions. The outbreak of conflict in the Rakhine State recently compounded the challenges faced by transitioning Myanmar. Therefore, any collaborative efforts at the bilateral level between these two states that have been undertaken and that will come up in the future will have to make a balance between short-term commercial interests and long-term policy of inclusive development that both countries need to undertake.

Overview of the chapters

Against this backdrop, using a bottom-up, locally grounded ethnographic perspectives from the borderlands, this book examines the prospects and challenges of India–Myanmar strategic partnership and analyzes further possibilities for bilateral ties between the two countries. Apart from the Introduction, the book is divided into three sections and each section deals with issues of ethnicity, security and connectivity between India and Myanmar.

The first section entitled 'India–Myanmar Relations: Ethnicity and Security Dimensions' has four chapters. Chapter 2 in this section authored by Pahi Saikia, Ingudam Yaipharemba Singh and Apurba K. Baruah is entitled *State-territoriality, circulation of socio-cultural relations and resistance in India–Myanmar borderlands*. The chapter argues that postcolonial border drawing and political boundary making in South Asia had an impact on ethnic ties, connectivity and people perceptions on security along the international borders in the areas surrounding Myanmar and the vicinity of India's eastern frontiers. State building in India and Myanmar failed to discern the complex patterns of historical mobility and construction of multiple identities in the peripheral regions of India's Northeast and Myanmar. Using fieldwork narratives from two border villages in the Moreh district of Manipur, this chapter examines the persistence of a range of transborder connections, power narratives and sociocultural boundaries. The chapter particularly looks at the establishment of border regimes and border pillars in India and Myanmar borderlands and ways in which village residents negotiate their ethnic identities. It uses the literature on ethnic identity and borderland studies and examine the local politics embedded in the borderland experiences of militarization. It argues,

> In post-colonial states, particularly South Asia, nation-state building practices since 1940s consolidated border regimes as a part of right sizing of borders and nation state making exercises and created new borderlands. Borders became a marker of identity within specific contexts through mapping, scaling, census making.

It also analyzes the reconstruction of ethno-political identities vis-à-vis state-territoriality in the emerging phase of global and translocal dynamics. The chapter points out that border restructuring in India and Myanmar redefine the 'mundane and localized ethno-politics' of cross-border communities in these two villages. The objective is to understand the power asymmetry created by border dynamics, problem of integration of borderland communities into the emerging political economy, resistance and politics of defiance in India–Myanmar borderlands.

Chapter 3, entitled *Crisis in the Rakhine State of Myanmar: bilateral relations with India in perspective* and authored by Mihir Bhonsale, examines the political, strategic and cultural implications of large-scale cross-border movement of ethnic groups such as the Rohingyas. It emphasizes that the Rohingya crisis has assumed a regional dimension and therefore the refugee crisis has to be analyzed in the light of contemporary relations between India and Myanmar. The chapter begins with a historical analysis of the origins of the Rohingyas, their settlement history in the Rakhine state and the evolution of the 'majority-minority relations in the Arakan.' The chapter moves on to discuss the postcolonial developments and the promulgation of the 1974 Emergency Immigration Act by the military regime in 1970s which subsequently led to waves of out-migration of the Rohingyas in Myanmar in the late 1970s, 1990s and 2000s to Bangladesh and other countries. The last of the phases of out-migration began in 2012 when communal riots took place in several places in Rakhine state. Also, in this phase, 'fleeing poverty, rampant physical abuse and statelessness, the Rohingyas took to sea in search of refuge, beginning in 2014.' Following the August 25, 2017 attacks on military outposts in the Rakhine state, the largest exodus of Rohingya people in postcolonial history of Myanmar has taken place. Yet as the author argues the international response to the humanitarian crisis involving the Rohingyas has been inadequate. The state of Myanmar too failed to take adequate measures to take the responsibility to protect the Rohingyas. India adopted a 'dual strategy,' as the author argues. The Indian state tried to 'maintain good political relations with both Myanmar and Bangladesh that are central to its 'Neighborhood First' and 'Act East Policy.' At the same time, India adopted a 'push back' policy toward the Rohingyas. India's 'two pronged approach' of 'deporting back the illegal Rohingya migrants while soft-pedalling on Myanmar and at the same time also assuring Bangladesh that India is for a long-term solution for resolving the crisis in the Rakhine state is an example of Indian realism in her eastern neighborhood.'

Chapter 4, *Reality on the Indo–Myanmar Border: field observations from Longwa and Hmaungbuchhuah on issues of ethnicity, connectivity and security*, authored by Rajeev Bhattacharyya, analyzes the changing realities in the India–Myanmar borderlands. The analysis in this chapter is grounded on field visits in two different border areas along the India–Myanmar borderlands: Longwa and Hmaungbuchhuah. Field visits indicate that the traditional notions about security, connectivity and ethnicity are undergoing a change that are specific to ethnic linkages, local perceptions on security and age-old connectivity across these border areas. The discussion in the chapter also reveals that the cross-border access to socioeconomic activities like primary education and informal economic exchanges are indispensable and have been historically followed out of necessity in the livelihoods of the borderlands. The chapter critically analyzes the literature on borders and borderland livelihoods to support the argument.

Chapter 5 on *Territoriality, ethnic contestation and insurgency in the Indo–Myanmar corderland* by Ngamjahao Kipgen is based on a case study of the Kuki-Chin people of the Indo–Myanmar borderlands. Identified by different names, Kuki and Mizo in India and Chin in Myanmar/Burma, the Kuki-Chin ethnic group is a fringe community and a non-state entity that has sustained a fluid identity under changing historical contexts. The chapter discusses the Kuki-Chin community, 'transborder peoples' who constitute the minority in the states they inhabit but have 'connected history.' It tries to understand how their notion of ethnic identity and territory had been displaced and fragmented by the colonial and postcolonial states boundaries. The current engagement of the government of India with various insurgent groups in the region makes it imperative to revisit certain problems related to the rise of ethnic nationalism and to explicitly tackle the issues of overlapping territorial demands. The article argues that such overlapping territorial claims, which have their roots in colonial processes of ethnicization and territorial demarcation, need immediate attention to bring durable solution. Such competing claims arose only after colonially constructed categories of local people who shared local living spaces began to claim exclusive ownership of the entire territory of certain administrative units. Drawing on archival sources and ethnohistory, this article examines the Kuki-Chin ethnic insurgents group operating in the Indo–Myanmar borderlands.

The chapters in the first section of the volume, therefore, understand the re-bordering practices, power asymmetry, resistance and changing perceptions of contemporary sociopolitical realities in the India–Myanmar borderlands. These chapters also examine how border restructuring in India and Myanmar redefine ground realities of cross-border communities and peripheral economies. The paradox of power asymmetries in India–Myanmar borderlands as the chapters in this part argue can be much attributed to the persistence of 'coloniality' and postcolonial boundary making and administrative structures. British administrators had drawn and redrawn the map of the South and Southeast Asia, integrating kingdoms and principalities under colonial administration. Redrawing of boundaries had an impact on ethnic categorization, belonging and political choices of border-land communities like Kukis, Chins, Mons and Shans. To understand these politi-cal choices Chapters 2, 3, 4 and 5 evaluate the local narratives of identity, security, connectivity and territoriality in the emerging phase of new phase of globalization and wider bilateral dynamics between India and Myanmar.

Section II of the volume entitled 'Proximity to Connectivity: India–Myanmar in Perspective' has three articles. Chapter 6 by Alana Golmei on *India–Myanmar Relations: a perspective from the border* highlights the 'strong historical and geographi-cal links' that the ethnic communities of the borderlands of India and Myanmar share with each other. These relations, as the author argues, are rooted in shared historical, ethnic, cultural and religious ties. The Chin and Mizo people for instance share common historical, cultural and religious backgrounds. These linkages were rejuvenated and opened the doors for cross-border migration of Chin people from the other side of Myanmar borderlands in search of economic security and survival to India. The estimated populations of the Chin state located in the western part of Myanmar, bordered by Bangladesh and India in the west, Rakhine state in the south, and Magwe and Sagaing Division in the east, is 500,000. According to the latest report from the staff of Chin Human Rights Organization, approximately 50000 Chin refugees have settled in different parts of the state of Mizoram in India's bor-derlands. What implications would the bilateral relations between the two countries have on these refugees who traverse these borderlands? In the context of increasing subregional cooperation, India and Myanmar conceptualized and proposed several bilateral ventures in the areas of 'infrastructural development, communications, road and rail connectivity.' However, the main question that needs to be addressed is how these connectivity projects impact the lives of people living in the India–Myanmar borderlands. In a nutshell, the chapter argues that these mega projects would have implications on the cross-border communities and would perhaps work in the favor of cross-border communities only if the two countries are able to establish 'vigor-ous and meaningful people-to-people contacts in the India–Myanmar borderlands.'

In Chapter 7 entitled *India–Myanmar borderland: pressing concerns in public health hazards*, Anasua Basu Ray Chaudhury and Sreeparna Banerjee discuss the problems of public health, particularly the threats 'posed by infectious border diseases like Malaria, Human Immuno deficiency Virus Infection and Acquired Immune Defi-ciency Syndrome (HIV AIDS) and Tuberculosis (TB),' in the borderlands of India and Myanmar. The chapter attempts to establish the correlation between migra-tion and the spread of diseases in the border areas. It also examines the 'status of diseases among the bordering states of northeast India and Myanmar.' The chapter argues that 'the India–Myanmar border is an artificial line which is superimposed on the socio-cultural landscape of the borderland.' Owing to 'historic ethnic link-ages,' people in the border villages particularly in places that share boundaries with Manipur and Mizoram, share cross-border land/property and have common 'socio-economic interests' across the borders. Migration of cross-border communities like the Chins trying to escape the violence persecuted by the Myanmarese army in the Chin state of Myanmar is visible in these areas. The Chins travelled to Mizoram and settled in the state in search of livelihood. The Mizos on the other hand feel threatened due to the migration of the Chins and their increasing settlement in the border areas. The Chins are considered to be 'illegal' by the people of Mizoram. Apart from increasing discrimination in the job markets, the Chins have been facing serious problems related to public health. The chapter therefore argues that HIV and TB are likely to be caused by unregulated movement of people across the borderlands. Unregulated drug-trafficking and involvement of refugee/migrant Chin/Kuki women in the flourishing sex industry adds to the problem of public health in the India–Myanmar borderlands. In conclusion, the chapter makes an attempt to address the problem of public health through collaborative efforts between both the nations for an effective border health infrastructure, management and disease control strategy.

Chapter 8, *Employing proximity: boosting bilateral ties between India and Myanmar* by Pratnashreee Basu discusses that regional connectivity can be viewed in terms of bridging domestic goals and geopolitical ambitions. The chapter begins by conceptualizing 'physical connectivity' and gradually proceeds to discuss how the 'political complexities, security issues, difficult physical terrain and deplorable road links' stood in the way of developing closer and faster connectivity and physical linkages between India and Myanmar. The chapter further examines the prospects of establishing 'bilateral engagements' between India and Myanmar in 'cross-border infrastructural development; trade and services; cooperation in technology and tourism.' The chapter reveals that nearly eight road connectivity projects were initiated by the governments of the two countries, yet except the Tamu-Kalewa-Kalemyo Friendship Road, none of these projects have advanced. The chapter highlights that these projects (especially road links) have faced difficulties due to protests over land acquisition, fear of displacement, environmental concerns and local politics. Delays in these projects have also led to the escalation of costs of these projects. The chapter also emphasizes on 'soft connectivity' projects between the two countries. It argues that 'cross-border fibre optic links providing high-speed broadband link for voice and data transmission have been set up between India and Myanmar. The first one, running for a distance of 500 km, was set up from Moreh (in Manipur) to Mandalay in 2009.' Finally, the chapter argues that 'being neighbors, sharing a common historical past and cultural similarities' the two countries have a wider scope to 'employ their geographical proximity to the greatest advantage.'

Section III of this volume focuses on Myanmar's changing political landscape and scope for strengthening cooperation between India and Myanmar. Chapter 9 in this section is titled *Political economy of subregional cooperation: 'interests' in reframing the peripheries of India and Myanmar*. In this chapter, Rakhee Bhattacharya explores the evolving dynamics and India's current stand on subregional cooperation in Asia in the context of both economy and security with emphasis on Myanmar. The chapter gives an elaborate landscape of India's ongoing bilateral engagement with new Myanmar, and its heightened economic diplomacy to support all physical, economic, social and educational infrastructures toward restructuring the nation, which is devastated due to prolonged military regime and China's extra activism.

As India aims to gain regional power, it has simultaneously started to shift the narrative of its Northeast periphery as a 'natural gateway' toward achieving the goals of subregional economic integration. In this context, the chapter also argues about the shifting geopolitical theater toward Myanmar's strategic Rakhine state, where a new regime of power and 'interests' of various stakeholders are aiming to explore the space for various economic activities. As Myanmar is also partnering with such new subregional dynamics for its own economic gains, the state has created a security perception by systematically targeting a particular community. The chapter therefore ends on a cautious note for the need of a democratization process in the approach of subregionalism where economic integration and gains can have a bottom-up approach and remains meaningful for the peripheries.

Chapter 10, titled *Act East policy and the importance of Myanmar and Northeast India Region*, authored by Nehginpao Kipgen, discusses Myanmar's importance to the Act East Policy (AEP), which, Kipgen argues, is defined by different factors, including shared history, culture, ethnic relations and religious ties. The chapter adopts actor-oriented approach to understand foreign policy making in International Relations. India and Myanmar share 1,643-kilometer border in four Northeast Indian states. They also share the waters of Bay of Bengal, including the strategically important Andaman and Nicobar Islands. Myanmar serves as India's gateway to other ASEAN countries and provides a geographical contiguity to the Asia-Pacific region. Due to its geographical proximity, Myanmar also provides India a transit route to Southern China. On the other hand, the idea of the inclusion of 'Northeast Development Concern' as an important component of AEP came up in 1997. The AEP rightly aims at the creation of an enabling environment so as to end the landlocked situation and isolation of the Northeastern region by opening up its borders and integrating the region's economy through improved trade and connectivity with Southeast Asian countries. However, looking at the ground reality, the growth of border trade and tourism between the region and ASEAN countries is still relatively insignificant, especially its visibility in Northeast India. This chapter analyzes the LEP-AEP's development and challenges and argues that Myanmar and Northeast India are crucial for the success of the policy.

Chapter 11 by K. Yhome, titled *India–Myanmar relations: political transition and shared borderlands* shows that Myanmar has witnessed a phenomenal political transition in recent years with huge implications on the country's internal political and socioeconomic landscapes as also on its foreign relations with the outside world. Internally, the change has brought about an end to the five-decade long military rule and set in motion a process of establishing a democratic system of government in the country. So far, the most significant outcome of this process has been the historic victory of the National League for Democracy and the coming to power of the party in March this year. Externally, it has opened up room in the country's foreign engagements as well as for multiple external players to enter and engage with the country. These internal and external changes have direct and indirect implications on India and Delhi's relations with Naypyitaw and the wider region. Within this context, as political changes further redefine Myanmar's politics and its future, a few pertinent issues that need assessment in India–Myanmar relations are: How does Myanmar's democratic transition impact India–Myanmar relations? In what ways do multiple political players shape India's ties with Myanmar? Do increased external players' engagement with Myanmar affect its ties with India? There are three areas where the implications of these changes will have a direct impact, namely security, connectivity, and ethnicity. Importantly, these issues are inter-related and the progress in one will have a positive impact on the other while the reverse is also equally true. This chapter takes up each of these issues and examines the changes, challenges and prospects.

In a nutshell, this volume analyzes the emerging relations between India and Myanmar. The focus of this volume is to highlight the enduring historical ties in the borderlands of the two countries. The chapters in the volume examine the prospects and challenges of cooperation in three key areas: ethnicity, security and connectivity between the two countries, a major focus of the chapters in the volume. One of the major objectives was to understand the transborder linkages in the India–Myanmar borderlands with the help of existing scholarly literature on borders and borderlands. The main concern is to look at bilateral ties beyond classical neo-realist visions of inter-state relations and in turn, generate ideas on the processes of transformations in the frontiers of Myanmar and India's Northeast. Besides new neighborhood policies on trade and economic ties, border crossings of goods and people, sanctuary provided to insurgent groups, transborder criminal networks, 'hot pursuit' counterinsurgency raids and the issue of territorial sovereignty have been the cornerstone of the diplomatic meetings concerning issues of subregional security. Therefore the attempt in this volume is to move beyond methodological nationalism and understand the diverse links, the ethno-geography and economic linkages that traversed these frontier regions through trade as well as culturally significant migrations. As analyzed in some chapters, cross-cultural encounters in the borderland regions surpassed the official perceptions of political boundary making reinforced by South Asia's geopolitics and contemporary security concerns. Based on secondary source literature review, local narratives and interviews, the arguments in the chapters of the volume are mostly couched in a rich body of literature on multidisciplinary approaches on border making and territorial governance of modern nation-states. The volume draws from various approaches on borders and borderlands (Passi 2009; Baud and van Schendel 1997; Scott 2010; Gellner 2013). While doing so, this volume adopts constructivist perspectives on inter-state politics to examine the transformation in a transborder subregion, the India–Myanmar borderlands. The borderlands gain salience and occupy a significant political space within this discursive transformation of bilateral ties between the two neighbors.

To conclude, this collected volume provides a comprehensive view of the India–Myanmar borderland covering ethnicity, security and connectivity dimensions. Each chapter of this book covering a specific case study helps the readers understand the gray areas of borderlands between India and Myanmar. The book may be used as reference and recommended readings in colleges and universities for courses in

International Relations or Foreign Policy. The volume has an international appeal in generating awareness regarding the presently prevailing opinion about Myanmar and its engagement with its immediate neighborhood. Given that connectivity and security are dominating the discourse on neighborhood studies, against the shared ethnicity of the region, this volume will add to the existing literature.

References

Agier, Michel (2016). *Borderlands: Towards an Anthropology of the Cosmopolitan Condition.* Chichester, West Sussex: John Wiley & Sons, p. 7.

Banerjee, Paula and Anasua Basu Ray Chaudhury (eds.). (2012). *Women in Indian Borderlands.* Delhi: Sage Publications, pp. 27–29.

Brubaker, Rogers (2009). *Citizenship and Nationhood in France and Germany.* Cambridge, MA: Harvard University Press, p. x.

Buzan, Barry, Ole Waever and Jaap de Wilde (1998). *Security: A New Framework for Analysis.* Boulder, London: Lynne Rienner Publishers.

Chalfin, Brenda (2016). "Border Security as Late-Capitalist 'Fix'." In *A Companion to Border Studies,* edited by Wilson and Donnan. Chichester, West Sussex: John Wiley & Sons, p. 284.

Cline, Lawrence E. (2015). "Insurgencies of Northeast India: Ethnic/Tribal Competition, State Responses and Underdevelopment." In *Ethnic Subnationalist Insurgencies in South Asia: Identities, Interests and Challenges to State Authority,* edited by S. Chima Jugdep. New York: Routledge.

Coleman, Mathew (2016). "From Border Policing to Internal Migration Control in the United States." In *A Companion to Border Studies,* edited by Wilson and Donnan. Chichester, West Sussex: John Wiley & Sons, p. 430.

Ford, Michele and Lenore Lyons (2016). "Labor Migration, Trafficking and Border Controls." In *A Companion to Border Studies,* edited by Wilson and Donnan. Chichester, West Sussex: John Wiley & Sons, p. 442.

Gastelum, Yvonne Aime (2005). "Borderlands and the Claims of Justice." Working Paper, Center for Comparative Immigration Studies University of California, San Diego.

Houtum, Henk van (2016). "Remapping Borders." In *A Companion to Border Studies,* edited by Wilson and Donnan. Chichester, West Sussex: John Wiley & Sons, p. 406.

The Indian Express (2015). "18 Army Men Killed in Manipur, Naga Rebel Outfit NSCN-K Claims Responsibility." June 5, https://indianexpress.com/article/india/18-army-men-killed-in-manipur-naga-rebel-outfit-nscn-k-claims-responsibility/(accessed May 14, 2019).

Lintner, Bertil (2012). *Great Game East: India, China and the Struggle for Asia's Most Volatile Frontier.* New Delhi, India: HarperCollins.

Megoran, Nick (2016). "Bordering and Biopolitics in Central Asia." In *A Companion to Border Studies,* edited by Wilson and Donnan. Chichester, West Sussex: John Wiley & Sons, p. 475.

Mountz, Alison and Nancy Hiemstra (2016). "Spatial Strategies for Rebordering Human Migration at Sea." In *A Companion to Border Studies,* edited by Wilson and Donnan. Chichester, West Sussex: John Wiley & Sons, p. 455.

Myint-U, Thant (2011). *Where China Meets India: Burma and the New Crossroads of Asia.* London: Faber & Faber, p. 3.

Ohmae, Kenichi (1995). *The End of the Nation State: The Rise of Regional Economies.* New York: The Free Press.

Pandey, Alok (2015). "7 NSCN-K Militants Killed by Indian Army in Nagaland's Tuensang." *NDTV*, August 28, www.ndtv.com/india-news/six-militants-of-the-nscn-k-killed-by-the-indian-army-in-nagalands-tuensang-1211982 (accessed December 12, 2018).

Passi, Anssi (2009). "Bounded Spaces in a 'Borderless World': Border Studies, Power and the Anatomy of Territory." *Journal of Power* 2 (2) (August): 213–234.

Press Release, Visit of External Affairs Minister to Myanmar (2018). *Ministry of External Affairs, Government of India*, May 11, www.mea.gov.in/pressreleases.htm?dtl/29889/Visit+of+External+Affairs+Minister+to+Myanmar+May+1011+2018 (accessed October 25, 2018).

Rosenau, James N. (2006). *The Study of World Politics: Volume 1: Theoretical and Methodological Challenges*. London and New York: Routledge.

Sharma, Sriram (2015). "NSCN-K Claims Responsibility for 18 Soldiers Killed in Manipur Ambush." *Huffington Post*, www.huffingtonpost.in/2015/06/05/manipur-ambush_n_7516380.html (accessed December 12, 2018).

Smith, Martin and Annie Allsebrook (1994). *Ethnic Groups in Burma: Development, Democracy and Human Rights*. A Report, London, Anti-Slavery International.

Strange, Susan (1996). *The Retreat of the State: The Diffusion of Power in the World Economy*. Cambridge, UK: Cambridge University Press.

Wilson, Thomas M. and Hastings Donnan (eds.). (2016). *A Companion to Border Studies*. Chichester, West Sussex: John Wiley and Sons.

Yhome, K. (2018). "The BRI and Myanmar's China Debate." July. Delhi, Observer Research Foundation.

PART I

India–Myanmar relations

Ethnicity and security dimensions

2

STATE-TERRITORIALITY, CIRCULATION OF SOCIO-CULTURAL RELATIONS AND RESISTANCE IN INDIA–MYANMAR BORDERLANDS

Pahi Saikia, Ingudam Yaipharemba Singh and Apurba K. Baruah

> *On January 11, 2018, a team of police officials along with Assam Rifles personnel in Moreh, 'foiled the attempt' of unidentified Myanmarese villagers to put fencing at no man's land located between ward no. 4 in Moreh and Myanmar.*
>
> (*The Sangai Express* 2018a)

> *The Manipur Police arrested two Rohingya Muslim men and a 20 year old woman, suspected to be a trafficking victim, from Moreh. Police identified the two men as Mohd Saifullah (34) and Mohd Salam (25) from Arakan province, which is now known as Rakhine. The woman's name was Toiba Hatu alias Nargis (20).*
>
> (*Hindustan Times* 2018)

> *On May 4, 2018, a combined team of Narcotics and Affairs of Border (NAB) and the police officials of Tengnoupal district of Manipur arrested the members of a family for their involvement in cross border illegal drugs trade between India and Myanmar border.*
>
> (*The Sangai Express* 2018b)

> *On June 12, 2018, unidentified gunmen open fired for half an hour at the residential areas of Gamnom Veng in the Manipur-Myanmar border town. Some houses and vehicles were damaged. Correspondent.*
>
> (*The Imphal Free Press* 2018)

The preceding incidents indicate how international borders and boundaries become securitized and are located at the interface between 'concrete manifestations of international law and cartography, tighter border regulation and controls' on the one hand, and 'newly developing frameworks of regional integration, cross-border mobility and cooperative arrangements,' on the other (Nugent 2012, 558). These incidents also represent the infringement of border controls in the contested borderlands of India and Myanmar. Porosity of the borders between India and

Myanmar that are often beyond the bounds of the state makes these transgressions easier. Smuggling of small arms, narcotic substances, human trafficking and infiltration of armed groups contribute to the complex and hybrid character of governance in the borderlands. In order to prevent such transgressions, the Indian state considered construction of fences along the border areas. Accordingly, in 2003 the government of India and Myanmar conducted a joint survey along the borders. Prior to this in 2001, a Group of Ministers (GOM) in India recommended the government to enact effective border management policies by 'converting all single fences into double fences with concertina coils' (Government of India 2001). In the recent decade, the government approved border fencing of about 404 kilometers along the Mizoram–Myanmar border but the plan has not been operationalized. Additionally, the government identified a stretch of 14 kilometers for fencing near the international boundary in the border district of Moreh in Manipur (Haokip 2015). The government made the decision to 'fence the area between border pillar no. 79 and 81 along the India–Myanmar borderlands' (Saddiki 2017).

These activities initiated by the states in India and Myanmar represent continuous nation-state making exercises mediated by ways in which the states institutionalize political and military control of the territory and the people in the marginal borderlands. A securitized border enacted by a variety of state and non-state actors is experienced in the everyday practices of communities in the India–Myanmar borderlands. The security check posts manned by the Assam Rifles along the base of the Kuki hills for instance, in the India–Myanmar border zones, symbolize the essentialized state presence and the complex nation-making practices. Bordering activities in these zones emphasize protection, reterritorialization and erection of segregated walls between lives, ethnicities and social relations of transborder communities. At the same time, these practices are challenged and become ruptured by a range of activities, everyday networks and connections between people who live on both sides of the international border.

Using fieldwork narratives from two border villages in the Moreh district of Manipur, this chapter examines the persistence of a range of transborder connections, power narratives and socio-cultural boundaries. The chapter particularly looks at the establishment of border regimes and border pillars in India and Myanmar borderlands and ways in which village residents negotiate their ethnic identities. We use the literature on ethnic identity and borderland studies and examine the local politics embedded in the borderland experiences of militarization. We also analyze the reconstruction of ethno-political identities vis-à-vis state-territoriality in the emerging phase of global and translocal dynamics.

The chapter argues that border restructuring in India and Myanmar redefine the 'mundane and localized ethno-politics' of cross-border communities in these two villages. The objective is to understand the power asymmetry created by border dynamics and the problem of integration of borderland communities into the emerging political economy, resistance and politics of defiance in India–Myanmar borderlands. As we argue further in this chapter, the narrative of everyday experiences and localized ethno-politics in the borderlands of India and Myanmar is intricately linked to the discourse of 'territorialization, a process, which Newman describes as the process of creation and construction of borders through the actions of states and individuals in the peripheries, located at the edges and beyond the reach of the state' (Gellner 2013, 4). Scholars have conceptualized territory as a 'political category, owned, distributed, mapped, calculated, bordered and controlled' (Elden 2013, 3).

Everyday actions and narratives across the border areas of India and Myanmar can be examined with the help of different sets of literature that emphasize (a) border reinforcement and territorial governance enacted in various forms of the state's bordering practices; and (b) everyday and mundane lives nested in local sociopolitical practices across borders. Often these practices challenge the sovereignty of the state. These approaches provide a useful lens to understand the circulation of sociocultural practices, people and trade across the borderlands in the Asian subregion. The mutual interactions and bordering practices in the Asian borderlands, including India–Myanmar borderlands, as this chapter argues, are grounded in a variety of historical constructions, geopolitical practices and cultural productions across the international borders. The empirical setting and examples in this chapter therefore requires detailed process tracing and historical analysis of the nature and creation of physical borders, construction of identities, institutions of governance and performativity in the borderlands. A historical analysis is crucial to evaluate the continuities and discontinuities of interactions between 'peoples and the states' in India–Myanmar borderlands.

Theoretical concerns

Scholarly debates on the study of borders and boundaries witnessed a shift in focus from understanding borders as political entities to borders as socio-territorial constructs. From a neoliberal perspective, the paradigmatic shift signifies lowering of concrete walls and borders and a move toward construction of a borderless and deterritorialized world defined by neoliberal economic principles, ideas, identities and deconstructed notions of citizenship. In the context of North America, Europe and Asia, serious advances have been made to construct a deterritorialized world by creating synergistic engagements between peoples, ideas and nation-states. We also witness perpetual increase in transborder interactions that transcend national borders and physical boundaries of modern nation-states.

Borders were conceptualized as 'the sites of social, political and cultural change that impact local and national politics' (Su-Ann 2016, 1). Borders have also been theorized as 'physical lines that manifest the end of a state's territorial power, geographical phenomena that demarcate the sovereign territories of states and are located in specific contexts known as borderlands' (Passi 2009, 7). From the perspective of political geography the spatial dimension of borders and the ideas of border landscapes were used 'to examine the physical and human environments contiguous to the state boundary' (Wilson and Donnan 2012, 8). From anthropological approaches, borders were reflected not merely as visible markers between states but were also related to symbolic boundaries of identity and socio-cultural categories such as ethnicity (Barth 1969). Studies on the anthropology of borders emphasized 'people's experiences at the international borders, the symbolic processes of culture and the ties of border peoples to other people in the neighboring states' (Wilson and Hastings 2012, 6).

Using diverse perspectives from social theories, border scholars also shifted their attention to the 'social, political and economic expressions' of borders, frontiers and boundaries in everyday lives as expressions of belonging or exclusion to ethnic and racial identities, postcolonialism, nations, gender and sexuality. Borders in this context are used as frames of reference to 'cultural constructions of everyday lives' and master narratives to challenge the hegemonic national symbols and changing power discourses on nations, states and other forms of individual and collective identity (Wilson and Hastings 2012). Ethno-nationalist movements, substate and minority nationalisms in Eastern Europe in 1990s, and the persistent rise in the number of new social movements and cross-border activities added new dimensions to border studies.

This study takes cues from existing literature on border landscapes, boundaries and borderlands and uses the perspective of borders as a metaphor and a physical construct. We use a multidisciplinary approach and use perspectives from 'critical and post-structuralist debates in International Relations, political geography and anthropology to describe a range of transborder connections, socio-spatial identities and how marginal groups negotiate the meanings associated with their identities as members of nation-states' (Passi 2009, 7). Borderlands as earlier scholars theorized is used to analyze the 'dynamics of place and space, a region, divided by physical boundary lines between nation-states' (Wilson and Hastings 2012, 8). Borderlands constitute multiple cross-border connections, social identities and relations, both legal and illegal (Baud and van Schendel 1997). Borderlands are created as a part of the nation-building exercise of modern states.

In postcolonial states, particularly South Asia, nation-state building practices since the 1940s consolidated border regimes as a part of right sizing of borders and nation-state–making exercises and created new borderlands. Borders became a marker of identity within specific contexts through mapping, scaling and census making. The intellectual turn is to understand territorial governance in South Asian borderlands. The attempt is to understand the divides between a 'functioning core' and disintegrated peripheries, between indigenous natives and immigrant communities, between those who believe that 'cultural and political boundaries are intertwined' and those who assertively sought for the reordering of local landscapes. Scholarly attention turned toward exploring various forms of governance in militarized borderlands including India–Myanmar borderlands, where governance is often informed by statist policies without much dialogue with the people in borderlands.

Militarization of the borderlands in postcolonial South Asia became crucial not for the prevention of traditional wars but nontraditional security threats. State-initiated bordering practices in South Asia, such as border fencing, are associated with restrictions and regulatory practices to control mobility and illegitimate border crossings. A *"physical"* border fence, as the study argues, is 'a barrier, a protective system together with other engineering construction objects and sensors designed to contend, detain or even destroy an adversary' (Golunov 2016). Border fences often supplemented by ditches, barbed wire, surveillance cameras, patrolling and sometimes even minefields and rigid control at checkpoints became visible sites of control (Golunov 2016).

Creation of borderlands and consolidation of border regimes in postcolonial South Asia had profound consequences on everyday lives of people living in the borderlands. These practices had profound effects on 'borderland social structures, local politics, culture and economy as demonstrated in the Bengal borderlands' (Baud and van Schendel 1997, 19). In the postcolonial period, regular cross-border economic and traditional commercial networks that were established and practiced by the borderland people in the India-Bangladesh border region, for instance, were disturbed and weakened due to restrictive state policies adopted by both India and Bangladesh. Older links gave way to modified practices and advance web of relations often outlawed by the newly created border regimes of the two states.

Militarized practices to prevent cross-border movements, however, met with local resistance. Borderland communities resisted against state directed protection and controls in these borderlands including the India–Myanmar borderlands marked by violence and resistance due to the imposition of state control and militarization. Unlike the performativity and stringent bordering practices along the borders between India and Pakistan, the India–Myanmar borders are marked by limited performativity and dearth of strict bordering practices like walls or border fencing. Instead the borderlands of India and Myanmar are characterized by porosity and special arrangements for the mobility of people under the Free Movement Regime (FMR). In the recent decades, however, the border between the two counties has been characterized by a complex web of relations, ranging from visible performativity in the form of border check posts and controls of illegal crossings of goods and people and continuous inter-exchanges of social relations and negotiation of border culture and ethnic identities of the borderlanders.

The next section contextualizes creation of borders, boundaries, re-bordering practices, circulation of socio-cultural relations and resistance in South Asian borderlands, particularly in India–Myanmar borderlands.

Strategic borderland regimes in South Asia: an overview

Borderland regimes have been central to the hegemonic nation-state building process in South Asia. Hegemonic nation-state-building in this study is understood as calculated attempts made by states to direct their functions toward strengthening the institutions and to increase their capabilities to manage and control the external territories. Scholars argue that in the late 1940s and 50s states in South Asia were 'deeply concerned with securing control of the borderland by means of expanding their bureaucratic power, beefing up paramilitary forces and homogenizing the borderland population' (Schendel 2005, 257). In the case of India, the postcolonial state-building process coincided with militarizing the borderlands, particularly on the western frontiers. Underlying tensions on border claims between India-Pakistan and India-China contributed to the shift in the official discourses on borderlands and managing the borderland polities. In Northeast India, after the Chinese occupation of the Thagla Ridge in September 1962 in Arunachal Pradesh, borderlands were transformed from 'neglected zones,' not so much from a political economy perspective but to a large extent from a military perspective, due to changing power dynamics at a geopolitical level (Verma 2016). Managing the strategic peripheral borderlands by allocating resources toward road construction became a priority and symbolized demonstration of military bureaucratic and administrative structures much to the discontent of people dwelling in the marginal borderlands where peripheralization was imminent. Since then, despite problems of difficult terrain, lack of adequate transportation and communication infrastructure and lack of support from the local population, Border Roads Organization constructed about 681.13 kilometers of roads along the international border in Arunachal Pradesh (PIB, MOD 2018). About 1110.83 Kilometers of road construction are in progress (PIB, MOD 2018).

India shares 4096 km long international borders with Bangladesh through Meghalaya, Assam and West Bengal. The physical demarcation of the border is based on the 1971 Treaty with Bangladesh. The India–Myanmar border based on colonial boundaries of 1940s and an Agreement signed in 1967 passes through the states of Nagaland, Arunachal Pradesh, Mizoram and Manipur. The India Nepal border based on Anglo-Nepal Treaty of 1816 passes through West Bengal, Uttaranchal and Bihar and the India-Bhutan border accepted through the Treaty of Friendship, 1950 passes through West Bengal, Arunachal Pradesh and Assam.

Borderlands in South Asia were created through the process of political partition of the subcontinent. Extreme forms of violence accompanied partition and created conditions for ethnic expulsion, breakdown in political order, flow of refugees across borders, threats and demands for further territorial divisions at the subnational levels. As a consequence, devising rigid boundaries both real and imaginary and border regimes became essential. External borders and security regimes were created while delimiting external sovereignties, through regulation of cross-border economic exchanges, securitization and militarization of borders along the eastern and western frontiers of India. Erection of barriers and border security regimes was to prevent not only the free flow of goods and people but also to put a check on internal security threats.

Borderlands in South Asia acquired significance in this particular context. These geographical margins were heavily impacted by partition. Cross-border networks such as socioeconomic activities were soon disrupted as Schendel notes due to erection of barriers:

> Before partition the Bengal-Assam-Arakan region had been integrated into a web of complex economic ties. The region inhabited by tens of millions of people, had a strong agricultural base and a large variety of industrial zones.

For many centuries it had been linked to global commercial networks, mainly through agro industries producing silk and cotton textiles, indigo, opium, tea, rice, sugar and jute fabrics. The events of 1947–48 precipitated what can perhaps best be described as the political assassination of this regional economy.

(Schendel 2005, 148)

At the same time, these regions became sites of illegal crossings of 'undocumented transactions and criminal networks,' which further necessitated the re-bordering practices like fences and security check gates. These practices continued until 1980s, 1990s and early 2000s. In late 1980s, the Government of India decided to construct concertina wire fencing along the 75-mile land border on the western frontier, between Punjab on the Indian side and Pakistan. Border fences were designed to restrain the movements of illegal weapons and insurgents. Border fences in the western zone however, failed to completely stop the transgressions. Illegal border crossings continue through other means like tunneling, bribery of border guards and use of forged documents to penetrate the protected territory. Unlike the western frontiers, postcolonial states on the eastern frontiers of South Asia have not been able to establish physical barriers or construct border fences. Precolonial kinship ties and everyday networks mark the spatial geographies of eastern borderlands. Cross-border ties continue to exist along the porous India-Bangladesh border and the India–Myanmar borderlands. On the Myanmar side, India had a special arrangement called the Free Movement Regime (FMR) that permitted free movement of ethnic tribes, within 16 km across the international boundary. The government in India recently took steps to build roads and also fence the area. The India–Myanmar Friendship Road, also called the Tamu-Kalewa-Kalemyo road, for instance, was initiated by India.

FIGURE 2.1   India–Myanmar Friendship Road.

Source: Fieldwork, April, 2016

FIGURE 2.2   Movement of people on the India–Myanmar Border (along FMR).

Source: Fieldwork, April, 2016

To sum up this part of the discussion, borderlands along the eastern frontiers in South Asia feature multifaceted cross-border networks that existed in the region since precolonial times. These networks contributed to a complex web of interdependence and shaped ethnic, local and translocal identities of people living across the borderlands. India and Myanmar used various strategies to integrate the borderlands. The attempts at integration, co-optation and coercion met with resistance and added to prolonged peripheralization. Often, these borderlands were converted into zones of extreme violence, disorder and defiance exhibited in various forms of anti-state resistance. Cynthia Enloe's work on ethnicity and state building perhaps rounds up this debate (Enloe 1980). Enloe's writing on ethnocentric, majoritarian and highly centralized policies adopted by state-building elites is illustrative of how political elites have a tendency to ethnicize the bureaucracy by creating ethnic security maps. Enloe argues,

> A wide-ranging survey of state militaries, past and present, reveals that in a majority of cases the military has served chiefly to divide the citizenry on either class of ethnic lines. In many instances the military's impact was even more deleterious for genuine nation-building in so far as the military became so intimately identified with one ethnic group, which controlled its policy making, that other social groups identify the state structure as the special resource of one community to the exclusion of the others.
>
> *(Enloe 1980)*

Where the conditions of enduring linkages between the state and nation are either unclear or weak and where the regime is highly involved in augmenting the political resources of the dominant ethnicity, distribution of economic resources and policies are skewed and strongly based on patron-client networks constructed around ethnic loyalties. These conditions were noticeable in Burma where the tatmadew regime sought ethnocratic nationalist policies to forcibly integrate peripheral ethnic communities (Enloe 1980; Ellinwood and Enloe 1981).

Circulation of violence and socio-cultural relations in India–Myanmar borderlands, with a focus on the two case studies chosen for this study is examined against the backdrop of these theoretical underpinnings and postcolonial developments.

Borderlands and ethnicity: historical background

India and Myanmar share an international land boundary of 1643 km. Mountainous ranges mark the terrain along the international boundary. The Alpine-Himalayan mountain belt turns southwards through Myanmar and forms the Patkai belt of mountains (Park 2018). Further south, the Patkai hills, also known as Patkai Bum in India, joins the Chin hills on the Myanmar side, the Lushai hills on the Indian side and the Naga hills along the Indian borderlands. These ranges are further subdivided into a 'number of parallel and sub-parallel ranges intervened by river valleys' (Dikshit and Dikshit 2013). The Manipur river flows southwards into Myanmar through 'a deep gorge between Lumbang and Falam and the Chin hills before it merges with the Myittha river, a tributary of the Chindwin and finally the Irrawaddy river in Myanmar' (Johnson 2007, 67). Similarly, the Tizu river passes through the Naga hills and flows northwest and joins the Chindwin river in Myanmar. The international border continues along the Kolodyne (pronounced as Kaladan) river, which originates in the Chin state of Myanmar, then takes a northward turn and forms the river boundary between the borderlands of India and Myanmar. Kolodyne flows further north, meets the Tio (Tyao) river and heads northwest into the state of Mizoram in India, where the river is locally termed as Chhimtuipui (Singh 2017). On the southern side of Mizoram, the Kaladan river, part of which forms a boundary between India and Myanmar, meanders through Chin and Rakhine states of Myanmar before it falls into the Bay of Bengal at Sittwe, the capital of Rakhine state (Seekins 2017).

The India–Myanmar border passes along the states of Manipur, Mizoram, Nagaland and Arunachal Pradesh. Manipur has a long porous international border of 398 km with Myanmar (Das and Thomas 2005, 1). The India–Myanmar border was originally an administrative line between the provinces of British India, Burma and Assam until April 1, 1937. The British colonial government separated the jurisdiction of Burma from British India, under the Government of Burma Act, 1935. A brief historical overview of the colonial occupation of the region reveals that the British established its commercial contacts with the kingdom of Ava (Burma) in 1619 and set up factories in Syriam (Rangoon) (Topich and Leitich 2013, 46–47). Formal occupation of the Arakan and Tenessarim on the Burmese side and Assam led by Ahoms, Manipur, Cachar and Jaintia on the British Indian side, took place by the British government in 1826. In 1834, the boundary was demarcated between

Manipur and Chin hills and in 1837, the Patkai range was accepted as a boundary between Assam and Burma (The Geographer 1968; Phanjoubam 2016). By 1852, the joint forces of the British army and navy annexed the port of Martaban, the city of Rangoon and Pegu. In 1886 the British government occupied Upper Burma and included it as a province of British India (Topich and Leitich 2013, 48).

Meanwhile, the British government sent expeditions to the Chin and Lushai hills in 1871. The expeditions were aimed to control the raids conducted by the tribes in the Lushai hills where the British had already established its commercial interests in the tea gardens. Due to these aggressions, in 1881, the British government under the Political Agent Colonel Johnston appointed a Commission to 'lay down a definite boundary between Manipur and Burma by replacing the imaginary line, known as the Pemberton line earlier drawn northwards from the Kubo (present Kabaw in Tamu region of Myanmar) valley' (Mackenzie 2012, 209). In 1882, the Commission completed the survey and marked the boundary of the eastern frontier between Burma and Manipur. The boundary stretched from the

> eastern slopes of the Malain range to Namia river, a few hundred yards east of Kangal Thanna and turns east to the Talain river and then proceeds down the Napanga river where it passes through a gorge in Kusom range. The boundary was marked with pillars and a road connecting Namia river and Talain river.
>
> *(Mackenzie 2012, 210)*

In 1901, the colonial government demarcated the Lushai-Chin hills boundary (The Geographer 1968; Phanjoubam 2016). The colonial boundary was inherited by India and Myanmar.

Although the British colonial government had less commercial interest in a geographically remote and relatively resource-poor Manipur valley, their control and regulatory practices had a deep impact on the precolonial institutions in the valley and the hills. British interest in the region was premised on grounds of opening a buffer state through Kabaw valley and that traversed the entire frontier region of Manipur and Burma. Distribution of power and authority during the colonial period created newer forms of asymmetry between the valley and the hills. These asymmetries between the Imphal valley and the disintegrated peripheries in the Naga and Kuki hills continued as legacies in the postcolonial period. In the postcolonial period the local polities in the hills witnessed resistance against incorporation into the larger Meitei nation and the dominant state-making enterprise. The postcolonial period also witnessed intense forms of resistance led by the politically dominant Meiteis in Manipur against the forcible merger of Manipur in 1949 with the Indian Union.

The land boundary agreement between India and Myanmar finally took place in Rangoon on March 10, 1967 (The Geographer 1968, 6). Both the countries agreed that there is a need to modify the traditional boundary that India and Myanmar inherited from the British period. The Instrument of Rectification was signed on

May 30, 1967 to bring modifications to the international boundary. However, the actual boundary has not been demarcated.

The preceding discussion reveals how colonial and postcolonial boundaries were reconstructed and negotiated as a part of the state-building practices in Myanmar and India. These hegemonic geopolitical practices affected the everyday lives of borderlands. The historical narrations of the border communities in the Imphal valley (Meiteis) and the hill tribes (Kukis and Nagas) also point toward the permeability and cross-border historical connections not only in the form of wars and conquests but also in the form of trade as well as marriages that were established in the precolonial period. Overlapping territories, and absence of distinctive ethnic identities as well as coherent political boundaries between groups who lived in these peripheries later contributed to intense discord on 'membership,' rights and group claims on power divisions and territorial identities. Cross-border Kukis in Manipur and Myanmar may fit this category. The Kuki-Chins are cross-border ethnic groups presently dispersed in the districts of Sylhet and Chittagong hill tracts of Bangladesh, parts of Myanmar, Manipur, Mizoram, Tripura and North Cachar hills (Dima Hasao) in Assam in Northeast India.

As far as origin and description of ethnic hills tribes are concerned, records suggest that the terms were used to mean closely allied clans with well-marked characteristics belonging to the Tibeto-Burman stock. As Lokendra notes, "The hills with their heterogeneous slash and burn ethnic populations, were incorporated into the political order in a patron–client relationship with annual presentation of tributes."[1] Shakespear's historical account on the Lushei Kuki reveals that the term 'Kukis was loosely applied to most of the inhabitants of the interior hills beyond the Chittagong hill tracts' (Shakespear 1912). He further noted that

> in Cachar the term generally meant some family of the Thado or Khawthlang clan, locally distinguished as old Kukis (who made appearances in Cachar in 1800) and new Kukis (Thadous who came to Manipur from the Chin-Lushai hills in the later part of the 18th century). In Lushai hills, the term was hardly ever employed, having been superseded by the term Lushai. In the Chin hills and generally on the Burma border all these clans were called Chins.
>
> *(Shakespear 1912)*

Similarly, J. Ware Edgar in his account on the Lushai and other Kookies (Kukis) written in 1871 notes, 'The Kookie villages were found in Manipur, Sylhet, Cachar, Tipperah and possibly in the hill tracks of Chittagong. These settlements came up after the Kookies were driven out of Lushai hills' (Mackenzie 2012, 426). 'The Kookies,' as Edgar wrote 'were divided into different clans ruled by chiefs from each clan such as the Paitoos, Thados, Saihreems and Hraltes amongst others' (Mackenzie 2012). Most of the tribes came under the influence of Christianity with traces of traditional practices. Kukis, as some scholars suggest, have overlapping identities undesirable to the cultural tradition when a dominant nation-state in the making tries to imagine and impose a common identity on the minorities living within its borders (Haokip 2014, 161). British colonial expansion and the bordering practices had implications on the popular imaginings and the integration of these minorities into the state-building projects of the colonial and (post)colonial state. The dilemma faced by the peripheral minorities was whether to assert their historical 'spaces of multiple sovereignties' or to submit to the dominant cultural identity (Scott 2010). The internal relations between the tribes in the bordering hills of Manipur is best described by Edgar in these words, 'All these were people of the same race, speaking dialects of the same language, wearing the same dress, and having same customs, form of polity and religious belief. But they were constantly at war with each other' (Mackenzie 2012, 426).

Mizoram shares a border of 410 km with Myanmar. The Chin state in Myanmar has contiguous land borders with the postcolonial state of Mizoram in India. The Mizo Hills district, currently, the federal unit of Mizoram was earlier known as Lushai Hills. British administrative records referred to the tribes in the Lushai hills as Kookies. The term Lushais as a distinct tribe acquired recognition in 1860s when the British Government took a policy to deal with the 'fierce and predatory tribes of the North-eastern frontier of India' (Woodthorpe 1873, 3). Existing historical accounts reveal that the Lushais belonged to three different tribes: the Lushais, Pois and Paites/Chins.[2] The Zoumis are mostly populated in the Chin state of Burma and the states of Mizoram and Manipur in India. The Chins in Burma in the pre-British period failed to maintain complete independence from the Burmese kings. The Chin people inhabiting the Chin Special Division of the northwestern part of Myanmar share a lot in common with the groups across the borders in Mizoram, especially the Chin sub-group known as the Pawi.[3] As George A. Theodorson argued, 'The major distinction is between the Northern Chins (called Mar) and the Southern Chins (called Pawi). The Northern Chins are more closely related to the Lushai and belong to the Lushai-Kuki tribes' (Theodorson 1964). In the 1890s the Chin-Lushai hills and the plains bordering the hills were annexed by the British, which further brought the 'transborder tribesmen' into the fold of the colonial state-building process.[4] The colonial project of annexation was also aimed at introducing law and order in the hills. Annexation of Lushai hills conducted in 1889 was followed by the spread of Christian missionaries in 1894.

Ethnic relations between cross-border communities in the Lushai borderlands between India and Myanmar can therefore be traced back to the precolonial history of the borderlands. Formal and informal networks between the borderland ethnic groups continued during the nation-state building process in India and Myanmar. Evidence of assertion of cross-border ethnic linkages can be drawn from the activities of the Mizo Union during the nation-state making process in India and the Zomi People's Convention after the formation of Mizoram as a separate state within India in 1987. These groups defy the official boundary demarcation between India and Myanmar. The First Zomi World Convention held in May 1988 in the border region of Champai in Mizoram reiterated the demand for the unification of Zo territories in Manipur, Mizoram in India and the Chin state of Burma (Pau 2007). State-building efforts in postcolonial Myanmar led to restrictions on civil liberties, forced labor, unlawful detention, intimidation, extrajudicial killings and targeted attacks on the Chin ethnic minorities.[5] Mobility of Chins continued in the wake of state-building efforts, under the former military regime in Myanmar. Chins were forced to cross borders and migrate to India, mostly bordering places like Mizoram, rejuvenating cross-border ethnicties.

(Post)colonial boundary making and the larger nation-building project of the Indian state therefore subsumed cross-border historical mobility of the ethnic tribes in the Lushai, Chin, Naga and Kuki hills in the borderlands of India–Myanmar. Self-governing asymmetrical power structures were created to integrate the diverse historical and cultural groups in these borderlands. While these power structures were created to accommodate local tribal interests, they subsequently unleashed intense forms of resistance embedded in the politics of defiance and violence of the larger nation-state project and demands for unification of cross-border ethnic tribal minorities across the borders in India and Upper Burma.

Recent initiatives of boundary demarcation further added to complexities of integration of the borderlands when the Indian government decided to construct the border fence in 2013. Borderland resistance became visible when the border pillar 78 was replaced by border pillar 21 erected in Moreh district and further when the government decided that 99 border pillars would be constructed in the border region (*The Sangai Express* 2016).

Re-bordering practices in India–Myanmar borderlands: an analysis of circulation of socio-cultural relations and resistance in Moreh

Moreh, a semi-urban settlement in the border region between India and Myanmar, attracted the attention of journalists, policy makers and researchers in the recent decades. Moreh, located in Chandel district of Manipur has a multiethnic population of about 16,847 persons as per the district census of 2011. The religious distribution of the settlement reveals that about 56.67 percent of the population comprises of Christians, 26.14 percent comprises of Hindus, 13.97 percent are Muslims and the rest of the population comprises of religious minorities like Sikhs, Jains and Buddhists (Moreh Religion Data 2011). Located at the interface of transnational interaction and state-territoriality, Moreh symbolizes inter-ethnic conflict and asymmetrical power relations in the borderlands. This remote town along the borders embodies complex and multifaceted networks and interdependencies between borderland communities including tribes, insurgents, drug and gemstone traders and commercial sex workers. The border town illustrates how these illegal networks in the borderlands are deeply embedded in the process of state control and state re-bordering practices.

In the recent years, the government of India decided to construct border fences between the India–Myanmar border. In 2010, the Ministry of Home Affairs, India approved the fencing of border between Border Pillars 79–81 in the Moreh sector in Manipur (Statement Made by Minister of State 2016). Accordingly, the wildlife/

forest clearance was obtained from the Ministry of Forests and Environment. The Ministry of Home Affairs approved the Detailed Project Report (DPR) with the cost estimates of Rs 35.99 crores for the proposed fencing project (*The Assam Tribune* 2018). By 2014 about 3.47 km of border fencing was subsequently completed in the first phase of border fencing between Moreh Gate no. 2 to Govajang, which started in 2010.

Govajang, which was selected as a microlevel field site for this study, is a border village located between border pillars 79 and 80 in Moreh.[6] As per the population census of 2011, the village comprises of 35 households with a total population of 123. Thadou Kukis constitute more than 98 percent of the total population of the village. The primary source of livelihood in the village is rice cultivation. The villagers mostly practice shifting cultivation. Border fencing that was initiated by the central government between pillar 79 and 80 passes through Govajang village. Once the border fencing gets completed Govajang would be divided between India and Myanmar. Villagers claimed that the village church, playground and acres of land in the hills would be merged with Myanmar. The village chief of Govajang expressed a similar situation during our fieldwork to Govajang.

Re-bordering practices, however, met with resistance at the local level in the India–Myanmar borderlands, especially in the border villages like Govajang. It was reported that the village residents showed defiance against the display of reterritorialization and control of the borderlands by the central government authorities. Fear of redemarcation of cultivable land, shifting of families to the Myanmar side and moreover the fear of being disconnected with ethnic kin across the border mobilized the residents to protest against the construction of border fencing through Govajang.

Village residents expressed how the erection of border fences would disrupt the socioeconomic ties and the circulation of cultural relations among the Kukis living on the other side of the border in Myanmar. A report suggests that local people complained about the disruption of cultural and economic relations between people residing on both sides of the fence. T.H. Thomsing, ex-president of Rural Peoples Development Federation, expressed, 'The fence will also divide the villagers, as it would be very difficult for them to meet for cultural and other village activities' (Thokchom 2013). The village residents revealed that

> the actual border was along the foothills, while the fence was being constructed further up the hill. They also expressed that there was a difference of 500 meters between the original border line and the line along which the border fence was actually being constructed.
>
> *(Thokchom 2013)*

Another interview narrative revealed the following:

> The construction of the fencing by the government security forces was made possible by the Govajang village chief who gave the permission to the construction authority and in return it is said that the chief got the compensation. The actual compensation is still awaited.[7]

Another participant added,

> The fencing was also done in a hasty manner with many irregularities
> which involves certain vested interests. Originally the fencing process was
> a localized issue of the Govajang village that was losing the land but now
> with the involvement of many civil society groups the issue has become
> larger and the media also reports it as a Manipur-Myanmar border pillar
> disputes and territorial land protection measures by constructing the bor-
> der pillars and fencing to demarcate the villages. In the process, the lives of
> the villagers and our age-old connections get affected.[8]

Student activist organizations and civil society groups such as the Rural Peoples
Development Federation, the Kuki Students' organization, the Hill Tribal Council
and the Kuki Chiefs Association among others also raised objections to the contested
border pillars and the way the borders are being demarcated without much con-
formity to the local interests. As a result of the local protests, the state government of
Manipur appealed the center to redemarcate the boundary in the contested villages.

Similar evidence has been collected from Kwatha Khunou, a small village located
near border pillar 81, along the borders of India and Myanmar in Tengoupal district.
Kuntaung, a Myanmarese village mostly inhabited by Kuki tribes, on the other side
of the border is a few kilometers away from Kwatha Khunou. Kwatha Khunou comprises of a population of about 120 villagers. The village comprises of both Meiteis
and Thadou Kukis. The village is located on a hilly terrain and the residents share
cross-border ethnic and social ties, including matrimonial ties with the people living
on both sides of the border. Local narratives suggest that people on both sides of these
border villages share traditional social norms and neighborly ties. They also share
common resources like water from a stream called Namjet Lok, which flows along
the boundary between Kwatha Khunou and Kuntaung.[9] The terrain on the other
side of river is covered with rubber plantations and vast tracts of agricultural land.

Kwatha Khunou has been a site of conflict and contestation between the state
of Manipur and between India and Myanmar on one side and the village residents
on the other. The conflict is based on the claims that the original border pillar no.
81 established in the late 1960s has been shifted to a location about 300 meters
away from the original position. Subsidiary pillars have also recently been erected in
March and June 2018, between border pillars 81 to 82 in Khunou to make it easier
for the construction of the newly demarcated border pillar. Villagers claimed that
the new location of these pillars would lead to encroachment of the village land on
the Indian side of the territory, particularly Manipur that would have to part away
with about 400 meters of forest area in the village. An interview participant added,

> Other than Khunou, half of Molphei, a Kuki village inhabited by Thadou
> Kuki community will be demarcated inside Myanmar after the subsidiary
> border pillar gets erected. The fixation of the pillar has taken place just beside
> the Mayokpha tree (Arjuna myrobalan), which is considered sacred and wor-
> shipped by the Meiteis of Kwatha Khunou, will now be divided due to the
> construction of the subsidiary pillar.[10]

FIGURE 2.3 Border pillar no. 81, Kwatha Khunuo (near Namjet Lok River).

Source: Fieldwork in Moreh, July 2018, Courtesy: NGO, United Committee Manipur

Moreover, temporary pillars have been constructed under the supervision of the Assam Rifles between border pillars 81 to 82 in these villages. The pillars have signs that demarcate the territory, written in both English and Devanagri scripts on the Indian side and Burmese script on the other side of the pillar. The claims and counterclaims of territorial occupation resumed and led to further conflicts in June 2018 when the District Commissioner visited Kwatha Khunou to oversee the construction of the subsidiary pillars.

On the other hand, the competing claims on some of the contested villages by the Myanmarese army and the villagers along the India–Myanmar borderlands added to the complexities of securitization and hybrid governance structures that prevail in these borderlands. Reports suggest that the village residents on the Myanmar side with the assistance of the Myanmarese army made attempts to forcibly occupy the territories of two border villages located in Moreh in the Tengnoupal district of Manipur. The encroachers tried to occupy the territory on the Indian side by dismantling and erecting their own border pillars between the border pillars no. 49 to 89 in Tengnoupal and Chandel districts in Manipur along the border.[11] The intruders also shifted the border pillars between 32 to 48 in Churachandpur and Pherzawl districts, and 90 to 130 in Ukhrul and Kamjong districts to demarcate their own territory by occupying the villages. The government of India earlier demarcated these border pillars.[12]

These incidents of encroachment by Myanmarese villagers demonstrate how borderland communities dispute statist claims on the borderlands. Borderlanders along the border villages in Moreh tried to resist and undo the re-bordering practices of the Indian state. This further adds to the complexities and hybrid governance in the India–Myanmar borderlands.

As a response to the growing protests, an all-party delegation from Manipur visited Delhi during the UPA government and raised the controversies on border fencing. The central government decided to send a team to visit the contested site. Accordingly, the Surveyor General of India visited the disputed villages. The team of ministers and government officials made the decision that the construction of the fencing along the contested border pillars would be stopped until further notice.

The protestors made further demands to conduct fresh surveys in the disputed villages. While responding to these demands, on December 21, 2015, the government of India sent a team of surveyors to Satang and Kwatha Khunou villages in Moreh, Manipur. The District Commissioner of Chandel district accompanied the central government official. Joint meetings were held several times in 2015. The Indian authorities and the authorities from the Myanmar side participated in the joint survey. The joint survey team was in favor of the construction of the border fencing. Nevertheless, the Congress government of Manipur led by Ibobi Singh supported the protests and the local issues raised by the village residents. The state government remarked in the following words,

> There is an apprehension that the border fencing work would affect 11 villages including Kwatha Khunou, Satang, Leibi, Lamlong, Wakshu, Chatong, Saivol, Morelthel and Chanringphai. The total population of these villages is around 4000 and all of them speak Manipuri (Meiteilon) fluently which implies none of them are immigrants from Myanmar. Now the border fencing work is all set to be resumed and subsidiary pillars have been already erected. As a consequence, people of all the 11 villages are facing a critical situation where they may lose Indian citizenship even though they possess voter cards, ration cards and job cards.
>
> *(The Sangai Express 2016)*

The agitation further delayed the process of construction that was decided upon by both the Indian and the Myanmarese authorities. In 2018, the NDA government resumed its discussions on border fencing, border security and management with its counterpart in Myanmar. Accordingly, the government sent a team of senior officials to Manipur to conduct the updated surveys and resume border fencing along the eastern borders. The team constituted of the Surveyor General of India, Lt Gen. Girish Kumar, the joint secretary (Border Management), Ministry of External Affairs Sripriya Ranganathan and joint secretary (Northeast), Ministry of Home Affairs, A. V. Dharma Reddy. The team of officials with the help of the BJP Chief Minister of Manipur, Biren Singh and the state government officials interacted with the village residents of Kwatha Khunou, members of political parties and civil society organizations in Manipur. The Joint Secretary remarked, 'Based on our records, the position of the border pillar is correct but the villagers said as per the historical data, it was located somewhere else. We will see the record and consider the villagers' complaint' (Singh 2018).

The preceding interview narratives and the fieldwork indicate how border fencing becomes a visible site of the presence of the state in the borderlands. These bordering activities in Moreh emphasize security, protection and the erection of border fences by the Indian government in an area where demarcation of concrete borders is yet to take place. They also indicate how these practices of border securitization and the display of power impact the livelihood practices of the borderlands not just once but in everyday forms. As the interview narratives conducted in Govajang and Kwatha Khunou villages in 2016 reveal, the erection of border pillars by the government impeded the everyday lives and livelihood practices of the village residents such as cross-border agricultural practices that are an important source of livelihood in these borderlands.[13]

Summary and final thoughts

This chapter draws on multidisciplinary perspectives on borders and borderlands to examine the state-territoriality, circulation of socio-cultural relations and resistance in everyday lives in the borderlands. The chapter uses borders to understand the continuous process of borderization and hegemonic nation-state building exercise that takes place in the borderlands. We tried to analyze how borderland people negotiate with the nationalist and hegemonic nation-making practices. This approach allows us to understand two perspectives, (a) territoriality, geopolitical traditions and the role of 'bounded territorial spaces' nested in statism and cartographic exercises and (b) cross-border interactions, socio-cultural ties, economic networking and de-bordering practices. The chapter uses these various perspectives to examine the inter-linkages between ethnicity, security and connectivity in the context of India–Myanmar relations. While using borders as a sociopolitical construct and a geopolitical necessity we adopt a bottom-up approach to examine the grounded realities of governance, territoriality and the circulation of relations including, the engagement of people through transborder activities and economic interdependence across border on an everyday basis in India–Myanmar borderlands.

The chapter argued that postcolonial nation-state building was associated with domestic policies to control mobility of border communities. It led to 'bordering in' and 'bordering out' of ethnic minorities within 'loosely' defined geographical entities. Sharper lines were being drawn between marginal groups located at the edges of the nation-state, in the India–Myanmar borderlands and the hegemonic interpretation of national identities. Border redrawing in colonial and postcolonial states as discussed in the chapter thus separated societies with varying cultural identities, created divides and barriers to movement and communication between kin and communities belonging to same ethnicity for instance, Kukis, Nagas, Meiteis and Chins in India–Myanmar borderlands. In the colonial period imaginary borders and military pillars were drawn that was necessary and premised on grounds of expanding British commercial interests and the opening of trade routes that traversed this region. Small wars were conducted to manage borders, to maintain peace in the borderland frontiers where the colonial rulers encountered guerilla uprisings led by the 'frontier tribes.' Colonial brute forces were deployed to manage turbulent borders. As one military historian puts it 'In North-East sector, four battalions of Assam Rifles including Gurkha regiment were deployed to contain Kuki rebellion in 1917' (Roy 2015, 60–70). Alexander Mackenzie who was instrumental in making the frontier policy during colonial India, traced the political relations of the British Government with the Hill tribes of the Frontier and noted in his report that a frontier policy was pertinent for 'the tract which embraced the whole of the hill ranges north, east and south of Assam valley, as well as the western slopes of the great mountain system lying between Bengal and independent Burma' (Mackenzie 2012, 1). These kinds of policies became more crucial in the postcolonial states, which inherited the colonial demarcations that 'were often carved up with little regard to the coherence of historic, cultural, and ethnic zones' (Schendel 2005).

Physical features of borders became more visible in the postcolonial period and were conceived in our mental maps in the form of fences and armed border security forces. Redrawing of borders of the Indian subcontinent in 1947 however acted a point of departure and disconnectedness. The important links of art, culture and commerce discontinued. Unlike the profound sociopolitical and economic transformations in the core owing to their incorporation into the colonial policies and philosophies, these regions were excluded from imperial patterns of legislation and were thus accorded a marginal standing. Distribution of power and local governance created newer forms of asymmetries. As another historian puts it in these words, 'these are regions that were disconnected fragments and victims of cartographic surgery.'[14] Local polities in these regions witnessed movements and resistance against 'incorporation into the framework of colonial state and postcolonial nation-building.'

These theoretical underpinnings were represented in this chapter and we briefly discussed how the India–Myanmar borderlands experienced postcolonial challenges of integrating marginal frontier communities and the local polities into the larger nation-state building exercises. Despite continuous re-bordering practices, the porosity of the borderlands and the cross-border connections historically shared by ethnic communities in these borderlands adds to the complexities of state-territoriality and the transnational strategic and security interactions that the two states are trying to create through these borderlands along the boundaries of India and Myanmar. Moreover, as the case study analysis reveals in this chapter the imposition of control and territoriality over the inherited borders from time to time marked with the erection of border pillars, military check gates and fences, by postcolonial states, evoked resistance from below. Borderland resistance as this study reveals was witnessed in the India–Myanmar borderlands. The microlevel analysis of fencing and the erection of border pillars in the Govajang and Kwatha Khunou villages further demonstrate how militarized borders have consequences on cross-border mobility and lives of borderlanders. The violent assertions of the borderlanders in the borderlands of India and Myanmar further indicate how border securitization practices may have consequences on postcolonial state formation and the problems of integration of borderlands into the national imaginings of socio-economic development.

While considering bilateral relations between India and Myanmar it is pertinent to emphasize the localized mundane encounters in the borderlands. We try to understand how the India–Myanmar borderlands negotiate with the transborder transitions in the newly developing political economy and how the state reordering practices leave the impact on the borderlands that are deep, profound and lasting. In the recent decades, the attempt has been to transform these 'disturbed peripheries' into productive centers of a flourishing and integrated economy through mega infrastructural projects such as the Trans-Asian Highway and the Kaladan multi modal project. The national objective is to rejuvenate older links. It remains to be seen how the postcolonial borderlands in India and Myanmar responds to these currents of transformations and engage in the transnational development projects in the face of complex governing structures, local incapacities and the politics of violent defiance.

Notes

1 Discussion with the eminent historian in Imphal, April (2016). Also see, Arambam (2004, 67).
2 One of the British historical accounts reveals that the Lushais are a mix of Kooki (Kuki) and Burmese tribes. Mackenzie (2012, 293).
3 The Chin tribal groups are subdivided into more than 60 ethnolinguistic categories, spread out in Chin villages in Chin Hills of Burma and the neighboring regions of Bangladesh and India's Northeastern states of Manipur and Mizoram.
4 A term used to describe the tribes in Lushai hills by Nirmal Nibedon. See Nibedon (2013).
5 The Chin state in Burma became the battleground during WWII, between the British forces and the Japanese forces allied with the Burmese nationalist leaders like Aung San. The nationalists formed the Burmese Independence Army, fought against the colonial forces during the late 1930s and early 1940s and took control of Burma proper in May 1942. The Chins supported the British. In 1943 the Japanese occupied Burma and declared Burma as an independent nation. Later, when Japanese forces refused to give away the power to the nationalists, the latter shifted their alliance and started negotiations with the British seeking assistance to expel the Japanese. Aung San, the nationalist leader also negotiated with the ethnic minorities including the Chins, Kachins amongst others and signed the Panglong agreement in February 1947, which guaranteed the establishment of the Interim government to be led to Aung San. The agreement also allowed

autonomy for ethnic minorities. Failure of implementation of the Panglong Agreement led to discontentment and set the stage for ethnic conflicts in the minority states.

6 These pillars are located at about 3 km north of Moreh.
7 Interview conducted (June 12, 2018) with Rajendro (Name changed), Moreh, Imphal.
8 Interview conducted (June 12, 2018) with Shivachnadra (name changed), Moreh, Imphal.
9 Interview conducted (July 22, 2018) with Iboyaima Kshetrimayum, Moreh, Imphal.
10 Interview conducted (June 12, 2016) in Moreh, Imphal.
11 Interview conducted (June 12, 2016). with N. Rajendro (Name changed), Moreh, Imphal. Also see, Chakraborty (May 11, 2011).
12 Interview conducted (June 12, 2016). with Rajendro (Name changed), Moreh, Imphal.
13 Interview (June 22, 2016) with Rajendro (name changed) conducted in Moreh, Imphal.
14 Schendel (December 2002). Cited in Misra (2011).

References

Arambam, Lokendra (2004). "Historical Organisation of Public Spaces: Ritual Theatre State in Pre-Colonial Manipur." In *Folklore, Public Sphere and Civil Society*, edited by Kaushal Molly and M. D. Muthukumaraswamy. New Delhi: Indira Gandhi National Centre for the Arts, p. 67.

The Assam Tribune (2018). "Centre Firms Plans to Fence Border Areas." April 12, http://www.assamtribune.com/scripts/mdetails.asp?id=apr1218/at057 (accessed September 10, 2018).

Barth, Frederick (1969). *Ethnic Groups and Boundaries: The Social Organization of Culture Difference*. IL: Waveland Press.

Baud, Michael and Willem van Schendel (1997). "Toward a Comparative History of Borderlands." *Journal of World History* 8 (2): 19.

Chakraborty, Sujit Kumar (2011). "Myanmar Pushes into Indian Territory, Occupies Manipur Villages." *Rediff News*, May 11, https://www.rediff.com/news/special/myanmar-pushes-into-indian-territory-occupies-manipur-villages/20180511.htm (accessed February 10, 2018).

Das, Gurudas and C. J. Thomas (2005). "Economy of Myanmar: Trends, Structure and Implications for Border Trade with India's Northeast." In *Indo-Myanmar Border Trade: Status Problems and Potentials*, edited by Gurudas Das, N. Bijoy Singh and C. J. Thomas. New Delhi: Akansha, p. 1.

Dikshit, K. R. and Jutta K. Dikshit (2013). *North-East India: Land, People and Economy*. Netherlands: Springer.

Elden, Stuart (2013). *The Birth of Territory*. Chicago: University of Chicago Press.

Ellinwood, Dewitt C. and Cynthia H. Enloe (eds.). (1981). *Ethnicity and the Military in Asia*. London: Transaction Publishers.

Enloe, Cynthia H. (1980). *Ethnic Soldiers: State Security in Divided Societies*. Athens, Georgia: The University of Georgia Press.

Gellner, David, N. (2013). *Borderland Lives in Northern South Asia*. Durham and London: Duke University Press.

The Geographer (1968). "International Boundary Study: Burma–India Boundary." Office of the Geographer Bureau of Intelligence and Research, No. 80, May 15, https://fall.fsulawrc.com/collection/LimitsinSeas/IBS080.pdf.

Golunov, Serghei (2016). "Border Fences in the Globalizing World: Beyond Traditional Geopolitics and Post-Positivist Approaches." In *Borders, Fences and Walls: State of Insecurity*, edited by Elisabeth Vallet. London: Routledge.

Government of India (2001). *Reforming the National Security System-Recommendations of the Group of Ministers*. New Delhi: Ministry of Defence.

Haokip, Jangkholam (2014). *Can God Save My Village? A Theological Study of Identity Among the Tribal People of North-East India with a Special Reference to the Kukis of Manipur*. UK: Langham Monographs, p. 161.

Haokip, Thonkholal (2015). *India's Look East Policy and the Northeast*. New Delhi: Sage Publications.

Hindustan Times (2018). "Two Rohingya Muslim Men Arrested in Manipur on Trafficking Charges," April 8, www.hindustantimes.com (accessed April 10, 2018).

The Imphal Free Press (2018). "UPF Condemns Moreh Firing, Says 'Peace Not Violence,'" July 13, www.ifp.co.in/ (accessed August 5, 2018).

Johnson, Robert G. (2007). *On the Back Road to Mandalay*. USA: Xulon Press.

Mackenzie, Alexander (2012). *History of the Relations of the Government with the Hill Tribes of the North*. Cambridge: Cambridge University Press, p. 209.

Misra, Sanghamitra (2011). *Becoming a Borderland: The Politics of Space and Identity in Colonial Northeastern India*. New Delhi: Routledge.

Moreh Religion Data (2011). www.census2011.co.in/data/town/801496-moreh-manipur.html (accessed February 12, 2018).

Nibedon, Nirmal (2013). *Mizoram: The Daggar Brigade*. New Delhi: Lancer Publishers.

Nugent, Paul (2012). "Border Towns and Cities in Comparative Perspective." In *A Companion to Border Studies*, edited by Thomas Wilson M. and Donald Hastings. Chichester: Wiley Blackwell, p. 558.

Park, Graham (2018). *Mountains: The Origins of the Earth's Mountain Systems*. Edinburgh: Dunedin Academic Press.

Passi, Anssi (2009). "Bounded Spaces in a 'Borderless World': Border Studies, Power and the Anatomy of Territory." *Journal of Power* 2 (2): 213–234.

Pau, Pum Khan (2007). "Administrative Rivalries on a Frontier: Problem of the Chin-Lushai Hills." *The Indian Historical Review* 34 (1): 187–209.

Phanjoubam, Pradip (2016). *The Northeast Question: Conflicts and Frontiers*. New Delhi: Routledge.

Press Information Bureau (2018). "Construction of Road Along the China Border, Government of India, Ministry of Defence." March 5, https://pib.gov.in/newsite/PrintRelease.aspx?relid=176947.

Roy, Kaushik (2015). *Frontiers, Insurgencies and Counterinsurgencies in South Asia: 1820–2013*. New Delhi: Routledge, pp. 60–70.

Saddiki, Said (2017). *World of Walls: The Structure, Roles and Effectiveness of Separation Barriers*, Cambridge, UK: Open Book Publishers.

The Sangai Express (2016). "Indo-Myanmar Border Fencing, Manipur CM Insists on Permanent Settlement." March 5.

The Sangai Express (2018a). "Fencing Attempt Halted," January 12, www.manipur.org/news/tag/moreh/ (accessed January 13, 2018).

The Sangai Express (2018b). "International Drug Cartel Busted, Members of Family Held," May 4, http://e-pao.net/GP.asp?src=11..050518.may18 (accessed May 10, 2018).

Schendel, Willem van (2002). "Geographies of Knowing, Geographies of Ignorance: Jumping Scale in Southeast Asia." *Society and Space*, December. Cited in Misra, Sanghamitra (2011). *Becoming a Borderland: The Politics of Space and Identity in Colonial Northeastern India*. New Delhi: Routledge.

Schendel, Willem van (2005). *The Bengal Borderland: Beyond State and Nation in South Asia*. London: Anthem Press, p. 257.

Scott, James (2010). *The Art of Not Being Governed: An Anarchist History of Upland Southeast Asia*. Singapore: NUS Press.

Seekins, Donald M. (2017). *Historical Dictionary of Burma (Myanmar)*. Lanham, MD: Rowman & Littlefield.

Shakespear, J. (1912). *The Lushei Kuki Clans*. London: Macmillan and Company.

Singh, Dhruv Sen (2017). *The Indian Rivers: Scientific and Socio-Economic Aspects*. Singapore: Springer.

Singh, Ngangbam Indrakanta (2018). "Delhi to Survey Manipur Pillars." *The Telegraph*, July 26, https://www.telegraphindia.com/states/north-east/delhi-to-survey-manipur-pillars/cid/1455914 (accessed September 15, 2018).

Statement Made by Minister of State, Home Affairs, Ministry of Home Affairs, Government of India (2016). November 16, https://mha.gov.in/MHA1/Par2017/pdfs/par2016-pdfs/ls-221116/1146.pdf (accessed January 20, 2018).

Su-Ann, Oh (2016). *Myanmar's Mountain and Maritime Borderscape: Local Practices, Boundary Making and Figured Words*. Singapore: ISEAS-Yusof Ishak Institute.

Theodorson, George A. (1964). "Minority Peoples in the Union of Burma." *Journal of Southeast Asian History* 5 (1) (March): 1–16.

Thokchom, Khelen (2013). "Fence Rips Through Manipur Villages-Indo-Myanmar Border Residents May End Up on Wrong Side of Barbed Wire." *The Telegraph*, July 29, https://www.telegraphindia.com/india/fence-rips-through-manipur-villages-indo-myanmar-border-residents-may-end-up-on-wrong-side-of-barbed-wire/cid/279446 (accessed February 18, 2018).

Topich, William J. and Keith A. Leitich (2013). *The History of Myanmar*. Santa Barbara, CA: Greenwood, pp. 46–47.

Verma, Shiv Kunal (2016). *1962: The War That Wasn't*. New Delhi: Aleph Book Company.

Wilson, Thomas M. and Hastings Donnan (2012). "Borders and Border Studies." In *A Companion to Border Studies*, edited by Thomas M. Wilson and Hastings Donnan. UK: Wiley Blackwell, p. 8.

Woodthorpe, Robert G. (1873). *The Lushai Expedition: 1871–1872*. London: Hurst and Blackett Publishers, p. 3.

3

CRISIS IN THE RAKHINE STATE OF MYANMAR

Bilateral relations with India in perspective

Mihir Bhonsale

The Southeast Asian country, Myanmar is at the center of the world's gravest humanitarian crisis. The exodus of an ethnic group known as 'Rohingya' the world over but referred to as 'Bengalis' in Myanmar has drawn global attention for the number of lives at stake and the severity of atrocities committed with alleged complicity of the Myanmar state. More than a million Rohingyas have fled the Rakhine state of Myanmar beginning from 1970 up to August 2018. Not recognized as citizens in Myanmar, these refugees have also taken to sea in search of safe shores and the countries they turned to in search of shelter have included Malaysia, Thailand and Indonesia. Through Bangladesh, Rohingya refugees have also entered India.

The cross-border movement of such a large number of people has political, strategic and cultural implications. The present chapter focuses on the Rohingya refugee crisis in the light of contemporary relations between India and Myanmar. Though, not strictly a bilateral issue between India and Myanmar, the Rohingya crisis has assumed a regional dimension. The Indian state's response to the Rakhine crisis needs to be assessed for two dimensions – one as a recipient of Rohingya people in the past one decade and second of its conduct of foreign relations with two neighbors crucial to her 'Act East' and 'Neighborhood First' policy – Myanmar and Bangladesh.

Background of the problem

On the eastern shores of the Bay of Bengal, cut off from the Irrawaddy valley by a series of near impassable Yoma mountains, lies the Rakhine state of Myanmar. It shares an international border with Chittagong Division of Bangladesh in the northwest. The northern Rakhine region and particularly the townships of Buthidaung and Maungdaw known till 1961 as the Mayu Frontier District that are adjoining to the Chittagong Division of Bangladesh are ethnically distinct from the rest of Rakhine state. Located approximately 120 kilometers from the state capital of Sittwe, these townships are home to a unique set of population who identify themselves as 'Rohingyas,' practice Islam and speak Rohingya, closely related to Chittagonian language spoken in parts of Bangladesh.

The 'Rohingya' identity is purportedly of a late origin. This ethnonym came to be used in the 1950s by a section of Muslims living in Arakan (present-day Rakhine state) though there exists to be a mention of this word in a precolonial English text (Leider 2014, 9). The said text is Dr. Francis Hamilton-Buchanan's article, 'A comparative vocabulary of some of the languages spoken in the Burman Empire' where the word 'Rohingya' is mentioned as among the three dialects spoken in the Burmese empire (Leider 2014, 5). The word 'Rohingya' or 'Roewengyah' in the Rakhine language means the 'dear ones' or 'compassionate ones' or mutilation of words 'rwa-haung-ga-kar,' 'tiger from the ancient village; which means brave and was a name given to Muslim soldiers who settled in Buthidaung (Yegar 1972, 69).

The Rakhine state that was earlier known as Arakan was independent till the Burmese kings conquered it in 1784 (Yegar 2018, 2). It had political and cultural contact with Islamic Bengal between the 14th and the 18th centuries (Yegar 2017, 2). Arakan had the influence of both Buddhism and Islam at different periods of time. The period from the 13th to 14th centuries saw the emergence of Arakanese kingship which was predominantly Buddhist. However, from 15th century through the 18th century the impact of the Mughal Sultanate of Bengal on Arakan was there (Bhonsale 2016, 631). While the Rakhine trace back their history to their Buddhist past, the Rohingyas highlight the strong influence exercised by Muslim Bengal on the Arakanese (Selth 2003, 12). The irreconcilable historical narratives and memory of distinct past of the same land, Arakan (Rohingyas), is the reason for the rift between the two communities.

At least two distinct positions have been taken by historians to classify the Mayu Frontier district or the northern strip of Arakan (Bhonsale 2016, 634). Citing British records, Aye Chan makes a claim that the Rohingyas are second or third generations of Bengali immigrants who came during the British period as agricultural labor and settled in Burma (Chan 2005, 402). At the advent of the British period, the region between the Lemro rivers and Kaladan rivers was thinly populated and only wild weeds grew in the land (Charney 1999, 279). Only after the exodus of Bengali immigrants did the population of Arakan swell, especially in the Mayu Frontier Area (Chan 2005, 397). Chan thus concludes that the region in Arakan populated by Muslims is an 'enclave' (Bahar 2010, 51). An enclave is part of a country geographically separated from the main part by surrounding foreign territory (Bahar 2010, 51). Civilian collaborators of the Burmese military claim of an existence of a Muslim enclave in the northwestern corner of Burma (Bahar 2010, 51). Chan cites occupational interest as the only interest behind migrating to Arakan first as seasonal migrants and who later settled over time (Chan 2005, 402).

The other position of the Mayu Frontier District in Arakan populated by Muslims by the Rohingya School is that of a 'Frontier Culture' (Bahar 2010, 34). This region geographically located at the intersection of South Asia and Southeast Asia oscillated between the influences of Burma and Bengal. Hence, this 'marginal land' clearly has a 'frontier culture' developed with people of two racial groups – the Rakhines and the Rohingyas (Bahar 2010, 34). Language and culture of the Rakines and the Rohingyas though has witnessed a separate evolution, but until recently, they have recognized one single history of Arakan (Bahar 2010, 34). The different positions taken by historians show the contestations among scholars on the identity of Muslims minorities in Arakan, while one school claims that Rohingyas are of Bangladeshi descent, the Rohingya school believes that the Rohingya have centuries old history of living in Arakan (Bhonsale 2016, 635).

The ethnic identity discourse in Arakan took a dramatic turn due to events during the Second World War (Bhonsale 2016, 635). These have a lasting impact on majority-minority relations in Arakan (Bhonsale 2016, 635). The period that ensued also saw the political assertion of the Rohingya identity and a secessionist Mujahid movement by a section of minorities who demanded the union of minority dominated northern Arakan with East Pakistan (Bhonsale 2016, 635).

Waves of Rohingya migration

The Rohingya migration from the Rakhine state of Myanmar to Bangladesh and subsequently to other countries has occurred in waves since 1979. This section outlines the cycles or waves of migration and the reasons that led to their migration. While historians claim that there have been antecedents to the first major flight of Rohingyas in 1979, four major waves of migration can be identified beginning from 1979 up to 15 August 2018, as shown in Table 3.1.

The first major wave of Rohingya refugees leaving Rakhine state in Bangladesh was in 1979. Prior to this (1979), Myanmar's then President, Ne Win had promulgated the 1974 Emergency Immigration Act that replaced National Registration Certificates with color-coded cards. Those residing lawfully in Myanmar were divided into four colors viz. pink for those who are full citizens, blue for those who are associate citizens, green for naturalized citizens, and white for the foreigners (Ahmed 2004). The Rohingyas were quickly told that they do not fall under any of these four colors and no such cards were issued to them (Ahmed 2004). There was

TABLE 3.1 Year-wise exodus of Rohingyas from Myanmar

Year	Number of Displaced
1979	200,000
1992	250,000
2012	1,20,000
2013–16	1,51,000
2017–18	7,20,000
Total	**15,41,000**

Source: Prepared by researcher based on figures quoted in (Yegar 2018, 201) (Tan 2016, 6) (UNHCR 2016) (Doctors without Borders, March 2018)

an exodus in the year following the Emergency Immigration Act, 1974. Rakhine Buddhist people had forced thousands of Rohingya Muslims to flee to Bangladesh in 1975 (Yegar 2018, 2). However, what led to the exodus in 1978 was a military operation named 'Naga Min' or 'Dragon King' launched by Myanmar army to recognize citizens and weed out foreigners from her land (Pugh 2013, 14). Allegedly, persecuted by the local Rakhines of Arakan and the Myanmar army failing to protect the Rohingyas from the violence directed by the Rakhine Buddhists, about a quarter of a million Rohingyas were forced to leave Burma in search of refuge in neighboring Bangladesh (Yegar 2002, 56).

The second wave migration of Rohingyas is said to have taken place in 1992. Another military operation Pyi Thar Ya or 'Prosperous State' in 1991 by the Burmese military was blamed to have led to the exodus of 250,000 Rohingyas to Myanmar (Tan 2016, 6). In 1988, the State Law and Order Restoration Council (SLORC) took charge in Myanmar after disavowing the results of general elections called by General Ne Win. Myanmar's military presence in northwestern Arakan was stepped up. Having violently put down the democratic movement, the military *Junta* that was in firm control of the government in Myanmar in order to give legitimacy to its rule among core constituencies that included the ethnic Rakhine minorities and Buddhist community, began to deprive anyone it considered Rohingya of citizenship chapters (Klinken and Aung 2017, 358). The army also forced the Rohingyas into road constructions and initiated settling of ethnic Rakhine in the townships of Buthidaung and Maungdaw leading to fresh confrontations between Rohingyas and Rakhine. This led to the second Rohingya exodus between April 1991 and May 1992 and the number rose to 250,000 (Nemoto 6).

The third major wave of migration of the Rohingyas took place in 2012. It is said to have killed over 192 people and displaced within Myanmar over 150,000 Rohingya Muslims. Though the migration was domestic i.e. within the Rakhine state of Myanmar, the violence of 2012 initiated a trend of violence in the following years leading to migration from Myanmar into Bangladesh. What began as an inter-communal conflict in four townships in Rakhine state in June 2012 had by October of the same year engulfed the whole nation including major urban centers of Yangon and Mandalay. A series of incidents are believed to have triggered the June 2012 riots – the primary one being an alleged gang rape and murder of a Rakhine Buddhist girl in Sittwe and subsequent arrests of three Muslims by the police as accused (The Guardian 2012; Klinken and Aung 2017). By official count, the first phase of violence killed a total of 98 people, injured 123 and destroyed some 5,300 houses (Republic of Union of Myanmar 2013, 19). The communal violence against Rohingyas resurfaced in October 2012. But, a large number of these attacks were allegedly orchestrated by local Rakhine political party cadres, section of the Burmese monks and common Rakhine in association with police (Human Rights Watch 2013). Another distinguishing feature of the violence that broke out in October 2012 was that the violence was not just directed toward the Rohingyas but against Muslims in general, an example being the Kaman Muslim; the latter are also recognized as an ethnic group of Myanmar (International Crisis Group 2013;

Human Rights Watch 2013). Killing of a Rakhine merchant by a mob for selling rice to Muslims in Mrauk-U on October 21, 2012 is said to have unleashed a wave of violence in a total of nine townships in three days (Physicians for Human Rights 2013). Mrauk-U Township, remained the worst hit in the second wave of violence that left 94 dead (68 Rohingyas and 26 Rakhine) and 42 Rakhine and 3,234 Rohingya homes destroyed (Republic of Union of Myanmar 2013, 19).

Fleeing poverty, rampant physical abuse and statelessness, the Rohingyas took to sea in search of refuge, beginning in 2014. Their arduous sea journeys in the Bay of Bengal and Andaman Sea in order to reach distant shores of Thailand, Malaysia and Indonesia were reported by media. By May 2015 more than 5,000 Rohingya migrants from Myanmar and Bangladesh were found stranded in the sea (UNHCR 2015). Purportedly, rings of trafficking lured to undertake journeys via sea route to reach foreign shores in search of a safe haven. The trafficking rings often left the migrants stranded on boats without food and water. With lack of food and water on the vessels ferrying the migrants across about 70 Rohingyas reportedly died in ships abandoned by traffickers in May 2015 (UNHCR 2015). The media also reported of mass graves off the Thailand coast at a captivity for illegal migrants before being smuggled into Malaysia (Aljazeera, 24 May 2015).

The year of hope when the first civilian government in about five decades assumed power in 2016 also unleashed brutality for the Rohingya, laying a foundation of the worst exodus in the history of Rakhine state. The incident that triggered the exodus was a coordinated attack on three border guard outposts near Maungdaw in Northern Rakhine, killing nine police officers and injuring five on October 9, 2016 (Myanmar Times, 10 October 2016). A statement from the office of Myanmar's President Htin Kyaw blamed the little-known 'Aqa Mul Mujahidin' with links to the Rohingya Solidarity Organization for the October 9th attacks (Reuters, 14 October 2016; President's Office, 15 October 2016). The government claimed that the attacks aimed at instigating the majority Muslim population of the area to engage in extremist violence. The military and the police forces launched search operations to apprehend the terrorists and seize arms. By November 17, 300 persons were detained by the army. The army allegedly carried out excesses on civilians, killing about 100 civilians and displacing many, some also fleeing to neighboring Bangladesh. The area was cordoned off from the media and human rights groups. Human Rights Watch (HRW) released images purportedly showing 1,250 destroyed buildings in three villages in the Rakhine (International Business Times, 21 November 2016). The military's True News Information Team also rejected claims that its soldiers had razed Rohingya villages (Lone and Lewis, 24 October 2016). Instead they released a statement on November 15, claiming that the buildings had been 'torched by members of the violent attackers in northern Rakhine' (Lone and Lewis 2016).

On August 24, 2017, a militant group by the name Arakan Rohingya Salvation Army (ARSA) staged attacks on a military base and up to 30 security outposts across the northern Rakhine state, killing 59 militants and 12 security forces (Reuters, 24 August 2017). The said attack took place within hours after a panel led by former U.N. chief Kofi Annan advised the government on long-term solutions for Rakhine (Myanmar Times, 10 October 2016). Beginning from August 25, the Myanmar army started 'clearance operations' in hundreds of villages in Maungdaw, Buthidaung and Rathedaung townships. The operation known as 'Scorched Earth' was targeted toward eliminating the Arakan Rohingya Salvation Army (ARSA) who had plotted and executed the attacks on the outposts. The number of dead between August 25 and September 24 was 6,700 due to the violence, including 730 children under the age of five (Doctors without Borders, March 2018). By September 7, the United Nations Refugee Agency (UNHCR) estimated that 164,000 Rohingyas had fled the Northern Rakhine state since the violence began August 25, 2017 (UNHCR, 8 September 2017). The figure of refugees fleeing to Bangladesh soared to 600,000 by the end of 2017 and reached 725,000 by August 15, 2018.

Response to the Rohingya crisis

The response to the humanitarian crisis in the Rakhine from the global community has been inadequate considering its nature and scale of the crisis. UN Secretary General Antonio Guetteres described it as the world's fastest growing refugee emergency and carefully worded statements accusing Myanmar of perpetrating 'Crimes Against Humanity' and guilty of 'ethnic cleansing' and genocide were issued. The failure of Myanmar state to fulfill her responsibility to protect the Rohingya minority group has been criticized. India's response is excluded in this section as it will be exclusively dealt with in the next section.

Political and economic reforms in Myanmar in 2010 had grabbed the attention of the European Union and USA in what they foresaw as the 'world's last frontier.' Despite calls by UN agencies and human rights watchdogs on deteriorating human rights in Myanmar, especially pertaining to the situation of Rohingyas following the 2012 attacks, in April 2013, the European Union lifted sanctions barring arms embargo. Southeast Asian countries Malaysia and Indonesia who were most vocal among the regional bloc Association of Southeast Asian Nations or ASEAN turned back boats of Rohingyas desperate to reach their shores. These two Muslim majority countries were joined by Thailand in refusing to Rohingya refugees to come ashore. Only after pressure mounted on the respective governments of the ASEAN countries did they allow Rohingya boats ashore.

Suu Kyi, the state counselor responsible for the Rakhine Affairs responded by ordering an enquiry and later by also forming an advisory commission under former UN Secretary General Kofi Annan after a worldwide criticism on the aftermath of the 2016 attacks in Rakhine state. Bangladesh, immediately after the 2016 military operations, is also believed to have prevented the Rohingyas from entering their territory by tightening the border controls but failed to prevent the exodus from entering Bangladesh (Holmes and agencies 2016). Around 21,000 Rohingya people had fled to Bangladesh between October 9 and December 2, 2016 (International Business Times, 21 November 2016).

Following the launch of army operations beginning from the end of August 2017, there was more talk and little action. Despite extensive reportage of the plight of the Rohingyas in the media, the response went little beyond condemnation and has failed to translate into concrete actions (Parikh 2017).

The U.N. Security Council on August 30, 2017 convened a closed-door meeting within a week of the August 24, 2017 attacks to discuss the situation in the Rakhine state. They again met on September 12 at the request of members Sweden and Great Britain when a statement was issued appealing to Myanmar to end violence against the Rohingyas (Reuters, 12 September 2017). Secretary General of United Nations Antonio Guterres described the situation in Rakhine state as 'ethnic cleansing' arguing that one-third of the Rohingya population had to flee the country.

Several world leaders assembled at the United Nations General Assembly in New York trained barbs at Myanmar for prosecution unleashed by the army on the Rohingya Muslims. Those who were reported to have prominently voiced their opinion included Turkish President Recep Tayyip Erdogan, who reportedly said the international community has failed in the Rohingya crisis similar to that it did in Syria (Daily Sabah, 19 September 2017). The Myanmar State Counselor Aung San Suu Kyi refrained from participating in the United Nations General Assembly in New York.

Suu Kyi, on September 19, 2017 in her first public address, said that her country does not fear international scrutiny and the state has to determine whether the allegations are based on evidence (McPherson 2017). She also said that conflicts and military operations had ceased on September 5.

The Association of Southeast Asian Nations (ASEAN) issued a Chairman's statement signed by ASEAN foreign ministers and unequivocally criticized the attack launched by Myanmar authorities on August 25 and atrocities that killed civilians, damaged houses and displaced Rohingya people. The 2017 ASEAN Chair, Philippines also underscored the importance of increased humanitarian access to the affected areas and assistance to be given to affected communities (Tempo.co, 25 September 2017).

Muslim majority countries including Malaysia, Indonesia, Pakistan, Turkey and Iran condemned the violence against the Rohingyas. The Maldives Foreign Ministry even announced severing of all trade ties with Myanmar. The Organization of Islamic Cooperation urged Myanmar to accept UN monitors to carry out 'a through and independent investigation of the violation of international human rights and bring those responsible to justice.'

President of France Emmanuel Macron announced that his country plans an initiative in the U.N. Security Council in relation to the crackdown on Myanmar's Rohingya population. In a joint statement issued by U.N. Principals called the pushing over of 500,000 refugees into Bangladesh as the fastest growing refugee crisis and a humanitarian emergency. The statement co-signed by Filippo Grandi, United Nations High Commissioner (UNHCR, 16 October).

A European parliament resolution called upon the military to immediately cease the killings, harassment and rape of the Rohingya people and burning of their homes. The European lawmakers also urged the European Union to clarify to Myanmar that it was prepared to impose sanctions on Myanmar if it did not halt human right abuses (DW, 14 September 2017). UK announced the suspension of courses offered to the Myanmar military, lest there was an acceptable resolution to the crisis (Coates 2017). The office of British Prime Minister Theresa May said that the actions of military forces in Myanmar against the Rohingya people looks like ethnic cleansing. Her spokesperson called it a major humanitarian crisis triggered by the Myanmar military (The Independent, 13 November 2017).

US President, Donald Trump supported efforts to end the violence, to ensure accountability for atrocities committed and to facilitate safe and voluntary return of refugees. He also added that the US welcomes commitments by Myanmar government and is ready to support the implementation of the Rakhine commission recommendations.

Despite attempts by Myanmar government to negotiate with China and Russia for blocking a UN Security Council censure over Rohingya exodus, China supported UN Security council's resolution to end violence targeting the Rohingyas (Reuters, 6 September 2017) (South China Morning Post, 14 September 2017). Reportedly China, expressing concern over the excessive use of force during security operations in the Rakhine state called for immediate steps to end violence, its first such agreement to the Council's statement on Myanmar after nine years. However, in a turn of events, China refused to interfere in other country's matters and extended support to Myanmar's efforts in safeguarding peace and stability in the region and hoped all areas will realize peace, stability and development (Worley 2017).

China even offered to mediate between Myanmar and Bangladesh to resolve the Rohingya refugee crisis. Chinese Foreign Minister, Wang Yi travelled to Dhaka and Nay Pyi Taw in succession and met leaders of both countries, proposing a three-phased solution to put a permanent end to the crisis. The three-phased solution had a ceasefire as the first step with no further displacement of local residents. Second, to encourage Myanmar and Banagladesh to keep communication in the bud to resolve the issue and third a commonly agreed long-term resolution (Hindu Businessline, 20 November 2017). Regional intergovernmental organization ASEAN in its statement made no mention of the Rohingya crisis except for highlighting the importance of humanitarian relief provided for victims of natural disasters in Vietnam, victims of a recent battle with militant in Philippines and affected communities in the northern Rakhine state (Reuters, 13 November 2017).

China along with Russia and eight more countries opposed a resolution put forward in the United Nations General Assembly urging Myanmar to end a military campaign against the Rohingyas and appoint a UN Special Envoy. It asked the Myanmar government to allow access to aid workers, ensure return of all refugees and grant full citizenship to the Rohingyas. It requests that UN secretary general

António Guterres appoint a special envoy to Myanmar (The Guardian, 24 December 2017). Russia opposed the labelling of Myanmar army's crackdown on Rohingya Muslims as 'ethnic cleansing' as unhelpful and warned that it could aggravate the situation. Moscow's approach, a Russian emissary said, was to solve Rakhine issue through politics (The Guardian 24 December 2017).

India's response

The nuances of India's response to the Rakhine humanitarian crisis is coded in the dual strategy adopted by the Indian state viz. firstly to maintain good political relations with both Myanmar and Bangladesh that are central to its 'Neighborhood First' and 'Act East Policy' and second as 'push back' policy adopted by the Government of India toward Rohingyas that has disregarded the earlier tradition of providing sanctuary to prosecuted minorities.

The public discourse on the Rohingyas within India in the recent years began almost a month prior to the attacks in Rakhine state on August 25, 2017. Reportedly, Kiren Rijiju, Union Minister of State for Home Affairs, Government of India in a reply to parliament called the Rohingyas illegal migrants and accused them of indulging in unlawful activities (Bharadwaj, 31 July 2017). The Minister noted that illegal migrants like the Rohingyas enter into the country without valid documents in a furtive manner, leaving the state agencies with no data (NDTV.com, 31 July 2017). India is also believed to have taken up the matter with Myanmar and has emphasized the need for safe, speedy and sustainable deportation of the Rohingyas (Bharadwaj, 31 July 2017; NDTV.com, 31 July 2017). The Indian Ministry of Home Affairs even directed the state governments to constitute task forces to identify and deport illegally staying foreign nationals (Chauhan 2017).

The Union government of India told the parliament that the illegal Rohingya population in India is 40,000 and has seen a fourfold rise within two years when the population of Rohingyas was 10,500 (Sharma 10 August 2017). The Indian government's indication that manifold increase in the influx of Rohingya refugees includes the post-October 2016 period i.e. following militant attacks in Rakhine state and following that intrusion to India. The government in an affidavit to the Supreme Court of India also said that the continued stay of the 'illegal migrants' posed 'serious national security ramifications' (Times of India 18 September 2017).

The Ministry of External Affairs, Government of India however had a nuanced position on the issue. A statement issued on August 26, 2017 following the attacks purportedly by Islamic outfits on army outposts in Rakhine state, India's foreign ministry's statement condemned the attacks by militants and expressed grief over the loss of lives of Myanmar's security personnel. There was no indication on the continuing exodus of refugees to Bangladesh or for that matter on repatriation of Rohingya refugees from host countries including India.

Closely on the heels of the August 25 attacks, Indian Prime Minister, Narendra Modi made his first three-day state visit to Myanmar from September 5, 2017.

The Indian Prime Minister is also reported to have raised the issue of Rohingyas illegally staying in India (Dutta 17 September 2017). During his visit, Modi also offered Myanmar assistance for developing the Rakhine state, which his government considered to be a medium-term solution for addressing problems in the Rakhine state (*Hindustan Times*, 6 September 2017b). However, the silence on the refugees was broken when Bangladesh intimated India of the tremendous strain that it has got itself into following the coming of Rohingya refugees (Roy, 14 September 2017a). India in a statement issued on September 9 called for Myanmar to restore peace and normalcy in the Rakhine state (Roy, 14 September 2017b).

India also launched 'Operation Insaniyat' that gave relief materials to affected refugees who entered into Bangladesh from Myanmar. Union Minister of External Affairs, Sushma Swaraj during her visit to Bangladesh urged Myanmar to handle the situation with restraint, keeping in mind the welfare of the population. In a press statement issued after her visit, Swaraj is said to have called for a return of the displaced persons to Rakhine state and that rapid socioeconomic development and infrastructure upgrade are the long-term solution to the Rakhine problem.

Indian Foreign Secretary, S. Jaishankar visited Myanmar on 20 December 2017. He inked the Memorandum of Understanding on the Rakhine State Development Program. This program was the first of its kind intended to help the government of Myanmar achieve its objective of restoration of normalcy in Rakhine State and enable the return of displaced persons. India proposes under the said program to take up, among others, a project to build prefabricated housing in Rakhine State so as to meet the immediate needs of returning people. During the Indian foreign secretary's visit to Myanmar, India also signed a $25 million MoU with Myanmar for development of the Rakhine State (*Hindustan Times* 2017a).

India's External Affairs Minister, Sushma Swaraj visited Myanmar on May 10–11, 2018, she stressed the importance of 'safe, speedy and sustainable return of displaced persons to Rakhine State' (Ministry of External Affairs- Government of India). This is a departure from the previous position when it called for 'restraint' in handling the situation in Rakhine (Yhome 2018). The shift in stance of the Indian Ministry of External Affairs from that of 'silence' to 'safe, speedy and sustainable return of refugees to Rakhine state' followed Bangladesh's nudge to put pressure on Myanmar to take back the refugees. Even the use of the word 'sustainable' suggests that India is echoing similar desires to Bangladesh (Bhattacharjee 2018). Bangladesh is insisting on the 'safe and sustainable return of the refugees,' thus urging the long-term resolution of the problem.

Since the early 1990s, India has consistently engaged Myanmar and India's response to the Rohingya humanitarian crisis and needs to be seen in this light. Having said this, the Indian response is also calibrated by a close neighbour, Bangladesh, who is the recipient of the maximum number of refugees and has sought India's intervention in tiding over the wave of refugees.

Behind India's response

The Rohingya crisis presents a 'dilemma' or 'test of diplomacy' to the Indian state (Vembu 2017; Chandran, 20 September 2017). The debate about the Rohingyas is being constructed as one between humanitarian obligations and national security (Mehta 2017). The discourse is mostly focused around implications rather than finding a solution to the crisis (Yhome 2018). India has ended a golden tradition of confirming with international comity and good treatment of refugees like in the past when it received refugees from every religion (Aiyar, 20 September 2017). But, for the first time, religion has become a reason for rejection of the Rohingya refugees, as Home Ministry's September 2015 notification under the Passports Act and the Foreigners Act exempts from usual entry and residential procedures 'Hindus, Sikhs, Christians, Jains, Parsis and Buddhists' facing persecution, wrote a former union minister (Aiyar 2017). Noticeably, in the notification excepting Muslims, people from all other religions have been given exemption. This line of argument also reminds that the Indian state cannot ignore the 1951 UN Convention on refugees and the 1967 protocol that mandates all United Nations member states to adhere to non-refoulement that bars a member state from expelling or returning a refugee to 'frontiers of territories where his or her life or freedom would be threatened on account of his race, religion, nationality, membership of a particular social group or political opinion' (Parthasarathy 2017).

In contradistinction to the earlier set of views is the opinion arguing against giving the Rohingyas refuge in India. An article points out that despite India having historically kept her doors open for persecuted minorities from many parts of the world and that India's sympathies lay with such refugees at this stage of development, keeping an open door for persecuted refugees is borderline madness (Vembu 2017). However, the article says that New Delhi must persuade Myanmar's military rulers and Aung San Suu Kyi to set its own house in order. Similarly, an article argues that India would eventually have to send the Rohingyas back to Myanmar and it is in India's interest to see peace in the Rakhine state (Unjhawala 2017).

Discernibly, two schools of thoughts explain India's approach toward the Rohingyas (Yhome 2018). The first school sees elements of consistency in India's traditional hesitation about automatically designating asylum seekers as refugees. According to the first school, India has created disincentives for refugees to stay permanently in India, citing the case of refugees from Bangladesh during the 1971 war (Jaishankar and Saraf 2017). This school also has advocates who have raised the concerns of security in not allowing the Rohingyas a permanent asylum in India. The second school argues that it is a departure from the past and analyzes it from the perspective of potential implications on India (Yhome 2018). According to this line of reasoning, the government's Rohingya approach has put at stake the lives of thousands of Indian Diaspora communities in different countries including Myanmar (Yhome 2018). The second school argues that the approach of the Indian government toward the Rohingyas is short-sighted and could lead to further radicalization of the oppressed and would have spill-over effects for India (Vishwanathan 2017).

As most opinions emerging within India turned inwards on India's decision to deport back the Rohingyas, a few commendations turned to the Indian state's external relations. A few commentators on India's position on the Rohingya have also examined the geostrategic importance of Myanmar to the Indian state in deciding her course of action over Myanmar. However, some also argue that the Rohingya issue is a test case for Indian's diplomacy to balance self-interest with protecting the interests of her neighbor (sic Bangladesh) (Bhattacharjee 2017).

Commentators pointed out that a threefold imperative lends perspective to India's initial silence on the Rohingya issue (Sahoo 2017). First, security in the North Eastern states, which have seen a niggling insurgency since India's independence. Second, Myanmar's importance as a land bridge to ASEAN countries, and last, to check China's increasing influence in South Asia, the latter New Delhi holds to be in its traditional sphere of influence.

Beginning from the early 1990s, Myanmar has assumed significance as India's springboard for the 'Look East policy,' a foreign policy strategy aimed at improving political relations and intensifying economic cooperation with Southeast Asian countries or the ASEAN bloc. When the military violently suppressed a democratically elected government and staged a coup in Myanmar in 1988, India criticized the military rulers and gave refuge to political dissidents from Myanmar. India's turn toward her eastern neighborhood and Southeast Asia in particular was to mitigate the global shift from a bipolar to unipolar world and adjust to the post-Cold War era. India's rapprochement with the military *Junta* in Myanmar through violent suppression of democratic parties had come to political power was a major watershed in the political relations between the two countries tethered into oblivion.

By launching joint operations with Myanmar military, India hoped to curb militancy and illicit trafficking in India's North east. India's connectivity with Southeast Asia was the backbone of the economic pillar of the Look East policy and Myanmar served as the natural bridge. India in the first decade of the 21st century took up projects like the Rhi-Tiddim road, Kaladan Multi Modal Transit Transport Project and the India-Myanmar-Thailand Trilateral Highway project. Myanmar was also rich in resources and Indian companies jointly engaged in tapping gas and oil at Shwe gas fields. Lastly, sanctions imposed by Western countries on the military regime in Myanmar had pushed the country to deepen its relations with China, with the latter emerging as Myanmar's largest donor and supplier of military hardware. India through its Myanmar outreach hoped to supplant China's influence in Myanmar.

As the world erupted following the security operations carried out by the Myanmar military following the August 25, 2017 attack, Suu Kyi led NLD and the military in a rare show of unity on the issue of the Rohingyas as both considered the Rohingya as a 'national security threat' (Naing and Lee 2017). This apparent unity of the two camps on the Rohingya issue might have pushed India to stand up for Myanmar in the period at a time when sanctions by the West are looming large on Myanmar.

Conclusion

The Rakhine crisis has not suddenly dawned upon the world but has been built through a history of alleged excesses and migration resulting there-from. It has become the world's longest running ethnic strife. This humanitarian crisis though has attracted attention from media the world over but has failed to illicit strong response from world community. There is little beyond statements issued by world leaders to address the humanitarian crisis. Also imposing sanctions as the European Union and USA have done has not helped bring the Myanmar state on the corrective course. The failure of United Nations Security Council to adopt a resolution on the Rohingya crisis has further shrunk the intergovernmental council's role in Myanmar. Regional powers, India and China in the pursuit of their own interests have been soft-pedalling on Myanmar's army's complicity in genocide. They have been insisting that any intervention from the world community would be an infringement on Myanmar's sovereignty.

The two-pronged approach of the Indian state in deporting back the illegal Rohingya migrants while soft-pedalling on Myanmar and at the same time also assuring Bangladesh that India is for a long-term solution for resolving the crisis in the Rakhine state is an example of Indian realism in her eastern neighborhood. But many questions could be raised at the diplomacy with Myanmar that India is engaged in. Is India, which claims to be the largest democracy in the world, ready to forego her leadership in espousing humanitarian causes in the region for some self-interest? Is the Indian establishment wary of losing Myanmar if it joined the global community in censuring Myanmar? While turning the focus to a long-term solution to the Rakhine crisis that is merely innovative and addressing the problem, has the Indian state chosen short-sighted interests and short-term gains and foregone long-term vision?

References

Ahmed, Imtiaz (2004). "Globalization, Low-Intensity Conflict & Protracted Statelessness/ Refugeehood: The Plight of the Rohingyas." *GSC Quarterly* 13 (Summer–Fall), http:// www.kaladanpress.org/images/document/ahmed_rohingya.pdf (accessed August 25, 2018).

Aiyar, Shankar Mani (2017). "On Rohingyas, Modi Regime Ends India's Golden Tradition." *NDTV*, September 5, www.ndtv.com/opinion/the-unacceptable-stand-of-modi-regime-on-rohingyas-1654650 (accessed September 12, 2018).

Aljazeera (2015). "Malaysia Finds Mass Graves of Suspected Migrants." *Alzajeera*, May 24, www.aljazeera.com/news/2015/05/malaysia-mass-graves-150524070422569.html (accessed September 2, 2018).

Anand, Utkarsha (2018). "Can't Ask Govt to Let Rohingya Enter India, Provide Refugee Cards: Centre to Supreme Court." *News18.com*, March 16, www.news18.com/news/

india/cant-ask-govt-to-let-rohingya-enter-india-provide-refugee-cards-centre-to-supreme-court-1691035.html (accessed September 12, 2018).

Bahar, Abid (2010). *Burma's Missing Dots: The Emerging Face of Genocide*. Xlibris, p. 34, 51.

Bharadwaj, Supriya (2017). "India Soft on Refugees, Protecting Citizens First Priority: Kiren Rijiju on Rohingya Deportation." *India Today*, July 31, https://www.indiatoday.in/india/story/india-soft-on-refugees-protecting-citizens-first-prority-kiren-rijiju-on-rohingya-deportation-1301857-2018-07-31 (accessed September 10, 2019).

Bhatia, Rajiv (2017). "Can India Ignore the Rohingya Crisis?" *The Hindu*, September 15, www.thehindu.com/opinion/op-ed/can-india-ignore-the-rohingya-crisis/article 19686341.ece (accessed September 16, 2018).

Bhattacharjee, Joyeeta (2017). "Rohingya Crisis a Test for India's Diplomatic Ability to Balance Self-Interest and Fulfil Neighbour's Expectation." *Outlook*, September 19, https://www.outlookindia.com/website/story/rohingya-crisis-a-test-for-indias-diplomatic-ability-to-balance-self-interest-an/301924 (accessed September 10, 2019).

———. (2018). "Bangladesh First Behind India's Changing Stance on the Rohingyas." *The Diplomat*, May 23, https://thediplomat.com/2018/05/bangladesh-first-behind-indias-changing-stance-on-the-rohingya/ (accessed October 2, 2018).

Bhonsale, Mihir (2016). "Evolution of the Arakan 'Problem' in Burma." In *Proceedings of the Indian History Congress – 76th Session-University of Gour Banga-Malda 2015⊗*. Aligarh: Indian History Congress, pp. 631–636.

Bintang, Roni and Al-Zaquan Amer Hamzah (2015). "Hundreds of Refugees Arrive in Malaysia and Indonesia After Thai Crackdown." *Reuters*, May 11, www.reuters.com/article/us-indonesia-rohingya/hundreds-of-refugees-arrive-in-malaysia-and-indonesia-after-thai-crackdown-idUSKBN0NV0PC20150511?feedType=RSS&feedName=topNews&utm_source=twitter (accessed August 22, 2018).

Chan, Aye (2005). "The Development of a Muslim Enclave in Arakan (Rakhine) State of Burma." *SOAS Bulletin of Burma Research* 3 (2) (Autumn): 396–420.

Chandran, Nyshka (2017). "The Refugee Crisis Gripping Asia is Make-or-break for Indian Leadership." *CNBC*, September 20, https://www.cnbc.com/2017/09/20/myanmars-refugee-crisis-is-a-test-for-india-and-narendra-modi.html (accessed September 10, 2019).

Charney, Michael W. (1999). "Where Jambudipa and Islamdom Converged: Religious Change and the Emergence of Buddhist Communalism in Early Modern Arakan (Fifteenth to Nineteenth Centuries)." PhD diss., Ann Arbor: University of Michigan.

Chauhan, Neeraj (2017). "Identify and Deport Illegal Immigrants, Centre Asks States." *The Times of India*, August 13, https://timesofindia.indiatimes.com/india/identify-and-deport-illegal-immigrants-centre-asks-states/articleshow/60046250.cms (accessed September 19, 2018).

Coates, Sam (2017). "Britain to Withdraw Support for Burmese Army Over Rohingya Violence." *The Times*, September 20, www.thetimes.co.uk/article/britain-to-withdraw-support-to-burma-3t763bbqz (accessed September 9, 2018).

Doctors without Borders (2018), "'No One Was Left': An MSF Special Report on Violence Against the Rohingya in Myanmar's Rakhine State." March 12, https://www.doctorswithoutborders.ca/article/no-one-was-left-msf-special-report-violence-against-rohingya-myanmars-rakhine-state (accessed September 11, 2019).

Dutta, Prabhash K. (2017). "How Rohingyas Reached India and Why Government Is Not Ready to Let Them Stay." *India Today*, September 7, www.indiatoday.in/india/story/rohingya-muslims-myanmar-india-aung-san-suu-kyi-narendra-modi-1039729-2017-09-07 (accessed September 22, 2018).

DW (2017). "Rohingya Crisis: European MPs Call on Myanmar to Halt Violence." *DW*, September 14, www.dw.com/en/rohingya-crisis-european-mps-call-on-myanmar-to-halt-violence/a-40513370 (accessed September 9, 2018).

The Guardian (2012). "Burma Ethnic Violence Escalates as Villagers Flee." *The Guardian*, June 12, www.theguardian.com/world/2012/jun/12/burma-ethnic-violence-escalates.

———. (2017). "China and Russia Oppose UN Resolution on Rohingya." *The Guardian*, December 24, www.theguardian.com/world/2017/dec/24/china-russia-oppose-un-resolution-myanmar-rohingya-muslims (accessed August 29, 2018).

The Hindu Businessline (2017). "Myanmar, Bangladesh Accept China's Mediatory Role to End Rohingya Crisis." *The Hindu Businessline*, November 20, www.thehindubusinessline.com/news/world/myanmar-bangladesh-accept-chinas-mediatory-role-to-end-rohingya-crisis/article9967524.ece (accessed September 12, 2018).

Hindustan Times (2017a). "India Commits $25 Million to Develop Myanmar's Rakhine State." *Hindustan Times*, December 21, www.hindustantimes.com/india-news/india-commits-25-million-to-develop-myanmar-s-rakhine-state/story-lpwndpPujIn1hCwBhJoqAJ.html (accessed September 12, 2018).

———. (2017b). "PM Modi Tells Suu Kyi India Is with Myanmar, But Skips Mention of Rohingya Issue." *Hindustan Times*, September 6, www.hindustantimes.com/india-news/modi-in-myanmar-pm-praises-suu-kyi-s-leadership-vows-to-fight-terror-in-joint-statement/story-vC4Pi9WL594NnRt8Oe430J.html (accessed September 19, 2018).

Holmes Oliver and Agencies (2016). "Myanmar Seeking Ethnic Cleansing, Says UN Official as Rohingya Flee Persecution." *The Guardian*, November 24, www.theguardian.com/world/2016/nov/24/rohingya-flee-to-bangladesh-to-escape-myanmar-military-strikes (accessed August 22, 2018).

Human Rights Watch (2013). "All You Can Do Is Pray- Crimes Against Humanity and Ethnic Cleansing of Rohingya Muslims in Burma's Arakan State." *Human Rights Watch*, www.hrw.org/report/2013/04/22/all-you-can-do-pray/crimes-against-humanity-and-ethnic-cleansing-rohingya-muslims (accessed August 15, 2018).

The Indian Express (2017). "Around 40,000 Rohingya Migrants in India: Kiren Rijiju Tells Lok Sabha." *The Indian Express*, December 19, https://indianexpress.com/article/india/around-40000-rohingya-migrants-in-india-govt-tells-lok-sabha-4989879/ (accessed September 13, 2018).

International Crisis Group (October 1, 2013). "The Dark Side of Transition: Violence Against Muslims in Myanmar." https://d2071andvip0wj.cloudfront.net/the-dark-side-of-transition-violence-against-muslims-in-myanmar.pdf (accessed September 12, 2019).

Jaishankar, Dhruva and Saraf Tushita (2017). "India's Traditional Refugee Policy Shows Why It's Unlikely to Give Rohingyas Sanctuary." *The Print*, September 30, https://theprint.in/opinion/indias-policy-refugees-rohingya/11232/ (accessed September 19, 2018).

Joshi, Manoj (2017). "Shunning Rohingya Refugees Is a Bad Geopolitical Strategy for India." *The Wire*, October 15, https://thewire.in/diplomacy/rohingya-india-myanmar-china-bangladesh (accessed September 22, 2018).

Klinken, Gerry van and Aung Su Mon Thazin (2017). "The Contentious Politics of Anti-Muslim Scapegoating in Myanmar." *Journal of Contemporary Asia* 47 (3). file:///C:/Users/abc/Downloads/The%20Contentious%20Politics%20of%20Anti%20Muslim%20Scapegoating%20in%20Myanmar.pdf (accessed August 25, 2018).

International Business Times (2016). "New Wave of Destruction Sees 1,250 Houses Destroyed in Myanmar's Rohingya Villages." November 21, www.ibtimes.co.uk/new-wave-destruction-sees-1250-houses-destroyed-myanmars-rohingya-villages-1592582 (accessed August 22, 2018).

Leider, Jacques P. (2014). "Rohingya- The Name. The Movement. The Quest for Identity." *Network Myanmar*, www.networkmyanmar.org/ESW/Files/Leider-Rohingya.pdf (accessed August 10, 2018).

Lewis, Simon and Wa Lone (2016). "Myanmar Blames Islamist Group for Attacks in Rohingya Muslim Region." *Reuters*, October 14, https://in.reuters.com/article/myanmar-bor der/myanmar-blames-islamist-group-for-attacks-in-rohingya-muslim-region-idINK-BN12E1SR (accessed August 15, 2018).

Lone, Wa and Simon Lewis (2016). "Death Toll in Arakan Higher Than Reported: Activists." *DVB*, October 24, www.dvb.no/news/death-toll-arakan-higher-reported-activ ists/71964 (accessed August 22, 2018).

Lone, Wa and Shoon Naing (2017). "At Least 71 Killed in Myanmar as Rohingya Insurgents Stage Major Attack." *Reuters*, August 25, www.reuters.com/article/us-myanmar-rohingya/ at-least-71-killed-in-myanmar-as-rohingya-insurgents-stage-major-attack-idUSKCN-1B507K (accessed August 27, 2018).

McPherson, Poppy (2017). "Aung San Suu Kyi Says Myanmar Does Not Fear Scrutiny Over Rohingya Crisis." *The Guardian*, September 19, www.theguardian.com/world/2017/ sep/19/aung-san-suu-kyi-myanmar-rohingya-crisis-concerned (accessed September 2, 2018).

Mehta, Pratap, Bhanu (2017). "A Few Sacks of Rice." *The Indian Express*, September 23, https://indianexpress.com/article/opinion/columns/a-few-sacks-of-rice-rohingya-ref ugees-myanmar-4856665/ (accessed September 22, 2018).

Ministry of External Affairs- Government of India (2017a). "Operation Insaniyat – Humanitarian Assistance to Bangladesh on Account of Influx of Refugees." *Ministry of External Affairs- Government of India*, https://mea.gov.in/press-releases.htm?dtl/28944/Operation_ Insaniyat__Humanitarian_assistance_to_Bangladesh_on_account_of_influx_of_refugees (accessed August 24, 2018).

———. (2017b). "Press Statement by External Affairs Minister During Her Visit to Bangladesh." www.mea.gov.in/Speeches-Statements.htm?dtl/29039/ (accessed August 23, 2018).

Myanmar Times (2016). "Rakhine Border Raids Kill Nine Police Officers." *Myanmar Times*, October 10, www.mmtimes.com/national-news/22992-rakhine-border-raids-kill-nine-police-officers.html (accessed August 14, 2018).

Naing, Shoon and Yimou Lee (2017). "In a First 'Ethnic Cleansing' Unites Suu Kyi Party, Army and Public." *Reuters*, September 14, www.reuters.com/article/us-myanmar-roh ingya-suukyi/in-a-first-myanmars-ethnic-cleansing-unites-suu-kyis-party-army-and-public-idUSKCN1BP205 (accessed September 29, 2018).

NDTV (2017). "Some Rohingya Migrants Involved in Illegal Activities: Rijiju." *NDTV*, July 31, www.ndtv.com/india-news/some-rohingya-migrants-involved-in-illegal-activi ties-says-centre-1892697 (accessed August 29, 2018).

Nemoto, Kei. "The Rohingya Issue: A Thorny Obstacle Between Burma (Myanmar) and Bangladesh." *Burma Library*, www.burmalibrary.org/docs14/Kei_Nemoto-Rohingya.pdf (accessed August 27, 2018).

Nichols, Michelle (2017). "U.N. Chief, Security Council Call on Myanmar to End Violence." *Reuters*, September 13, www.reuters.com/article/us-myanmar-rohingya/u-n-chief-security-council-call-on-myanmar-to-end-violence-idUSKCN1BO0B1 (accessed August 20, 2018).

Parikh, Tej (September 14, 2017). "The Rohingya Don't Want Our Anger – They Want Our help." *CNN*, September 14, https://edition.cnn.com/2017/09/14/opinions/how-to-help-rohingya-opinion-parikh/index.html (accessed September 10, 2019).

Parthasarathy, Suhrith (2017). "At Home and in the World: On the Rohingya Issue." *The Hindu*, September 15, www.thehindu.com/opinion/lead/at-home-and-in-the-world-on-the-rohingya-issue/article19685778.ece (accessed October 2, 2018).

Physicians for Human Rights (2013). "Patterns of Anti-Muslim Violence in Burma: A Call for Accountability and Prevention." August, https://phr.org/wp-content/uploads/2013/08/Burma-Violence-Report-August-2013.pdf (accessed September 12, 2019).

President's Office, Republic of the Union of Myanmar (2016). "Press Release Regarding the Attacks on the Border Guard Police Posts in Maungdaw Township." *Republic of the Union of Myanmar- President's Office*, www.president-office.gov.mm/en/?q=briefing-room/statements-and-releases/2016/10/15/id-6678 (accessed August 12, 2018).

Pugh Cresa L. (2013). "Is Citizenship the answer? - Constructions of Belonging and Exclusion for the Stateless Rohingya of Burma." *Centre for Migration, Policy and Society Working Paper No. 107*, https://www.compas.ox.ac.uk/wp-content/uploads/WP-2013-107-Pugh_Stateless_Rohingya_Burma.pdf (accessed July 24, 2018).

Republic of the Union of Myanmar (2013). "Final Report of Inquiry Commission on Sectarian Violence in Rakhine State." July 8.

Reuters (2016). "Myanmar Blames Islamist Group for Attacks in Rohingya Muslim region." October 14, https://in.reuters.com/article/myanmar-border/myanmar-blames-islamist-group-for-attacks-in-rohingya-muslim-region-idINKBN12E1SR (accessed September 10, 2019).

———. (2017). "Southeast Asia Summit Draft Statement Skips Over Rohingya Crisis." November 13, https://in.reuters.com/article/asean-summit-myanmar/southeast-asia-summit-draft-statement-skips-over-rohingya-crisis-idINKBN1DD0CT (accessed August 22, 2018).

Roy, Suhhajit (2017a). "After Dhaka SOS on Rohingyas, New Delhi to Send Relief Flight." *The Indian Express*, 14 September, https://indianexpress.com/article/india/after-dhaka-sos-on-rohingyas-delhi-to-send-relief-flight-muslim-4842642/ (accessed September 9, 2018).

———. (2017b). "Rohingya Crisis: At UN, India Calls for Restraint in Rakhine, Praises Bangladesh." *The Indian Express*, September 19, https://indianexpress.com/article/india/rohingya-crisis-at-un-india-calls-for-restraint-in-rakhine-praises-bangladesh-4851517/ (accessed September 9, 2018).

Sabah, Daily (2017). "World Leaders Condemn Myanmar's Violence Against Rohingya Muslims." *Daily Sabah*, www.dailysabah.com/asia/2017/09/19/world-leaders-condemn-myanmars-violence-against-rohingya-muslims, September 19, (accessed August 29, 2018).

Sahoo, Niranjan (2017). "India's Rohingya Realpolitik." *Carnegie Endowment for International Peace*, https://carnegieendowment.org/files/Sahoo_Rohingya_final.pdf (accessed October 2, 2018).

Selth, Andrew (2003). *Burma's Muslims: Terrorists or Terrorised?* Strategic and Defence Studies Centre - The Australian National University.

Sharma, Neeta (2017). "Rohingya Population Shot Up Four-Fold in 2 Yrs to 40,000, Parliament Told." *NDTV*, August 10, www.ndtv.com/india-news/40-000-rohingyas-living-illegally-in-india-says-government-1735673 (accessed September 13, 2018).

South China Morning Post (2017). "China Backs UN Security Council's First Myanmar Statement in Nine Years as Ethnic Bloodshed Forces 380,000 Rohingyas to Flee." *South China Morning Post*, September 14, www.scmp.com/news/asia/diplomacy/article/2111097/un-chief-and-security-council-call-myanmar-end-violence-against (accessed August 29, 2018).

Spencer, Richard (2015). "Thousands of Burmese Migrants Feared Adrift at Sea as South-East Asian Governments Refuse Landing." *The Telegraph*, May 14, www.telegraph.co.uk/

news/worldnews/asia/indonesia/11598908/Thousands-of-migrants-feared-adrift-at-sea-could-die-unless-they-are-rescued-UN-warns.html (accessed August 14, 2018).

Tan, Vivian (2017). "An Estimated 164,000 Men, Women and Children Have Fled Violence in Myanmar's Northern Rakhine State in the Past Two Weeks, Many in Fishing Boats." *UNHCR*, www.unhcr.org/news/latest/2017/9/59b11b634/rohingya-sea-search-safety-bangladesh.html (accessed August 14, 2018).

Tempo.co. (2017). "ASEAN Issues Chairman's Statement on Rohingya Crisis." *Tempo. co*, September 25, 2017, https://en.tempo.co/read/news/2017/09/25/074911769/ASEAN-Issues-Chairmans-Statement-on-Rohingya-Crisis (accessed August 22, 2018).

The Times of India (2017). "Supreme Court to Take a Call on Rohingyas: Rajnath." *The Times of India*, September 18, https://timesofindia.indiatimes.com/india/supreme-court-to-take-a-call-on-rohingyas-rajnath/articleshow/60733405.cms (accessed September 15, 2018).

UNHCR- The UN Refugee Agency (2015). "Mixed Movements in South-East Asia." *UNHCR- The UN Refugee Agency*, https://www.unhcr.org/554c6a746.html (accessed October 12, 2018).

———. (2016). "Mixed Movements in South-East Asia." *UNHCR- The UN Refugee Agency*, http://reporting.unhcr.org/sites/default/files/UNHCR%20-%20Mixed%20Movements%20in%20South-East%20Asia%20-%202016%20--%20April%202017_0.pdf (accessed June 3, 2019).

———. (2017). "Joint Statement on the Rohingya Refugee Crisis." *UNHCR- The UN Refugee Agency*, www.unhcr.org/59e4c17e5.html (accessed August 14, 2018).

Unjhawala, Yusuf (2017). "India Needs to Help Rohingyas Without Letting Them in." *The Economic Times*, September 29, https://economictimes.indiatimes.com/news/politics-and-nation/india-needs-to-help-rohingyas-without-letting-them-in/articleshow/60757610.cms (accessed September 21, 2018).

Vembu, Venky (2017). "India's Rohingya Dilemma." *The Hindu Businessline*, September 12, www.thehindubusinessline.com/opinion/columns/from-the-viewsroom/indias-rohingya-dilemma/article9856323.ece (accessed September 11, 2018).

Vishwanathan, Shiv (2017). "There's a Rohingya in All of Us." *The Hindu*, September 6, https://www.thehindu.com/opinion/lead/there-is-a-rohingya-in-all-of-us/article19626127.ece (accessed September 29, 2018).

Watts, Joe (2017). "Downing Street Says Burma's Treatment of Rohingya Muslims Looks Like Ethnic Cleansing." *The Independent*, November 13, www.independent.co.uk/news/uk/politics/downing-street-burma-rohingya-muslims-theresa-may-ethnic-cleansing-military-forces-a8052031.html (accessed August 29, 2018).

Wescot, Lucy (2015). "Who Are the Rohingyas and Why They Are Fleeing Myanmar." *Newsweek*, November 5, www.newsweek.com/who-are-rohingya-and-why-are-they-fleeing-myanmar-330728 (accessed August 13, 2018).

Worley, Will (2017). "China Refuses to Condemn Burma Over Rohingya Crisis and Says Foreign Intervention Does Not Work." *The Independent*, October 21, www.independent.co.uk/news/world/asia/rohingya-burma-refugees-myanmar-china-refuses-to-condemn-persecution-genocide-burning-foreign-a8012961.html (accessed August 29, 2018).

Yegar, Moshe (1972). *The Muslims of Burma: A Study of a Minority Group*. Wiesbaden: Otto Harassowitz.

———. (2002). *Between Integration and Secession: The Muslim Communities of the Southern Philippines, Southern Thailand, and Western Burma/Myanmar*. Lanham, MD: Lexington Books.

———. (2018). "The Plight of Rohingya in Myanmar." *Israel Journal of Foreign Affairs*. https://doi.org/10.1080/23739770.2018.1515713 (accessed August 11, 2018).

Yhome, K. (2018). "Examining India's Stance on the Rohingya Crisis." *ORF Issue Brief 247*, www.orfonline.org/research/examining-indias-stance-on-the-rohingya-crisis/ (accessed September 15, 2018).

———. "Suu Kyi Focuses on Neighbourhood Diplomacy." *www.orfonline.org*, www.orfonline.org/research/suu-kyi-focuses-on-neighbourhood-diplomacy/ (accessed August 23, 2018).

4

REALITY ON THE INDO–MYANMAR BORDER

Field observations from Longwa and Hmaungbuchhuah on issues of ethnicity, connectivity and security

Rajeev Bhattacharyya

The region known as the Indo–Myanmar border is a long stretch of land spanning 1643 km that mirrors the diversity in India's Northeast and Myanmar. It is inhabited by communities speaking different languages and following disparate customs and religious practices since time immemorial. The borderland had remained outside the active sphere of the colonial regime since it was not considered necessary for a variety of reasons. The border, which was hurriedly delineated in 1947, divided the homelands of many ethnic groups although both the countries also agreed to maintain the 'free-border regime' ensuring the unhindered movement of people from both sides. A large chunk of the border region remained inaccessible during the subsequent decades owing to factors ranging from poor connectivity to disturbed conditions that have also discouraged research and detailed reporting. But undercurrents of change in all spheres of life are now palpable in the region in varying degrees. The slew of policies unleashed by the governments, coupled with the changed aspirations of the younger generation and the onset of improved modes of communication have engendered a situation different from the earlier times. This chapter makes an attempt to analyze the changing realities in the India–Myanmar borderlands based on field visits in Longwa and Hmaungbuchhuah.

Field visits indicate that the traditional notions about security, connectivity and ethnicity are undergoing a change that are specific to ethnic linkages, local perceptions on security and age-old connectivity across these regions. The discussion in the chapter reveals that the cross-border access to socioeconomic activities like primary education and informal economic exchanges are indispensable that have been historically pursued due to the livelihood patterns of the borderlands. The chapter also critically evaluates the literature on borders and borderland livelihoods to support the argument.

Borders and borderlands: a theoretical overview

Borders are defined as 'institutions and symbols that are used by states to reproduce territorial power' (Passi 2009). Borders are considered as dynamic and crucial, related to 'changing societal power relations and have to be analyzed critically in context' (Passi 2009). An analysis of the literature on border studies suggests that the persistence and disappearance of borders is a heavily contested domain. In Asia, the studies show that an important aspect of borders in the region is 'the way people imagine the border as modern or pre-modern' (Gellner 2013, 7). Asia inherited both these types of borders, pre-modern as they are 'fuzzy and contested and also because the local population in many places have strong ties across borders'(Gellner 2013, 7). Daily lives are carried on across these borders. This applies to the India–Myanmar border areas where the local population can move across the border on a daily basis. The nature of interaction displays 'ground level realities' and the variations of economic and cultural relations over time in these borderlands.

Unlike the integrated borders in parts of Asia or Europe, the local economies in these regions display unofficial forms modeled on local governance structures where the regulatory practices of the state were missing. In the recent decade, there has also been a change in the attitudes and perceptions of especially the younger generation in these borderlands. More specifically, the perceptible changes in the agricultural practices and the involvement of the younger generation in the Konyak region as the rest of the chapter reveals demonstrated the 'newer paradigm of change' in these borderlands. Perhaps the new generation has increasingly realized the realities and benefits of becoming a part of the expanding market on either side of the border regions in India and Myanmar. In the backdrop of this perspective, borderlands seem to have created a niche to strike a reasonable balance between the formal and informal provisions that have long been the prevailing features of these domains.

In this chapter we define borders as a physical marker that allows the movement of people, goods and information through acceptable means. Inter-exchange of culture and identity allows us to examine the 'symbolic and material processes of social experiences' that take place on both sides of the borders between the residents. Cultural constructions are normal and a routine process that goes into the making of the lives of the people in the borderlands. Similar to Walker's analysis of the contemporary processes of development, cross-border exchanges and processes in the upper-Mekong region, the India–Myanmar borderlands also exhibit 'contradictions, disillusionment and provides unevenly distributed benefits and opportunities' (Walker 1999, 5). Walker also argued that there are variations and differences in characteristics in different borderlands. This analysis can also be applied to understand the day-to-day socioeconomic interactions between people and changes in the India–Myanmar borderlands.

Although the focus is not so much on a borderless world as some scholars suggest, in this chapter, we move away from a focus on state-centric analysis of borders and the pragmatic relations between the India–Myanmar borderlands. State-centric analysis examines the existence of strict security surveillance and bounded territories that prevent cross-border relations on a normal basis. These institutions are suggestive of state regulated movement of goods and people across borders. The complexity of these approaches on borders can be explained in Passi's words, who argued,

> States are changing, but they are not disappearing. State sovereignty has been eroded, but it is still vigorously asserted. Governments are weaker, but they can still throw their weight around. At certain times publics are more demanding, but at other times they are more pliable. Borders still keep out intruders, but they are more porous. The cultural roles of borders received more attention around 1990, but scholars were still mostly concerned with concrete border landscapes, which also implied that the complex roles of borders in the constitution of the power relations sedimented in state-territoriality were very much taken for granted.
>
> *(Passi 2009, 2–7)*

This chapter draws from both these approaches and shows the coexistence of check posts and people-to-people exchanges in both formal and informal ways in the India–Myanmar borderlands. With the change of regime in Myanmar, alternative forms of livelihood have unfolded in the recent decades in these borderlands. Mobility has increased and is much more visible not so much as a part of the integrated economy but as peripheral agents of contemporary changes and exchanges in the changing political economy of the borderlands.

Observations in Longwa

At the trijunction of Nagaland, Arunachal Pradesh and Myanmar is the border village of Longwa straddling the international border. It is inhabited by the Konyak, the largest among the Naga tribes, who were more famous for headhunting, which primarily entailed fetching the decapitated heads of adversaries from neighboring villages. According to oral history, the village originated sometime in the 16th century after being occupied by immigrants whose place of origin is still a topic of debate.[1] Due to the remoteness of the habitat, the pace of social change had been slower which was similar to the situation in some Naga inhabited regions of Myanmar in contrast to the trend discernible among the tribes in Nagaland where Christianity and government policies had brought about a vast transformation. No wonder the current social and economic indicators point to a wide gulf between the eastern and other districts of Nagaland (Nagaland Vision 2030).

Besides remoteness, insurgency has also been a contributing factor to the backwardness of Longwa and the adjoining areas of Phomching Circle in Nagaland's Mon district. Although the separatist movement in Nagaland began from the late 1940s, the Konyak region became intensely associated after the birth of the National Socialist Council of Nagaland (NSCN) in 1980. For the first time, NSCN brought a greater number of Naga leaders from both sides of the border on a common platform, which included several Konyak functionaries. Mention may be made of the venerable Khole Konyak, who ensured the support of almost all the villages inhabited by his community and the contiguous regions in both the countries after being assigned the role of deputy chief of the army in the new organization. However, in 1988, the outfit split into the Khaplang and Isak-Muivah factions and a deadly turf war ensued between the two groups for the control of territory. The turnout of events in the subsequent years ensured a greater control of the Khaplang faction (NSCN-K) over the Konyak region and the Naga inhabited more areas of eastern Nagaland and Myanmar than the Isak-Muivah group.

Nestled at a strategic location, Longwa has a population of around 7,000 people and is considered one of the bigger Konyak villages in the region.[2] It is concentrated within a stretch of 1.5 kilometers with the highway running close to the international boundary at several points. As in the previous decades, the border has never been a barrier in the continuation of social and economic ties among the villages, which is similar to the situation along the entire border that touches as many four states in India's Northeast. The 'free-border regime' allows residents from one country to cross the border and journey to a distance of 16 km but the travel sometimes entails reaching destinations at far-off places for different reasons. Longwa has long served as a crucial link to important centers on both sides of the border. It was connected to Challam Basti in Myanmar, the headquarters of NSCN, until it was raided by the army in the mid-1980s.[3] This was one of the first camps

FIGURE 4.1   A village in Longwa.

Source: Fieldwork, September 2016

of NSCN with a combined presence of rebel cadres from different states of India's Northeast and Myanmar, which was replicated at other places in northern Sagaing Division.[4] Years later, Longwa continued to be an important link with Taga where the central headquarters of the Khaplang faction of NSCN is located and other places like Lahe and Hkamti where Naypyidaw has a presence.[5] And it is from Longwa that the district headquarters in Mon can be reached and beyond to other towns in Nagaland and Assam. A major attraction is the civil hospital at the district headquarters at a distance of 42 km for treatment of ailments like tuberculosis since the primary health center at Longwa is nonfunctional. The hospital's infrastructure received a boost after *Medicins Sans Frontieres (MSF)* was engaged by the government between 2010–14 when a pharmacy, operation theater and a new state-of-the- art delivery facility came into being.

This researcher has visited Longwa on several occasions during the past one-and-a-half decades but a different situation was observed during the last assignment in 2016. While a section continued to engage in the conventional methods of agriculture including shifting cultivation, there was greater concern among the younger generation for alternate sources of livelihood and avenues of earning money. The evidence was discernible in the plots of cardamom cultivation at regular intervals on both sides of the road between the district headquarters and Longwa. There were cultivators enquiring about the market price in Guwahati and elsewhere and details of the network for faster transportation of the item. Many of them rued about the lack of government support in providing access to markets, which could have nullified the role of middlemen (Bhattacharyya 2017). A major portion of the produce is purchased by traders at the neighboring town of Sonari in Assam at prices which the farmers claim ought to have been much higher. Unlike the more commonly found green cardamom, the variety grown in Mon is black cardamom which is darker and larger, which is also grown in Sikkim, Darjeeling, and in parts of Nepal and Bhutan. Its aromatic seed capsules have a great demand in the domestic and international market: a kilogram is sold at rates ranging between Rs 800–1,200 which is several times more than the existing rates for rice, maize or vegetables grown in the village. About 600 kilograms are harvested from one bigha of cultivation every season in September. The success has also motivated the village elders to encourage more farmers to take the plunge into cardamom cultivation (Bhattacharyya 2017).

The change in the mindset was striking given that joining the rebel ranks was considered a viable option until recently by a sizeable number of the youth in such militancy-ravaged pockets in the Northeast. The transformation can be attributed to a combination of factors including war weariness, changed aspirations of the younger generation, easy access to information through technology and efforts made by the government to promote development in the eastern districts of the state. More young men and women are venturing out to the neighboring towns in the state in search of jobs and those that have stayed back are looking for avenues of gainful employment. Residents are also keen to attract more tourists for the annual Aoling festival, which celebrates the arrival of spring and

FIGURE 4.2   Cardamom farming, Longwa.

Source: Fieldwork, September, 2016

the Konyak new year.[6] Some families (from Nagaland) have even enrolled their children in a Myanmarese school named Amaka Longwa Theinka Primary School in the village with the hope of getting jobs in the neighboring country. Interestingly, the trend is being noticed in spite of the presence of two schools under the Nagaland government and a school run by missionaries in the village. Free education in the Myanmarese school is an incentive but there is also the belief that passing out of the school could offer employment in the development projects to be launched by *Naypyidaw* in the Konyak region in Myanmar. A newly built non-concrete road meandering through the hills from Longwa was visible that will soon link up with Loji and beyond to more settlements in Myanmar.[7] Interestingly, this trend seems to be concurrent with the increase in the number of young men from Myanmar arriving in Nagaland either for menial jobs or treatment of diseases.[8] The changed policy of *Tatmadaw* that has led to cordial ties with the Nagas is undoubtedly a factor contributing to the increased and unhindered movement of people across the border.

Gone are the days when *Tatmadaw* was viewed as a tyrant that would frequently descend on the villages to loot and burn. Its policy toward the Naga inhabited region underwent a marked change from 2001 when an informal understanding was firmed up with the NSCN (K) which was later converted into a written agreement in 2012 (Bhattacharyya 2014, 286). It may be mentioned that *Tatmadaw* has concluded ceasefire agreements with numerous rebel groups in the country since 1989 but only a few were written agreements, which proves the importance accorded to the Nagas. This also explains why the army has been reluctant to demolish the rebel camps and training facilities in Sagaing Division in spite of repeated pleas from New Delhi. For the first time, the *Naypyidaw* distributed solar panels at several villages in the region including Longwa, which was unthinkable two decades ago.[9] Even doctors were dispatched to some villages when news broke out about people dying from a mysterious disease, which showed symptoms similar to measles (Myint Kay Thi 2016). Myanmar government officials have also been spotted on a couple of occasions in the past six years interacting with the inhabitants at Longwa and gathering data on various aspects of the settlement.[10]

But there is hardly any awareness about border trade either among the inhabitants or government officials despite the fact that Longwa has been cropping up in academic discourses and government sponsored workshops from time to time. Residents were totally ignorant about 'Act East Policy,' and about the plans by the Indian government to link up with the neighboring country. A building was also hurriedly constructed some years ago at the outskirts of the village for promotion of trade, which now lies in a dilapidated condition. Electric poles were erected decades ago but they were never connected to the grid for transmission of electricity. The region across the border is even more backward, where modern traits of civilization like roads, schools, hospitals and power are yet to be seen and where money as a mode of exchange is just beginning to take root (Bhattacharyya 2014, 60). Villages in the Naga region were known as "Little Republics"; they were usually self-sufficient although scarcity of food sometimes becomes acute for some months every year. Their needs are few and items like salt, rice, clothes and medicines are imported through an informal mechanism from different centers in Mon. Of late, residents from neighboring villages in Myanmar like Hoyat, Thailo and Loji have also been noticed purchasing cellular phones from Mon town.[11] Incidentally, the network of cellular phones available in Mon also reaches several villages across the border. In the given circumstances, the immediate prospect of border trade in Longwa appears to be extremely dim which is also true of most villages along the state's border with Myanmar (like Pangsha) already earmarked as hubs of border trade. But trade through the informal channels could grow albeit at a slow pace, which is directly proportional to the increase in the income levels and growth of population.

More items are exported from Mon but opium seems to be a commodity that has been constantly imported since a long time from Myanmar. It is cultivated in the remote hills covering a wide expanse of territory in the Konyak, Lainong and Pangmi regions. It was also reported to be grown in certain pockets of Nagaland, Arunachal Pradesh and Manipur but the government agencies have been destroying the cultivated tracts at regular intervals, which contrast sharply with the scenario in the neighboring country. In Myanmar, NSCN (K) imposes a tax on opium, which is a primary reason why its cultivation would continue to flourish at least for some more time. During 2008–12, this researcher travelled to some Naga villages in Myanmar but opium was found to be banned only in Hoyat. Opium is a key ingredient for the manufacture of heroin but whatever is produced in

Myanmar is consumed locally and the surplus exported to villages in Nagaland and the eastern districts of Arunachal Pradesh. Addiction to opium continues to be a bane among the people in this region, which originated during the colonial era. Groups sitting around the hearth and inhaling long puffs of opium from a bamboo pipe is not an uncommon sight in the evening in these villages. Addicts were unequivocal that smoking of opium causes no harm and it cures stomach ailments. There were varying estimates about the number of addicts in the village but the majority view is that they were to be found in more than 50 percent of the households.

However, the church and some civil society organizations are convinced that addiction to opium causes long-term diseases. Some among them are also of the opinion that the high incidence of tuberculosis in the region is the result of continuous smoking of opium. Incidentally, *Medicins Sans Frontieres* treated a large number of patients suffering from the disease at Mon Civil Hospital with newly created facilities like special chest ward and designated microscopy center during 2010–14 (Nagaland India). Some groups in the village have also started a campaign against opium and it is not unusual for teenagers to check the vehicles on the road between Mon and Longwa for confiscation of the commodity meant for different destinations across the hill state. They were of the view that disruption in the supply chain between the production and consumption centers could contribute vehemently toward checking further addiction. They explained that their efforts to eradicate the menace have found support among organizations active in other parts of the eastern districts in the hill state.

The network of local groups is fast expanding facilitated by technology, cellular phone and social media, which are breaking traditional cultural barriers. The impact is perceptible among the inhabitants of Longwa who not only take pride in identifying themselves as Konyak but also for being part of a larger community residing on both sides of the border. The *Ang* (chief) of Longwa exercises jurisdiction over 30 villages with his deputies stationed in every settlement. There are councils in every village headed by an elder that keeps a tab on the progress of development schemes sponsored by the government among other functions. The movement for unity began decades ago, which picked up momentum in the early 1980s due to the campaign unleashed by the NSCN. Some residents claimed that plans were firmed up to erect a fence on the border in and around the village after the ambush by separatist rebel groups in Manipur in 2015 which resulted in the death of 18 army personnel. Subsequently, representations were made from the village to the Assam Rifles and the legislator voicing opposition to the proposal, which was soon dropped. Some residents were even heard toying with the idea of making a representation to the government with the demand to declare Longwa a 'special zone' without a border. Greater connectivity has reinforced ethnicity among the Konyak themselves and has also contributed toward forging a larger identity as 'eastern Nagas' which is evidenced from the unstinting support of the community and its leaders to the demand of a separate state by the Eastern Naga People's Organization (ENPO).

ENPO is demanding that the districts of Mon, Kiphire, Tuensang and Longleng be carved out from the state of Nagaland to form a separate state called *Frontier Nagaland*. ENPO is the apex organization of six Naga tribes – Konyak, Khiamniungan, Chang, Yimchunger, Sangtam and Phom –inhabiting the four districts. It had submitted a memorandum to Prime Minister Manmohan Singh in 2010 urging him to accept the demand while asserting that only a separate state for the six tribes would bring about socioeconomic development in the border region. Prior to Nagaland's attainment of statehood in 1963, the entire area was under the Tuensang Frontier Division of NEFA and Mon, Kiphire and Longleng emerged as separate districts after Nagaland was carved out of Assam. The demand was rejected by the UPA government but it offered a special economic package, which came only months after an autonomous council was proposed by the state government. ENPO has refused to accept the package and has been persistent with its demand for a separate state. A public rally was held on September 14, 2018 in Tuensang to reaffirm the demand for a separate state, which was unanimously supported by the representatives of village council associations, *gaonbura* (village chief) associations, senior citizens and other groups.

Observation in Hmaungbuchhuah

Separated from Longwa by hundreds of kilometers along the circuitous border is another village called Hmaungbuchhuah in Lawngtlai district of Mizoram which displays a pattern of lifestyle and socioeconomic conditions which are similar and dissimilar to other settlements. Located on the banks of the Sekul river in Bumthlang subdivision, the hamlet is inhabited by the Zakai or Rakhine Budhists as they are called by other local communities. Like other border settlements, they have ties with members of their community across the border in Myanmar's Chin State. The settlement is located 3 km ahead of the international boundary and separated by a distance of 87 km from the district headquarters of Lawngtlai. According to one estimate, the population of the Zakai in Lawngtlai would consist of around 2000–2500 out of a total population of 60,000 Budhists in Mizoram.[12] Data about Hmaungbuchhuah is extremely scarce and there is hardly any information available on the internet. Interaction with the inhabitants reveals that they are heavily dependent upon jhum cultivation where a range of vegetables are grown throughout the year. Only shrubs and grass are visible in the hillocks surrounding the village with intermittent patches laid completely bare for cultivation. Occasionally, there is a change in the vegetables that are grown although a few items like rice and maize are grown every year. The gap between demand and production is fulfilled by importing food items from Myanmar where cultivation is reportedly done on a larger scale.

Many settlements on the borderlands are deprived in terms of education and medical facilities and Hmaungbuchhuah is no exception. Perhaps it would figure among the hamlets with the least access to such facilities, which is similar to the condition of some Lisu inhabited villages in Arunachal Pradesh's Changlang

FIGURE 4.3   Hmaungbuchhuah village, Mizoram.

Source: Fieldwork, March 2018

district.[13] A school that was constructed at Hmaungbuchhuah some years ago now lies abandoned and the district administration does not have any answer to resolve the issue. There are no teachers who know the Zakai language, nor any books or syllabus designed specifically for the community. There are no schools across the border where the children could have enrolled themselves. The few monks stationed at the monastery in the village sometimes gather the children around them for informal classes but they are irregular and inconsistent. Families who can afford to bear the expenses have begun to send their children for studies to far-off locations in Arunachal Pradesh where residential schools have been established by Chakmas.[14] There was also a young monk in the village who was stationed in Bangalore but such cases were more an exception than the rule. Education is considered a privilege, which only a few families can afford for their children.

There is a high incidence of diseases like malaria and jaundice at Hmaungbuchhuah besides the ailments related to the stomach. Every year, these diseases take a toll in the absence of either health centers or hospitals in close proximity. The civil hospital is located at the headquarters in Lawngtlai but availing its services could depend upon availability of transport. Cases were heard when patients died on the way to the hospital or within days after being admitted. There was also a patient who breathed his last as he needed a surgery to be done but there was no surgeon in the hospital. So, in the village, the adage goes that 'Prevention is better than a cure' as there may not be a cure at all to some diseases. In terms of preventive measures, some pills that are imported from Myanmar are kept handy, which are popped whenever there are symptoms like fever and weakness. Besides the local methods of filter for drinking water using sand and coal, some families also resort to boiling the water fetched from the Sekul river before consumption. In the absence of electricity, firewood is the fuel for all the households, which also become scarce during the rainy season.[15] Electric poles were erected early in 2018 but there was no supply of power.

On a comparative note, the differences between Longwa and Hmaungbuchhuah are more glaring than the similarities. The Rakhine or Zakai Budhists in Mizoram are a minority in the district where the Lai have the maximum numbers. The Lai are Christians, speak a different language and belong to the Kuki-Chin-Mizo ethnic group that inhabits a wide expanse in Mizoram, Manipur's Churachandpur and the Chin State in Myanmar. The district has an autonomous council under the Sixth Schedule to the Constitution, which is one among three such bodies in the hill state. These councils are called 'state within a state' and are meant exclusively to promote development and protect the interests of local communities. But there has hardly been any representation in the council from the Zakai since their numbers are too small to really matter in the politics of the district. Nor is the village visited by politicians asking for votes during elections, unlike other border settlements in Mizoram and the Northeast.[16] Under such circumstances, the dependence of the Zakaion the government in Mizoram or its agencies is almost nil as they have developed their own strategies of sustenance and livelihood. Two shops located at the heart of the village offer a glimpse of the ties between the village and the settlements across the border. These shops were found to sell a range of items including shawls, bed sheets, blankets, trousers, hats, footwear, vegetables, dried fish, pickle, chocolate, etc. manufactured either in China or Myanmar. A shopkeeper disclosed that even large orders were accepted during certain events, which could take about a week to deliver. He receives his supplies from locations across the border where large volumes of all items are stored and which are regularly replenished through routes linked to far-off cities in Myanmar.

But unlike the Naga inhabited region where an inhabitant can freely travel on both sides of the border, the movement of the Zakai is restricted on due to disturbed conditions on the other side of the border. In October 2017, at least 11 soldiers of the Myanmar Army were killed at Paletwa on the Kaladan river following an ambush by the Arakan Army along the border of Chin and Rakhine States (Weng and Naing Zaw 2017). The Arakan Army is a rebel group of ethnic Buddhists and part of the Northern Alliance consisting of insurgent outfits from the northern region of Myanmar. The army retaliated with the same ferocity witnessed on several occasions earlier at different conflict-ridden zones in the country. Zakai inhabited villages suspected to have given asylum to the militants were burnt, bombed and hundreds forced to flee their homes in different directions. A month later, a large group of 1484 refugees including women and children streamed across the border into Mizoram. Most of them who did not have relatives in these villages were put up in school buildings and community halls in Zochachhuah, Laitlang, Dumzaut-lang and Hmawngchhuah across the district. Relief in terms of food, medicine and

FIGURE 4.4 A Local shop in Hmaungbuchhuah village, Mizoram.

Source: Fieldwork, March 2018

clothes was distributed by the district administration, Assam Rifles and local organizations such as the Young Lai Association (YLA) and Mizoram Thalai Kristian Pawl (MTKP), the youth wing of the Baptist Church of Mizoram (Press Trust of India 2017). Continuous efforts were also on by the government agencies to ensure their return; the Assam Rifles held a series of meetings with the Myanmar Army but the task was easier said than done. By March 2108, only 996 refugees could be persuaded to return while the others preferred to stay back at the refugee camps in Mizoram. Weeks later there were conflicting reports from across the border but all of them pointed toward an enhanced presence of the army combating to erode the adversary's support bases. According to some inputs, severe restrictions have been imposed on the villages similar to some Rohingya settlements in the neighboring Rakhine State of Myanmar. Resettlement has been permitted with a warning to all residents to abstain from supporting the rebel group (Bhattacharyya 2018a). Inhabitants from the villages in Mizoram have to produce identity cards and await permission sometimes to visit neighboring destinations in Myanmar.[17]

Security forces in Mizoram are alert along the southern border of the state following reports and inputs from the Myanmar army that functionaries of Arakan Army often take refuge at the Buddhist villages. During the rainy season, there are areas along the border that remain disconnected for several weeks from the district headquarters due to dearth of roads and bridges. Efforts are on to eradicate the gaps and ensure greater surveillance along the entire stretch of the border.[18] Another area of huge concern for Mizoram is the increasing flow of synthetic drugs (like *Yaba* and *World is Yours*) from Myanmar. The most prolific route is through Champhai on the eastern flank but there are reports that Arakan Army is also involved in the illicit trade. A section of officials are apprehensive that the rebel group could make efforts to lure and engage the poor residents of Hmaungbuchhuah and Zochachhuahto peddle the contraband item.[19] However, it must be borne in mind that proliferation of drugs and weapons depends to a great extent upon connectivity and routes that must remain hidden from security forces. Under the existing circumstances, it remains to be seen if the Budhist villages in Lawngtlai can replicate the role of some settlements in Champhai, which are engaged in the illicit trade.

Residents of Hmaungbuchhuah have pinned high hopes on the multi-crore Kaladan Multimodal Transit Transport Project envisaged as a key component of the Act East Policy and aimed at providing an outlet for the landlocked Northeast to Kolkata through Myanmar. They feel that they would be able to avail alternate and lucrative sources of income after the project is completed. Their expectations may not be based on false assumptions but hurdles in both countries have impeded the project. Work on the project had been stalled many a time following an agitation from landlords in Lawngtlai who are demanding compensation from the government. The uproar is over a plot of 40 acres near a border outpost of the Assam Rifles at Zochachhuah through which the Kaladan highway would pass through to Myanmar. Officials are of the view that the impasse would soon be resolved since the government is keen to offer a package to the landlords. No wonder, the budget for the 87 kilometers highway between Lawngtlai and Zorinpui which is financed by the Ministry of Road, Transport and Highways has been revised for the third time with the initial estimate of Rs 507 crore swelling to Rs 1011 crore. Two deadlines have already been missed and officials are reluctant to give the next date for completion of the highway. In March 2018, only 70 percent of the project was found to have been completed as per official records (Bhattacharyya 2018b). It is not precisely known if any scheme has been sanctioned so far for widening National Highway 54 from Lawngtlai to the state's border with Assam, which covers a distance of 515 kilometers via Aizawl and Kolasib. Although road conditions were found to be better than the other hill states such as Nagaland and Arunachal Pradesh, it is unlikely that the highway would be able to handle a large volume of traffic in the current conditions. There were bumpy stretches and potholes along the entire stretch considered the lifeline of Mizoram. At some places, it was difficult for two vehicles to cross without caution and deft maneuvering. The state government has submitted a proposal to the ministry for widening the highway till Silchar in Assam, which is also the point where the East-West Corridor begins.

In Myanmar, the construction of the Sittwe Port connecting the Kaladan river in Rakhine State, construction of a river terminal 158 km upstream at Paletwa and dredging of the river have been completed so far. There are reports indicating that the impasse over the 109-km road project that connects Paletwa river terminal to Zorinpui on the Mizoram border in Myanmar has drawn to a close. The 1,600-crore project has been awarded to Delhi-based C&C Constructions in June 2017. But the contractor had to wait till the next year for the mandatory clearances from the Myanmar government to start the groundwork (Ranjan Bose 2018). The Myanmar government might have been dragging its feet over the scheme owing to the disturbed conditions in the region and the increasing activities of Arakan Army. The road from Zorinpui to Paletwa passes through several strongholds of the rebel group, which has already launched an offensive against the army. Conflict had erupted again toward the fag end of 2018 after the army retaliated against the rebels in northern Rakhine State (Hnin Pwint 2018). It remains to be seen if the construction of the highway from Zorinpui to Paletwa takes off soon or if it remains stalled due to the disturbed conditions. Therefore, under the prevailing circumstances, it is hazardous to envisage an early timeframe for the completion of the Kaladan Multi-Modal Transit Transport Project.

Conclusion

In retrospect, the issues of security, ethnicity and connectivity are found to be interlinked in varying degrees along the Indo–Myanmar borderland, which have been shaped by a gamut of factors ranging from the historical to the current developments. Longwa and Hmaungbuchhuah depict different scenarios where the interplay of these factors has engendered different strategies of subsistence and adaptation. The observations also reveal that the pace and direction of social change depend much upon the nature and extent of social, economic and political ties with power centers and social groups on both sides of the border. But irrespective of these factors, awareness about Act East Policy and the plan to link up with Myanmar so assiduously promoted by New Delhi are extremely low along the border which points to the inescapable conclusion that there exists a wide gulf between the ground reality and the declared policies and objectives.

Notes

1 John Hutton's view is that the Nagas immigrated from Borneo while other theories suggest that they came from southeastern China. See Hutton (1921).
2 The Census of 2011 recorded 5132 inhabitants at Longwa in Nagaland. Also based on interview (September 20–22, 2016) with Tongyei, the king (Ang) of Longwa and other residents in Longwa (India & Myanmar).
3 Interview (December 2011–January 2012) with PareshBaruah, ULFA chief of staff, Sagaing Division, Myanmar. Interview (December 23–24, 2011) with S S Khaplang, NSNC (K) Chairman, Sagaing Division, Myanmar. Also see, Lintner (1996).
4 For more details, see Bhattacharyya (2014).
5 Based on a visit to northern Sagaing Division (13 October 2011–31 January 2012) to interview ULFA Chief of Staff Paresh Baruah and NSCN-K Chairman S.S. Khaplang at Hukwang Valley. The author returned through a route that began at Taga and ended at Longwa.
6 Interview (September 20–22, 2016) with residents of Longwa.
7 Ibid.
8 Interview (September 20–22, 2016) with Abon Konyak, resident of Loji village in Myanmar who stays in Longwa.
9 Interview (September20–22, 2016) with Abon Konyak, resident of Loji village in Myanmar who stays in Longwa. Solar panels were also seen by the author at Longwa in September 2016.

10 Interview (September 20–22, 2016) with residents of Longwa.
11 Interview (September 23, 2016) with a government official, Mon.
12 Interview (March 1–3, 2018) with government officials in Lawngtlai, Mizoram.
13 The author visited a Lisu village near Namdapha National Park at Changlang in Arunachal Pradesh in November 2013.
14 Interview (March 3, 2018) with residents of the Hmaungbuchhuah village, Mizoram.
15 Interview (March 3, 2018) with residents of the Hmaungbuchhuah village, Mizoram.
16 Interview (March 3, 2018) with residents of the Hmaungbuchhuah village, Mizoram.
17 Interview (March 3, 2018) with residents of the Hmaungbuchhuah village, Mizoram.
18 Interview (March 5, 2018) with a police official, Aizawl.
19 Interview (5 March 2018) with a police official, Aizawl.

References

Bhattacharyya, Rajeev (2014). *Rendezvous with Rebels: Journey to Meet India's Most Wanted Men*. New Delhi: HarperCollins Publishers.

———. (2017). "Cardamom Cradle: Longwa Village in Nagaland Adopts Spice Farming to Beat Drugs, Terror." *Firstpost*, May 6, www.firstpost.com/india/cardamom-cradle-longwa-village-in-nagaland-adopts-spice-farming-to-beat-drugs-terror-3425974.html (accessed May 7, 2017).

———. (2018a). "Buddhist Refugees in Mizoram Begin Journey Back to Myanmar, but Unconfirmed Tales of Horror Keep Them on Edge." *Firstpost*, March 9, www.firstpost.com/india/buddhist-refugees-in-mizoram-begin-journey-back-to-myanmar-but-unconfirmed-tales-of-horror-keep-them-on-edge-4383481.html (accessed March 10, 2018).

———. (2018b). "Road to Nowhere: Agitating Mizoram Landowners, Escalating Costs, Dearth of Records Stall Kaladan Project." *Firstpost*, March 15, www.firstpost.com/india/road-to-nowhere-agitating-mizoram-landowners-escalating-costs-dearth-of-records-stall-kaladan-project-4388959.html (accessed March 16, 2018).

The Census of 2011 Recorded 5132 Inhabitants at Longwa in Nagaland, India. www.census2011.co.in/data/village/267051-longwa-nagaland.html (accessed September 30, 2016).

Gellner, David N. (2013). *Borderland Lives in Northern South Asia*. Duke University Press.

Hutton, John H. (1921). *The Angami Nagas*. Macmillan & Co.

Lawi Weng and Htet Naing Zaw (2017). "Tatmadaw Troops Killed and Wounded in Arakan Army Ambush." *The Irrawaddy*, November 9, www.irrawaddy.com/news/tatmadaw-troops-killed-wounded-arakan-army-ambush.html (accessed November 15, 2017).

Lintner, Bertil (1996). *Land of Jade: A Journey from India Through Northern Burma to China*. Orchid Press.

Myint Kay Thi (2016). "Measles Vaccine Drive Launched to Stem Naga Outbreak." *Myanmar Times*, August 9, www.mmtimes.com/national-news/21840-measles-vaccine-drive-launched-to-stem-naga outbreak.html (accessed January 2, 2017).

Nagaland India (2010–14). "Medicins Sans Frontieres: Doctors Without Borders." www.msfindia.in/supporting-district-hospital-mon-nagaland (accessed February 14, 2017).

Nagaland Vision (2030). www.nagaland.gov.in/Nagaland/UsefulLinks/Nagaland%20Vision%20Document%202030.pdf (accessed October 12, 2018).

Nan Lwin Hnin Pwint (2018). "Tatmadaw, Arakan Army Clash in Buthidaung Township." *The Irrawadday*, December 6, www.irrawaddy.com/news/burma/tatmadaw-arakan-army-clash-buthidaung-township.html (accessed December 8, 2018).

Passi, Anssi (2009). "Bounded Spaces in a 'Borderless World': Border Studies, Power and the Anatomy of Territory." *Journal of Power* 2 (2) (August).

Press Trust of India (2017). "Mizoram's Lawngtlai District Starts Registration of Over 1,600 Myanmar Refugees Along Border." *Firstpost*, December 4, www.firstpost.com/india/mizorams-lawngtlai-district-starts-registration-of-over-1600-myanmar-refugees-along-border-4241429.html (accessed December 20, 2017).

Ranjan Bose, Pratim (2018). "India Starts Construction of INR1,600-cr Mizoram-Myanmar Kaladanroad." *Business Line*, April 17. www.thehindubusinessline.com/news/india-starts-construction-of-1600-cr-mizoram-myanmar-kaladan-road/article23577107.ece (accessed November 20, 2018).

Walker, Andrew (1999). *The Legend of the Golden Boat: Regulation, Trade and Traders in the Borderlands of Laos, Thailand, China, and Burma*. University of Hawaii Press.

5

TERRITORIALITY, ETHNIC CONTESTATION AND INSURGENCY IN THE INDO–MYANMAR BORDERLAND

Ngamjahao Kipgen

In October 2016, the External Affairs Minister of India, Sushma Swaraj requested the Myanmar Government to take steps in order to protect a banyan tree at Khampat in Sagaing region of northwestern Myanmar, which is regarded as the Mizo (Lushai) family tree (*Assam Tribune*, 13 October 2016; Barooah Pisharoty 2016). About 60 miles from Kalemyo on the road to the border town Tamu lies astride a small and insignificant town called Khampat,[1] a walking distance from Muolcham, the nearest village on the Indian side of the border. Much of the Kuki-Chin[2] legends are indeed associated with Khampat – it has been known and recognized as one of the earliest sedentary settlements of the Kuki-Chin people. Legend has it that before the dispersal from the Kale-Kabaw valley,[3] they planted at Khampat a banyan tree (*buong thing* or *bung pui*) and took a pledge that they would return to Khampat, their permanent home, when the sapling had grown into a tree and its hanging roots had turned into new stems (Vumson 1986, 58–59). The myths of the Khampat banyan tree were fostered by the Buddhist monks, and Kuki-Chin people who have emigrated to the Kale-Kabaw valley have used the legend as justification for their migration to the area (Lehman 1979). The legend depicts the Kuki-Chin people lebensraum. The geographical divisions of the Kuki-Chins initially created by the British colonialists, and were later reinforced by international boundaries in the postcolonial era.

Often, the Indo–Myanmar borderlands have been seen only from the perspective of the colonial and postcolonial states which see the border as the "outer land limits" (Nail 2016; Newman 2003). Cederlof (2014) situates the Indo–Myanmar borderland at the crossroads of old commercial trade routes between India, Burma, and China. Sanjib Baruah (2005) also strongly argued that Northeast India's ties – historical, cultural, social, and economic – do not stop at these international boundaries. Far from this, the people of the Indo-Burma borderland share more commonalities and have closer affinities with those of the Southeast than with their fellow men and women in the Indian mainland. According to Baud and van Schendel (1997) borderlands are home to 'borderland societies' with a distinctive socio-cultural, linguistic, economic, and political character. In fact Baud and van Schendel argue that the 'borderland people' are so different from everyone else that they feel 'ethnically and emotionally part of another, nonstate entity' (1997, 227, 233).

Drawing upon recent trends in historical researches, this chapter deals with a marginal 'hill people' in Northeast India and Upper Burma who did not themselves form a state, but had both resisted and collaborated with different state-building projects in Burma/Myanmar and India. van Schendel (2005) has argued that if we are to understand the state effect, we need to take seriously the experiences and history of the people whose lives were turned upside down by the creation of new international borders where none had existed before. The 'ethnohistory' (Dirks 2007 [1987]) and 'ethnogenesis' (Anderson 1999) of a fringe group like the Kuki-Chin ethnic group demonstrates the nature of community–state relations in an Asian borderland across the colonial and postcolonial periods. Reduced to an ethnic minority, the Kuki-Chin had been at the imperial edge of the British *Raj* before it got sandwiched between the two modern nation states – India and Burma (Myanmar). The chapter is a case study of the Kuki-Chins, known by different names in the region and its neighboring states. Generally identified as Kuki in other Northeastern states of India, they are called Mizo in the Mizo Hills (Mizoram) and Chin in Myanmar/Burma. In general, it represents the perspective of 'transborder people' (Weiner 1985; Campion 2017), who constitute the minority in the states in which they live (Asiwaju 1985, 1–2) today but have 'entangled histories' (Randeria 2006).

The chapter tries to understand the Indo–Myanmar borderlands as a space where colonial and postcolonial borders have had serious repercussions on the relationship of people of the same ethnic community, and on the other hand the revival of relationships across the border through the efforts of the people themselves relatively recently with the assertion and expression of ethnic nationalism. In other words, it is an attempt to examine the connected history of 'transborder' people within the broad framework of border and relationship. The emergence of Zomia, coined by Willem van Schendel, as a culturally distinct area comprising upland/highland of Northeast India and Southeast Asia against lowland civilization (van Schendel 2002; Scott 2009) has set a new paradigm and perspective of area study beyond border.

Colonial record and rule: open borderland and fixed boundaries

Colonial ethnographers and British officers who served in Burma (Myanmar), Chittagong Hill Tracts (Bangladesh) and Northeast region of India have written about the Kuki, Lushai (Mizo) and the Chins. They have emphasized the linguistic affinities among these groups. A remarkable feature among them is that members of different groups can converse with one another while using their respective dialects. The Kuki-Chins[4] are an ethnic people comprising numerous clans.

These clans share a common past, culture, customs and traditions (Shakespear 1912; Hutton 1929; Shaw 1929; Gangte 1993).

In colonial records, the first reference to the Kukis was made in 1777 A.D., when these tribesmen attacked the British subjects in Chittagong when Warren Hastings was the Governor General of Bengal (Shakespear 1912, 1). E.T. Dalton (1872, 44) traces the use of the term to an article written by Surgeon McCrea in the Asiatic Researcher (24 January 1799) who described the Kukis as a 'nation of hunters and warriors.' C.A. Soppitt (1976 [1893]) in his book *A Short Account of the Kuki-Lushai Tribes on the North East Frontier* wrote that all the tribes grouped under 'Kuki' had much in common, both in terms of language, manners, customs, and in terms of the system of traditional governance.

Similarly, Carey and Tuck, who were the first to bring the Chin under the system of British administration recorded that the term *Chin* is 'the Burmese corruption of the Chinese 'Jin' or 'Jen' meaning 'man or people'' (Carey and Tuck 1976, 3). The Chin and several of its synonymous names generally means 'People' and the name Chinland is generally translated as 'Our Land' reflecting the strong fundamental relationship they maintain with their land (Lian Uk 1968, 2). Evidently, the word 'Chin' had been used from the very beginning not only by the Chin themselves but also by neighboring peoples, such as the Kachin, Shan and Burman, to denote the people who occupied the valley of the Chindwin River.[5]

In Assam and Bengal, the Chin tribes who live close to that area were known as 'Kuki.' The term *Kuki* is Bengali word, meaning 'hill-people or highlanders,' which was, as Reid described in 1893:

> [O]riginally applied to the tribe or tribes occupying the tracks immediately to the south of Cachar. It is now employed in a comprehensive sense, to indicate those living to the west of the Kaladyne River, while to the west they are designated as Shendus. On the other hand, to anyone approaching them from Burma side, the Shendus would be known as Chiang, synonymous with Khyen, and pronounced as "Chin."
>
> *(Reid 1893, 238)*

G.A. Grierson (1904) in his monumental work, *The Linguistic Survey of India* has classified the Kuki-Chin as a sub-family of the Tibeto-Burman family. In 1912, Lt. Colonel Shakespear declared that the term Kuki refers to a group of closely allied clans, having well-marked cultural characteristics and belonging to the Tibeto-Burman stock. He stated that 'on the Chittagong border, the term is loosely applied to most of the inhabitants of the interior hills beyond Chittagong Hill Tracts.' He concluded by writing, 'Nevertheless, there is no doubt that the Kukis, Lushais and Chins are all of the same race' (Shakespear 1912, 8). William Shaw (1929, 16), a British civil servant who served in Assam wrote that 'the Koms, Aimols, Khotlangs, Thadous, Lushais, Chins, Pois, Suktes, Paites, Gangtes and so on are undoubtedly all connected,' and are Kukis. If we analyze their customs, there is a 'common principle'[6] running through them all (Shaw 1929, 16).

When the British colonizers suddenly intervened on the historical scene, the process for the formation of paramount chiefs had been set in motion in the Chin Hills and the Lushai Hills. The traditional territorial base of the Kuki-Chin was in the Northern Chin Hills till large parts of this tract were ceded to the jurisdiction of Manipur by the Boundary Commission of 1894. It is important to note that prior to the advent of the British colonialists, Kukis were an independent people ruled by their chieftains. In order to understand the territorial distribution and relative political standing of the Kuki-Chin at the end of the 19th century AD, it is imperative to look into the practices of Boundary Survey and administrative arrangement under British colonial rule. On September 28, 1892, the Political Officer of Chin Hills submitted "a scheme in detail for the future administration of the Chin Hills"[7] (and entered the number of tribes inhabiting the Northern Chin Hills as five in number, namely, Nwite (Guite), Yoe (Zou), Thadou, Kamhow (Kamhau) and Siyin (Sihzang). The first four mentioned are the northern most and the last the southern most.

The separation of British India and Burma in 1937 and the Partition of India in 1947 created arbitrary boundaries, dividing many ethnic groups such as the Kuki-Chins and placed them into different nation-states. These borders were created by uninformed and indifferent colonial overlords, who took decisions from a distance by ignoring geographical and historical realities, ethno-demography and economic interdependence, resulting in disorder to their lifeworld. This colonial geopolitics has been exacerbated by the hardening of international borders ever since 1947. Here, I concur with van Schendel that 'borders not only join what is different but also divide what is similar' (2005, 9).

The Kuki-Chin ethnic groups have more in common with the population living across the boundary than with their own nationals. So long as the national boundaries which separated the different civilizations were relaxed, the ethnic groups in the region lived in peaceful coexistence with each other and acted as a buffer against the intrusion of people from the other side (Nongbri 1995, 53). The affinity of groups with their kin groups across the border and the sense of support (both material and non-material) they derive from them have had serious implications (Datta 2000). Furthermore, after 1947, there came into existence a bounded nation-state due to endeavours by national governments and popular movements to close off, regulate and suppress mobility across national borders more rigorously than ever before, with a goal to defend national territory against foreign threats and to secure national territory against internal disruption that might be fed by forces across the border (Ludden 2003, 12). All these brought about the regulation and restriction of mobility across borders in India's northeast and worked against the interests of the transborder communities such as the Kuki-Chins, who, despite these divisions and restriction of movements, continue to maintain their age-old ties. According to Karin Dean (2005), these communities have 'creatively adjusted to the dominating international system of the states' and despite being citizens of different states, they are 'united through a tight unique kinship lineage network of various spatial trajectories and social bonds, a commonly recognized *lingua franca* and a variety of tangible ethnic features.'

In the next section, the chapter discusses that the Kuki-Chin are one people, a nation, and were always independent before the British annexed part of their territory—and may be regarded as part of the process of constructing an 'ethnie.' Here, my analysis corroborates Anthony Smith's seminal observation on formation and maintenance of ethnie, ethnic and nationalist identities (1986, 16).

Invoking an 'Ethnie': historical connection and territoriality of the Kuki-Chins

Ethnic identification among the tribal groups in Northeast India and elsewhere has centred on territorial affiliation (Sarkar 2006, 8) and claims for ancestral land based on past history (myths, songs and lores). Traditional accounts of the origin of the Kuki-Chin people have been obscured by myths and mythologies that together with symbols, values and other collective memories are important elements of what Clifford Geertz (1983) called 'primordial identities,' which so often define and differentiate the Kuki-Chin as a distinctive people and nationality throughout history. Here I follow Baud and van Schendel's (1997) bottom-up perspectives on borderlands, using oral history, by considering the experiences of the Kuki-Chins of India and Myanmar. In their self-perception, the Kuki-Chin groups believe that all of them originated from the same place, they have a common social origin and share descent. All sources of Kuki-Chin traditions maintain that their ancestors originated from 'Chinlung' or 'Sinlung' or 'Khul' which always means 'cave' or 'hole' no matter what the dialect.[8] This myth of social origin from a *khul* is well-documented in the writings of Shakespear (1912, 91–94), Shaw (1929, 24–26), Carey and Tuck (1976 [1896], 142), Parry (1976 [1932, 4), and Gangte (1993, 14–16), who stressed that the present day clans are descendants of the same progenitor.

This myth of social origin is narrated even today and is the subject of folk songs and stories. The location of the particular *khul* is uncertain, but its enlivening significance continues even today. The Kuki-Chin nomenclature acquired functional administrative utility during the colonial period. Nevertheless a mythology of common brotherhood has affirmed kinship among all these cognate groups. Kuki-Chin comprises numerous agnate clans with shared cultural roots. For instance, Mizo became an official terminology when the Lushai Hills district of Assam was changed in 1954 to the Mizo Hills district.

Territorial habitation has strongly defined Kuki-Chin identity and representation in colonial discourse. According to Volume 13 of the 1962 edition of the *Encyclopaedia Britannica* (1962, 15), Kuki is the 'name given to a group of tribes inhabiting both sides of the mountains dividing Assam and Bengal from Burma, south of the Namtaleik River.' In this sense, the term Kuki is used as a reference for a group of people living in a specific geography.

Captain R. B. Pemberton (1985 [1835], 16–18) made a remark that the Kukis, inhabiting the inaccessible broad belt between Tipperah and Chindwin River, lived in a state of splendid isolation.[9] The Kuki-Chin claimed to have their own state in the Chindwin Valley from where they fled the advancing Shan and Burman state-building projects.[10] That they might at some point have settled in the valley and lived in a walled city possibly under a ruler of their own, is corroborated by their deep-seated oral traditions. Captain Lewin (1870) described the Kukis as 'men who live in the interior part of the hills.' Later when he became the Deputy Commissioner of Chittagong Hill Tracts in 1870, he stated,

> The Looseis [Lushais], commonly called the Kookis [Kukis] are a powerful and independent people, who touch the borders of Chittagong Hill Tracts. They extended in numberless hordes north and north-east until they reach Cachar on the one hand, and the frontiers of Burma on the other.
>
> *(Lewin 1870, 130)*

Dalton wrote, 'The hill country occupied by them [Kukis] extends from the Valley of the Koladyne, where they touch on the Khumis to Northern Kachar and Manipur; a distance of about 300 miles' (1872, 44). An excerpt that provides a glimpse of the Kuki territory is available in the writing of G. A. Grierson (1904):

> The territory inhabited by the Kuki tribes extends from the Naga Hills in the north down into the Sandoway District of Burma in the south; from Myittha River in the east, almost to the Bay of Bengal in the west . . . From here a great mass of mountain ridges starts southwards, enclosing the alluvial valley of Manipur, and thence spreads out westwards to the south of Sylhet. It then runs almost due north and south, with cross-ridges of smaller elevation, through the districts known as the Chin Hills, the Lushai Hills, Hill Tipperah, and the Chittagong Hill Tracts.

The British managed to colonize Burma and thus the Chin Hills after invading as many as three times before they finally defeated it in January 1886 (Donnison 1953, 28). Like much of Southeast Asia, the Chin Hills were subjected to colonial rule, which lasted from 1824 to 1947. The Chin Hills were administered as part of Arakan Division and the American missionaries began arriving in the 1890s and, by the middle of the 20th century, most of the Chin people had converted to Christianity.

The ancestral domains of the Kuki-Chins were brought into British India and British Burma after the 'Anglo-Kuki war 1917–1919' or 'Kuki rising 1917–1919'[11] (also recorded as Kuki Rebellion). Borders were drawn dividing the Kuki-Chin into India, Chittagong Hill Tracts (Bangladesh) and Burma (Myanmar). There is some consensus that they are now known in Burma/Myanmar, Bangladesh and India as Chin, Kuki or Bawm and the Lushai or Mizo respectively (Lehman 1963). Subsequently the British employed these terms to christen these 'wild hill tribes' living in the 'unadministered area.' Colonial administrators eventually made these assigned titles legal.

The Kuki-Chin ethno-nationalist movement

The Kuki-Chin ethnic nationalist movement has continually raised issues of ethnicity and identity. The origins of the Kuki-Chin movement can be traced back to the

Anglo-Kuki wars of 1845–71. This was a time when the British Empire expanded its hegemony in various parts of India. British incursions into the Kuki territories threatened the Kukis' local self-regulatory powers and led to hostilities between them and the British. Haokip (1998, 73) summarizes how, faced with threats to their supremacy, the Kukis led by their chiefs held meetings at various places in the hills to organize a concerted campaign against the British and drive them out from their ancestral land (*Zale'n-gam*). They fought the British as early as 1845 and until 1871. The British themselves, who recorded it as the Great Kuki Invasion of the 1860s, have chronicled accounts of this Great War.[12] A series of further battles in 1872 and 1888, followed by the Anglo-Chin war of 1889–90 in Burma, preceded the Anglo-Kuki war of 1917–1919 in British India known as 'The First Kuki War of Independence.'[13] After this Great War, the Kukis of this area were subjugated, like the other communities, to British control and they dispersed to many more places.

Historically, it can be argued that the Chin Hills formed an independent state entity, which was never part and parcel of the ancient kingdoms of Burma and India (Stevenson 1943, iv–x).[14] When the area was merged into the Union of Burma in 1947, the Panglong Conference Agreement with Burman leaders, sought to secure some degree of continued autonomy for the Chin people. With the partition in 1947, the Panglong Agreement formed the Union of Burma,[15] and the Chin state leaders headed by Vumkhohau Thuantak, with Burman, Shan and Kachin leaders, participated in the Panglong Conference which discussed the future of an independent Union of Burma.[16] The members of this conference believed that the Shans, Kachins and Chins would more speedily achieve freedom by giving immediate cooperation to the interim Burmese government. The members attending the conference agreed to cooperate without any dissent.[17]

The Chin Hills representatives produced a Charter of Demands, to be presented to His Majesty's Government of Burma, submitted on 19 April 1947 at Maymyo to the Frontier Enquiry Commission, signed by all 19 representatives from the four subdivisions of the Chin Hills (Khupzago 1988, 114–119). Numerous demands related to equal rights for the Chin people after federation with Burma, appropriate representation of their voices and needs, financial provisions for local entities and adequate community representation at central level. There was even a demand for some form of affirmative action for access of tribal people to education and employment. Significantly, item (xv) still refers to the possibility of secession in case of severe disagreement, though there was a desire to become an integral part of Burma (Furnivall 1960, 111–113).

However, the draft constitution was amended, betraying both in letter and spirit of the Panglong agreement (Vumson 1986). Neither the Panglong Agreement of February 12, 1947 nor the Frontier Enquiry Commission of April 19, 1947 yielded any positive results and benefits for the Chins as expected by them. The hope of the Shan, Kachin and Chin people that freedom would be more speedily achieved if immediate cooperation was extended to the interim Burmese government was a far cry (Maung 1961, 229). Much discontentment arose among the Chin leaders at the obstinate attitude of the Burmese government, while poverty and underdevelopment in the region continued. Poverty led many Chins to serve in the Myanmar

Armed Forces (Tatmadaw), instead of devoting themselves to local politics or other activities. Indeed, this became the only career open for them (Fredholm 1993, 180).

The administration of free Burma soon fell into chaos, however, partly because various ethnic minority nationals were preparing to severe ties with Burma, hoping to declare independence for themselves. As ethnic insurgency grew in Burma, in 1948, Captain Mang Tung formed the Chin People's Movement for the Rights of the People. This challenged the hereditary community leadership and led to the birth of the Chin National Day on February 20, 1948. In 1957, the Chin People's Freedom League and the Chin Union were amalgamated to protect the rights of Chin people under the constitution. In 1964, after General Ne Win's military coup in 1962, an Anti-communist Freedom Organization was formed to struggle for the Chin people.[18] In 1969, Pu Tial Khal formed the Chin Liberation Front and became its president, with Thawmluai as vice-president and Thong Sei (Thawng Sai) as secretary of foreign affairs.[19]

Also, in India, the Kuki National Assembly (KNA) was formed in 1946 with the primary objective of fostering consciousness of common identity and making a single political unit of the Kukis. KNA also planned to establish a pan-Kuki platform for the Kuki-Chin groups of Manipur. The Kuki National Assembly had submitted a representation to the then Prime Minister of India, Pandit Jawaharlal Nehru, wherein it demanded the creation of a Kuki state way back in 1960 (*Kuki State* 1960). Similarly, the Chins have launched an agitation in support of their demand for the creation of an independent 'Chinland' comprising parts of India, Burma [Myanmar] and Pakistan [Bangladesh].[20] The Mizo National Front (MNF) formed in 1963 adopted a similar map projection as Grierson's (1904) Kuki country during its movement from 1960s to 1986. The MNF demand creation of 'Mizoram' as an independent and sovereign state. It was a major political movement of the ethnic people since India gained independence. In 1964, Kuki National Assembly supported the Manipur Mizo Integration Council (MMIC) for a single administrative unit.[21] The Mizo People's Convention was held at Kawnpui in Churachandpur from 15–18 January 1965. The main agenda was 'Territorial Integrity' and creation of one Administrative Unit for the Kuki-Mizo people called 'Mizoram State' (Vumson 1986, 278).

In 1986, the Mizo Accord was signed between the MNF and the Government of India. However, the Accord failed to achieve the principal objective of 'Territorial Integrity' and one Administrative Unit. However, as mentioned above, the Mizo Accord, signed with the Government of India in 1986, relates only to the erstwhile Lushai Hills, which represents a fraction of Kuki country. Only the former Lushai Hills became the state of Mizoram. The fall out of this lack of MNF leaders' political vision is immense, particularly in Manipur. Just six years after 1986, from 1992, the NSCN (IM)-led Nagas carried out a massive pogrom against the Kukis, which lasted until 1997.

On the Burmese side, official reluctance to grant more autonomy prompted the reorganization of various Chin insurgent groups. Prominent among these are the Chin National Front/Chin National Army (CNF/CNA) and Chin Liberation

Army (CLA). As discussed, by 1947–48, they were divided into three new postcolonial nation-states in their traditional territory. However, since amalgamation of the Kuki-Chin territories of India, Burma/ Myanmar and Bangladesh is clearly not possible across the various international boundaries, at present, the CNF/CNA are India-based Myanmar movements and the KNA/Kuki National Organization (KNA/KNO) is an India-based movement operating partly in Myanmar and mainly in India.

Mention may be made here that the institution of church plays a fomenting role in forging the Kuki-Chin ethnic group. Kuki-Chin Baptist Union (KCBU) was formed as a federal union among the Baptist denominations. It began as a consultation of the Kuki-Chin Baptist leaders. The constituent members were Kuki Baptist Convention (KBC), Chongthu Baptist Association (CHBA), Chin Baptist Association (CBA), Gangte Baptist Association (GBA), Thadou Baptist Association (TBA), Vaiphei Baptist Association (VBA) and Kom-Rem Baptist Association (KRBCA) etc. The outcome of the various consultations was the publication of a research book entitled *In Search of Identity* (Haokip 1986, 1–2) in 1986 and also the holding of a Conference from February 25-March 1, 1993 at Keithelmanbi village in Manipur (Haolai 1994, 19). The KCBU has greatly contributed to the unification of Kuki-Chin ethnic people spiritually, emotionally and politically.

The Kuki-Chin insurgency

The failure of the central and state governments to acknowledge the peaceful demand of the Kukis for a separate state in the 1960s (Kuki National Assembly, *Memorandum*), betrayal of Mizo National Front (MNF) in the 1980s and the territorial acquisitiveness and hegemonic policies of the Meitei and Naga insurgents in the past few decades have led to the emergence of Kuki revolutionary movement. The attainment of Mizoram statehood by the MNF not only frustrated but also greatly inspired the Kuki-Chins, at first especially in Burma. Within three to four months, on June 20, 1987, the Zomi Liberation Front (ZLF) was formed to strive for a free state for the Zomis in Burma, as done by the MNF for the Mizos.

In post-independent India, many tribal communities in the Northeast region gained separate statehood in due course, while most Kuki communities were left out which led to various insurgency movements. In response to this, on May 18, 1987, the Kuki National Front (KNF) was formed under the leadership of (Late) Pu Nehlun Kipgen at Molnoi village (Myanmar) to secure a separate 'Kuki state' within the Indian Union by integrating all KUKI INHABITED areas of Manipur.[22] In a statement, Pu Nehlun wrote that:

> The long sufferings and sacrifices of the Kukis, the pains and the agony of our forebears, are however not put into oblivion by the younger generation today. Having witnessed and experienced the step-motherly attitude and treatment from the Government of India for many decades since India's independence, the young generations of the eighties pledged to take up arms and resolved to

fight until a separate state for the Kukis is carved out within the framework of Indian constitution.

(The Shillong Times, 1 October 1993)

The birth of Kuki revolutionary organizations in the late 1980s was seen as a continuation of the unfulfilled aspiration that was initiated by the Kuki National Assembly (KNA). According to T. S. Gangte, the KNF was established to accelerate the demand earlier raised by the KNA in the 1960s for creating a Kuki state (Gangte 2007, 136).

The other group called the Kuki National Army (KNA) was founded in 1988 under the leadership of (L) Pu Thangkholun Haokip. Since then the KNA has been fighting to carve out a separate homeland for the Kukis living in Myanmar. Noted journalist Phanjoubam has observed that 'the underground KNA aims at achieving an independent sovereign Kuki state by carving out the Kuki-populated areas of Myanmar and portion of Kuki inhabited districts of Manipur' (2004, 171). Since the late 1980s, the Kuki National Organization (KNO) and its arm wing KNA have redrawn the map of *Zale'n-gam* by expanding the boundaries including some other parts of NORTH EASTERN India.

Zale'n-gam is an ideological concept propounded by P. S. Haokip (Haokip 2008), which means 'freedom of the people in their land.' It encapsulates and expounds the essence of Kuki history and nationalism and the restoration of the erstwhile Kuki territory in the precolonial period.[23] To understand *Zale'n-gam*, I have drawn upon Benedict Anderson's (1991) concept of 'imagined community.'[24] As discussed, the Kukis (India/Manipur), the Chins (Myanmar), the Mizos (Mizoram), although separated by different political boundaries, share the same social origin as evident in their common folklore, myths and legends. The motive and the intention behind *Zale'n-gam* is their desire to unify all the Kuki inhabited areas into a single administrative unit.[25] Oommen had argued 'some nations are subjected to ethnification as a result of a division of their ancestral homeland into two or more territories, thereby endangering their integrity as nations' (1997, 14). The KNO, under the leadership of, has propagated the ideology of *Zale'n-gam* which will unite the erstwhile ancestral domain of the Kukis prior to British rule and restore the Kuki nation (*23rd KNO Raising Day Message*, 24 February 2010).

The next section discusses the ethnic conflict arising from the question of "land" and claims for "exclusive territory" vis-à-vis "identity" in the context of Manipur state in India.

Politics of contiguous homeland and ethnic contestation

Fraser (1995) has rightly argued that the contention that the 'struggle for recognition' is fast becoming the paradigmatic form of political conflict since the later part of 20th century. And one of the most obvious aspects concern articulations of ethno-nationalist identities, groups seeking recognition and rights on the basis of being a people, an ethnic group or a nation (Baruah 2005). Contestations over claims and counter claims over territory on ethnic lines have been building up since the British rule in the Northeast region of India. With such overlapping and sometimes opposing territorial claims, it can hardly come as a surprise to anyone that ethnic mobilization and identity politics, more generally, easily take on a violent and socially destructive character (Vandenhelsken and Karlsson 2016). The growth of political consciousness among the hill people in contemporary Manipur, ethnic belonging too has got tangled with the claims over territory. The present political map of the state of Manipur is based on the creation of the British. In fact the term Manipur 'is not used at all until the British period' (Parrat 2005, 14). As much as the Kukis (KNF and KNA) claimed a Kuki homeland, the Nagas claimed large parts of Manipur as Naga territory. Like the Kukis demand, the Nationalist Socialist Council of Nagalim–Isaac Muivah (NSCN-IM), a Naga insurgent group established in 1980 also has the agenda of bringing the Nagas under one common political entity.

The history of inter-ethnic relationship in Manipur reached a turning point when the ethnic clashes between the Nagas and the Kukis broke out in the early 1990s. These ethnic clashes have promoted ethnic nationalism. The territorial claims of the Kukis pursued by the Kuki insurgents overlap the territorial demands of the Nagas (NSCN-IM) in Manipur. In short, it is this overlapping territorial interest which has embroiled the two communities and led to violent clashes during the 1990s. The Nagas see the Kukis as an obstacle to their long cherished goal of ethnic unification of all Naga inhabited areas. While the Naga insurgents have been consistently demanding the integration of all Naga inhabited areas in north east India (including the hill districts in Manipur), the Kuki insurgents have upheld a separate Kuki state (Kukiland) with Manipur as its bastion within the Union of India (*Memorandum* of KNF submitted to Prime Minister of India on August 2006).

A memorandum submitted by the Delhi-based Kuki Students' Organization (KSOD) to the Prime Minister of India on June 27, 2001, highlighted how the landholdings of the Kukis on their ancestral land are greater than those of the Nagas (Gangte 2007, 96). However, the Naga ethnic armies under the aegis of NSCN (IM) made strategic attempts to wipe out the Kukis from their place of habitation through 'ethnic cleansing' to strengthen their claims of a sovereign Nagalim.

It is worth recalling that the NSCN (IM) 'ethnic cleansing' policy against the Kukis during the 1990s had killed more than 900 Kukis, uprooted more than 350 villages while over 50,000 Kukis had been displaced (Haokip 2004). Tarapot Phanjoubam, a senior representative of Press Trust of India (PTI) based at Imphal, has given the statistics that 534 persons, including 391 Kukis and 143 Nagas were killed and 4900 houses, of which 2649 belonged to the Kukis and 2251 to the Nagas, were burnt down. The highest toll occurred in 1993 wherein 320 persons including 260 Kukis and 60 Nagas were killed, 138 others injured inclusive of 69 Kukis and Nagas each were injured, and 3520 houses inclusive of 2144 for Kukis and 1376 for Naga were also burnt down (till the day of December 10, 1995). He further added that during 1992 to 1999, more than 900 people inclusive of 534 Kukis and 266 Nagas were killed while others (257 Kuki and 223 Naga) sustained injuries, and 5724 houses of which 3110 belonged to the Kukis and 2614 to the Nagas were set ablaze (Phanjoubam 2007 [2004], 200). The Naga–Kuki clashes throughout Northeast India have left hundreds dead in the 1980s and 1990s. This indicates, in principle, how conflicting homeland demands could lead to ethnic cleansing in pursuit of 'pure ethnic states' (Bhaumik 2004, 231).

The issue of Manipur's territorial integrity divides the Meiteis (Hindu-valley dwellers), Nagas and Kukis. The Kukis and Meiteis protested the extension of Naga ceasefire (NSCN-IM with the Government of India) to Manipur in 2001 for different reasons. While the Meiteis perceived it as a threat to the territorial integrity of Manipur, the Kukis considered it as a significant step toward the Naga territorial unification (of all Naga inhabited areas) process that would affect their territory (ethnic homeland). The Kukis vehemently opposed NSCN (IM)'s ethnic cleansing policy and communal war to create a Greater Nagaland. The Meiteis very often question the need for separate states for both the Nagas and Kukis by citing the existing provisions for protecting them. The Meiteis have persistently made an attempt to abolish chiefship right over land, extension of Manipur Land Revenue and Land Reforms Act 1960 (as amended in 1989) in the hill areas, opposition of Sixth Schedule status to the present Autonomous District Councils (ADCs) have created a deep sense of insecurity among the Kukis and Nagas. The Meiteis opposed the tribes' demands for more autonomy and constitutional protection on the ground that these will usher the route to the formation of a Kuki state and Nagalim. In the process, the Kukis have ended up fighting both the Nagas and Meiteis, although more with the Nagas because of overlapping claims in the hill areas.

Political negotiations and challenges

As discussed, the political mobilization of the members of the Kuki community in support of a 'Kuki homeland' has revived their ethnic nationalism under the aegis of Kuki National Organization (KNO) and the United People's Front (UPF) (Kipgen and Roy Chowdhury 2016; Arora and Kipgen 2017). However, things have changed in the past few years. One important factor is the 'Suspension of Operations' (SoO) [Ceasefire] signed on August 10, 2005 between the Army and Kuki National Organization (KNO), followed by another SoO on August 22, 2008 signed between Government of India, KNO and the state Government of Manipur (*The Sangai Express*, 23 August 2008; *The Imphal Free Press*, 3 August 2008).[26] The United People's Front (UPF), formed in 2006, which is another umbrella organization comprising Kuki-Chin revolutionary groups, also signed the same SoO on August 22, 2008. Both UPF and KNO's political objectives are identical and focus on the demand for separate statehood for the Kukis. In my personal interview (May 2010) the President of KNO, P. S. Haokip, asserted the following:

> Kuki identity and nationalism is rejuvenated under the aegis of KNO and UPF (a conglomeration of several Kuki ethnic armed groups). The formation of the UPF and the KNO as a common bi-platform for all the existing Kuki

armed groups has shown a new sense of hope for the political movement of the Kukis once again.

According to Seilen Haokip, the spokesperson of the KNO, '[with the formation of UPF and KNO] . . . Kuki identity refashioned nearer to its historical status also set grounds for tangible deliberations for a stable political future for the people' (Haokip 2010). It may be mentioned here that the Kuki insurgency movement began in the late 1980s. Since then, many revolutionaries have sacrificed their precious lives. The biggest challenge is whether the signing of SoO would lead to a political dialogue and address the problems of the Kukis. Some of the Kuki communities are optimistic that the present SoO would find a lasting solution, while other sections are skeptical. They are apprehensive because such SoO or ceasefires, as seen in other parts of the region have not resulted in any effective resolutions of conflict and decline in violence. Will the Indian Government be able to tackle and resolve the ethnic conflict and restore peace in the region?

Current border impasse and conclusion

Since the early 1990s, under the new geopolitics of the region, India has dropped its general attitude of neglect toward its eastern bordering countries. In the process India and Myanmar has renewed their relationship – chiefly cooperation in developmental projects and trade, plus growing concern about counterinsurgency. These two policy concerns are evidently connected, since India launched several institutional and development projects through its 'Look [Act] East Policy' which would be beneficial to both countries on both counts. However, a related result of such concerns has been a quite aggressive effort to engage in border fencing between the two countries. Time and again, the construction work of the border fence by the Myanmar Army encroaches on Indian Kuki settlements. While the Government of India has voiced its concerns over this with the Government of Myanmar, India seems more concerned about controlling the insurgent groups in the region rather than safeguarding its territorial integrity. In all these new developments Kukis are again becoming victims by way of surreptitious ceding of their territory to Myanmar by India. There is an emerging concern on the part of the Kukis as the situation is becoming increasingly volatile.

For instance, just around 3 Km away from Moreh Township in Haolenphai, the Myanmar Army intruded and prevented the villagers from constructing a house. The villagers alleged that on March 3, 2017 the Myanmar Army had not only vandalized the village saw mill and took away the machinery but even looted their houses too.[27] There have been apprehensive on the part of the Kukis that the disputed land may be acquired by Myanmar very soon as they have already been carrying out construction work in the area and has repeatedly claimed Haolenphai to be their territory. The villagers of Haolenphai alleged that the Indian Army, which is guarding the international boundary area, is not providing any security as they remain mute spectators to the Myanmar Army who are constantly carrying out construction work at the area. In the last two years the Indian Authority have not taken any steps to stop the process of construction work such as shifting of boundary pillar to Manipur territory and construction of cannel. The villagers fear that they might lose the land of Haolenphai to Myanmar.

The border issue is a serious one but it has been rendered much graver by the government of India's unwillingness to acknowledge the border dispute. The border village (namely border number 75 and 76) like Haolenphai is a living testimony wherein the incursion by Myanmar soldiers into India is witnessed on a regular basis. 'The Burmese army personnel come to our village and keep loitering in the streets when it is dark, sometimes they come in vehicles. We are afraid to go out in our own village,' said L Haokip, a resident of Haolenphai village.[28] The said area is originally the ancestral land of the Kuki village and is claimed by Myanmar as their territory. The area Chairman of Lhangcham decried the step-motherly treatment by the Union government authorities and ignoring the woes of the villagers. 'We have been living in this land peacefully like our forefathers, we will not allow and resist the Burmese intrusion in any possible manner and even at the cost of our lives,' he said.[29]

Mention may be made that way back in 2003, the then Prime Minister Atal Bihari Vajpayee proposed holding an India–ASEAN car rally at the ASEAN–India Summit in Bali in 2003, to draw attention to India's geographical proximity with ASEAN countries. The ASEAN–India car rally became a reality on November 22, 2004, which was flagged off in Guwahati by Vajpayee's successor, Manmohan Singh. In his speech, the Indian prime minister referred to the 'Northeast' as a gateway to 'Asian Century.' The ASEAN–India car rally clearly reflects the existence of land route connectivity that could facilitate free flow of trade, investment and tourism between ASEAN and India. During the Second ASEAN–India car rally in 2012, the Kukis, who are mainly settled in the Indo–Myanmar border region, under the banner of Kuki State Demand Committee (KSDC), called for an indefinite blockade to press their demand for the creation of a separate Kuki state to be carved out of 'Kuki traditional lands' (*The Telegraph*, 12 December 2012). KSDC also 'threatened to block the entry of the Bangladesh, China, India, Myanmar (BCIM) Car Rally into "Kuki areas" of Manipur' (*The Times of India*, 13 February 2013). This agitation has pointed out the existence of a number of ethnic groups who have been ethnified by the British colonial rulers and the dissenting voices for their rights and autonomy in the postcolonial period.

The present central government policy of making agreements with different communities looks like 'appeasement policy' or 'divide and rule' and in the process delays justice, through prolonged silence regarding the bones of contention between different conflicting ethnic groups. On the other hand, the recent construction of border fencing which actually cedes landholdings of the Kukis to appease Myanmar does not augur well for ethnic minority people such as the Kuki-Chin group. This kind of policy may create more political unrest in future.

Notes

1 The present-day Khampat is a big town inhabited by the Kuki-Chin tribes, each tribe occupying different localities.

2 According to G. A. Grierson (1904, 126) the words Kuki and Chin are synonymous and are both primarily used for many of the hill tribes in general. Kuki and Chin are, then, like both sides of the same coin, combined as Kuki-Chin to cover a large internally diverse ethnic group which, to make things even more difficult, lives interspersed with other communities.

3 According to K. Zawla (1964) the Kuki-Chin people came to the Chindwin belt about 996 A.D.

4 In his *Linguistic Survey of India* (1904), G. A. Grierson gives a vivid account of the Kuki country during the colonial period. Grierson has grouped the Kuki-Chin in family of the Tibeto-Burman languages – largely based on historical, anthropological and linguistic affinities of the ethnic group.

5 In Burma, according to the Chin Hills Regulation of 1896, by a notification in the *Burma Gazette* (Christian 1942, 87), the term *Chin* includes Lushais, Kukis and Burmans domiciled in the Chin Hills and any person who has adopted the customs and language of the Chins and is habitually resident in the Chin Hills.

6 By 'common principle,' Shaw (1929) meant that all the groups under the Kuki fold have common ancestry, similar custom and language.

7 National Archives of India, New Delhi, Foreign Department, External Affairs, October 1893, Nos. 33–34, dated Camp Falam, September 28, 1892.

8 The literal meaning of *Chinlung* is 'the cave or the hole of the Chin,' the same meaning as the Burmese word for *Chindwin,* as in 'Chindwin River,' also 'the hole of the Chin' or 'the river of the Chin' (Lehman, 1963, 20). According to Rev. Liangkhaia, the inhabitants of Chin Hills, Manipur, Mizoram and Cachar all came from the traditionally conjectured place that is Chinlung (1976, 1). 'Sinlung,' according to Pu Rohauvung is a mythological rock fortress from which no one could escape (cited in Sonpate, 1977, 13–14).

9 See also Macrae (1801, 197), Mackenzie (2005 [1884], 287), Carey and Tuck (1976 [1896], 228).

10 For Kukis' settlement in Chindwin valley, see for instance, Lehman (1963), Vumson (1986, 26–105), Lalthangliana (1976, 1–26).

11 Scholars such as Bhadra (1975), Chishti (2004), Dena (1984, 1991), Gangte (1993) have written extensively on the Kuki Rising of 1917–1919. Also see Burma and Assam Frontier, Kuki rising, 1917–1919, L/PS/10/724, Oriental and India Office Collections (OIOC), British Library, London.

12 For details see Elly (1978 [1893]), reports about a series of raids and counter-attacks, p. 8.

13 This war is discussed in great detail by Kuki scholars who stress the sacrifices that their heroes made to safeguard the community's best interests, only to be defeated. See especially Haokip (1998, 75–160, 2008, 139–239); Guite and Thongkholal 2019.

14 Ethnically and historically, Chins and Burmans considered each other as different people, with a distinct language and culture.

15 For the actual document see: www.ibiblio.org/obl/docs/panglong_agreement.htm (Retrieved October 10, 2009).

16 In fact, the Shan, Kachin, Karenni and Chin States were referred to as frontier areas and were administered separately by the British. In other words, the ethnic minorities, literally, were neither present nor participated in political discourse with the British nor with the Burman.

17 An excerpt of the Panglong Agreement, signed on 12 February 1947, reproduced by Furnivall (1960, 94–96) and Khupzago (1988, 111–113).

18 It arose under the initiation of Colonel Son Kho Pau, Pu Dam Kho Hau, Pu Mang Khan Pau, Pu Hrang Nawl, Pu Son Cin Lian and Pu Thual Zen.

19 Fredholm (1993, 180) provides much further details of various Chin groups active in Burma.

20 See "Chins of Three Nations Want Free Homeland." (April 20, 1967). *The Times of India*, p. 9.
21 Document for Manipur Mizo Integration Council, signed by Holkhomang Haokip (now Ex-MP) and General Secretary and KT Lalla, Chairman of the Council.
22 Interview with S.T. Thangboi, the President (since 1993) of KNF in Ebenezer camp, Sadar Hills (Senapati district) during March 2009.
23 A nation may continue to be in its ancestral homeland and yet it may be ethnified by the native dominant collectivity transforming the original inhabitants of a territory into a minoritized and a marginalized collectivity (see Oommen 1997).
24 As Anderson explained, by 'imagined' he did not necessarily mean 'invented'; rather, people would define themselves as members of a nation 'who will never know, most of their fellow-members, meet them, or even hear of them, yet in the minds of each lives the image of their communion' (1991, 6).
25 Interview with P. S. Haokip, the President of KNO in Churachandpur, during June 2010.
26 Also see *Agreed Ground Rules for Implementation of the Suspension of Operations (SoO) with the United Peoples Front (UPF) in Manipur*, pp. 1–4, August 22, 2008, New Delhi.
27 "Haolenphai Fears of Losing Land to Myanmar," *Imphal*, April 2, 2017, www.imphal-times.com/news/item/8172-haolenphai-fears-of-losing-land-to-myanmar, accessed November 20, 2017.
28 Interview with a resident of Haolenphai village during May 2017.
29 Interview with the Chairman of Lhangcham area during May 2017.

References

Anderson, B. (2006 [1991]). *Imagined Communities: Reflections on the Origin and Spread of Nationalism*. London and New York: Verso.

Anderson, C. (1999). *The Indian Southwest, 1580–1830: Ethnogenesis and Reinvention*. Norman: University of Oklahoma Press.

Arora, V. and Ngamjahao Kipgen. (2017). "Demand for Homeland and Kuki Ethnic-Nationalism." In *Democratization in the Himalayas: Competing Interests, Conflict, and Negotiations*, edited by V. Arora and N. Jayaram. New Delhi: Routledge, pp. 161–185.

Asiwaju, A. I. (ed.). (1985). *Partitioned Africans: Ethnic Relations Across Africa's International Boundaries 1884–1984*. Lagos: University of Lagos Press.

Assam Tribune (2016). "Sushma Writes to Myanmar for Protection of Mizo Family Tree." *Aizawl: Assam Tribune*, October 13.

Barooah Pisharoty, S. (2016). "India Writes to Myanmar Seeking Help to Protect Mizo Family Tree." *The Wire*, October 20. www.nelive.in/mizoram/news/sushma-writes-myanmar-protection-mizo-family-tree (accessed November 20, 2017).

Baruah, S. (2005). *Durable Disorder: Understanding the Politics of Northeast India*. New Delhi: Oxford University Press.

Baud, M. and W. van Schendel (1997). "Toward a Comparative History of Borderlands." *Journal of World History* 8: 211–242. doi:10.1353/jwh.2005.0061.

Bhadra, G. (1975). "The Kuki (?) Uprising (1917–1919): Its Causes and Nature." *Man in India* 55 (1–4): 11–56.

Bhaumik, S. (2004). "Ethnicity, Ideology and Religion: Separatist Movements in India's Northeast." In *Religious Radicalism and Security in South Asia*, edited by Satu P. Limaye, Mohan Malik and Robert G. Wirsing. Hawaii: Asia-Pacific Center for Security Studies.

Campion, M. (2017). "The Construction of the Amazonian Borderlands Through the Longue Duree: An Indigenous Perspective." *Journal of Borderlands Studies* 13: 1–18.

Carey, B. S. and H. N. Tuck (1976 [1892]). *The Chin Hills: A History of the People, Our Dealings with Them, Their Customs and Manners, and a Gazetteer of Their Country*. Aizawl: Printed and Published by Firma KLM Pvt. Ltd., Calcutta, on Behalf of the Tribal Research Institute.

Cederlof, G. (2014). *Founding an Empire on India's North-Eastern Frontier, 1790–1840*. New Delhi: OUP.

Chishti, S. M. A. W. (2004). *Kuki Uprising In Manipur 1919–1920*. Guwahati: Spectrum Publications.

Christian, J. L. (1942). *Modern Burma: A Survey of Political and Economic Development*. Berkeley and Los Angeles: California University Press.

Dalton, E. T. (1872). *Descriptive Ethnology of Bengal*. Calcutta: Firma KLM.

Datta, S. (2000). "Security of India's Northeast: External Linkage." *Strategic Analysis* 24 (8): 1495–1516.

Dean, K. (2005). "Territorialities Yet Unaccounted." *Seminar*, 550 (June).

Dena, L. (1984). *British Policy Towards Manipur 1891–1919*. Churachandpur, Manipur: L&R Printing Press.

_____. (ed.). (1991). *History of Modern Manipur, 1826–1949*. Imphal: Orbit Publishers & Distributors.

Dirks, N. B. (2007 [1987]). *The Hollow Crown: Ethnohistory of an Indian Kingdom*. Cambridge University Press.

Donnison, F. S. V. (1953). *Public Administration in Burma: A Study of Development During the British Connexion*. London: Royal Institute of International Affairs.

Elly, E. B. (1978 [1893]). *Military Report on the Chin-Lushai Country*. Calcutta: Firma KLM Private Ltd.

Encyclopaedia Britannica (1962). Volume 13: 1–1009.

Fraser, N. (1995). "From Redistribution to Recognition? Dilemmas of Justice in a 'Post-Socialist' Age." *New Left Review* 212: 68–93.

Fredholm, M. (1993). *Burma: Ethnicity and Insurgence*. London: Praeger.

Furnivall, J. S. (1960). *The Governance of Modern Burma*. New York: Institute of Pacific Relations.

Gangte, T. S. (1993). *The Kukis of Manipur: A Historical Analysis*. New Delhi: Gyan Publishing House.

————. (2007). "Struggle for Identity and Land Among the Hill Peoples of Manipur." *Eastern Quarterly* 4 (2): 91–100.

Geertz, C. (1983). *Local Knowledge: Further Essays in Interpretive Anthropology*. New York: Basic Books, Inc.

Grierson, G. A. (ed.). (1904). *Tibeto-Burman Family: Specimens of the Kuki-Chin and Burma Groups, Linguistic Survey of India, Vol. III, Part III*. Published by Office of the Superintendent. Calcutta, India: Government Printing.

Guite, J. and H. Thongkholal (eds.). (2019). *The Anglo-Kuki War, 1917–1919: A Frontier Uprising Against Imperialism During the First World War*. New York: Routledge.

Haokip, H. (1986). *Kuki-Chin Baptist Union Khoppi len akichaitai* (KCBU Conference Is Over). A Report. Imphal: KBC Press.

Haokip, P. S. (1998). *Zale'n-gam: The Kuki Nation*. Zale'ngam: KNO Publication.

_____. (2008). *Zale'n-gam: The Kuki Nation*. Revised edition with additional text. Zale'ngam: KNO Publication.

_____. (2010). *Presidential Address on 23rd Kuki National Organisation Raising Day on 24 February*. Camp Salem, Mongbung: Manmasi.

Haokip, S. (2010). *Rhetorics of Kuki Nationalism: A Treatise*. New Delhi: Lustra Print.

Haokip, T. (2015). "India's Look East Policy: Prospects and Challenges for Northeast India." *Studies in Indian Politics* 3 (2): 198–211.

Haokip, T. T. (2004). *Naga Integration: Problems and Prospects*. Imphal: The Sangai Express, 26–28 February.

Haolai, Alun (1994). *Kuki Baptist Church Diary*. Imphal: KBC Press.

Hutton, J. H. (1929). Preface, in William Shaw, Notes on The Thadou Kukis. Aizawl: Published on Behalf of the Government of Assam.

The Imphal Free Press (2008). "State Government Authorizes Principal Secretary to Sign SoO Agreement with Kuki Militants." *Imphal: The Imphal Free Press*, August 3.

Khupzago, R. (1988). *The Chin Chronicles*. Churachandpur: L&R Printing Press.

Kipgen, N. and Arnab Roy Chowdhury (2016). "Contested State-Craft on the Frontiers of the Indian Nation: 'Hills-Valley Divide' and the Genealogy of Kuki Ethnic Nationalism in Manipur." *Studies in Ethnicity and Nationalism* (Wiley) 16 (2): 283–303.

Kuki National Assembly (1960). *Kuki State*. A Memorandum of the Kuki National Assembly to the Prime Minister of India.

Lalthangliana, B. (1976). "History of Mizo in Burma." Unpublished M.A. thesis, Mandalay University.

Lehman, F. K. (1963). *The Structure of Chin Society*. Urbana: University of Illinois Press.

———. (1979). "Review of History of Mizo in Burma, by B. Lalthangliana." *Thu le Hla* 6 (9): 13–26.

Lewin, Capt. T. H. (1870). *Wild Races of South-Eastern India*. London: W. H. Allen & Co.

Lian UK. (1968). "Chin Customary Law." Unpublished L.L.B. thesis, Rangoon University.

Ludden, D. (2003). "Where Is Assam? Using Geographical History to Locate Current Social Realities." *CENISEAS Papers 1*, OKDISCD, Guwahati.

Mackenzie, A. (2005 [1884]). *The North-East Frontier of Bengal*. New Delhi: Mittal Publications.

Macrea, T. (1801). "Account of the Kookies or Lunctas." *Asiatic Researches* 7 (6): 163.

Maung, M. (1961). *The Constitution of Burma*, 2nd Edition. The Hague: Martinus Nijhoff.

Nail, T. (2016). *Theory of the Border*. New York: Oxford University Press.

Nehlun. (1993). "Why not Kukiland for Kukis?" *The Shillong Times*, Shillong: dated October 1, 1993.

Newman, D. (2003). "On Borders and Power: A Theoretical Framework." *Journal of Borderlands Studies* 18 (1): 13–25.

Nongbri, T. (1995). "Ethnicity and Political Activism in North East: Tribal Identity and the State Policy." In *The North-East and the Indian State: Paradoxes of a Periphery*, edited by P. S. Datta. New Delhi: Vikas.

Oommen, T. K. (1997). *Citizenship, Nationality and Ethnicity*. Cambridge: Polity Press, Blackwell Publishers.

Parrat, S. N. (2005). *The Court Chronicle of Manipur* (The Cheitharol Kumpapa). London and New York: Routledge.

Parry, N. E. (1976 [1932]). *The Lakhers*. London. Repr. Aizawl: Tribal Research Institute.

Pemberton, R. B. (1985 [1835]). *Report on the Eastern Frontier of British India*. Government of Assam.

Phanjoubam, T. (2007 [2004]). *Bleeding Manipur*. New Delhi: Har-Anand Publication.

Randeria, S. (2006). "Entangled Histories: Civil Society, Caste Solidarity and Legal Pluralism in Postcolonial India." In *Civil Society: Berlin Perspectives*, edited by J. Keane. New York: Berghahn Books, pp. 213–242.

Reid, A. S. (1893). *Chin-Lushai Land*. Calcutta: Thacker, Spink and Co.

The Sangai Express (2008). "Cabinet Nod to SoO Deal." *Imphal: The Sangai Express*, August 23.

Sarkar, R. M. (2006). *Land and Forest Rights of the Tribals Today*. New Delhi: Serials Publications.

Scott, J. C. (2009). *The Art of Not Being Governed: An Anarchist History of Upland Southeast Asia*. Agrarian Studies Series. New Haven, CT: Yale University Press.

Shakespear, J. Lt. Col. (1912). *The Lushei Kuki Clans, Part I & Part II*. London: Macmillan & Co, Ltd.

Shaw, W. (1929). *Notes on the Thadou Kukis*. Aizawl: Published on Behalf of the Government of Assam.

Smith, A. D. (1986). *The Ethnic Origins of Nations*. Oxford: Basil Blackwell.

Smith, M. (1999). *Burma: Insurgency and the Politics of Ethnicity*. London: Zed Books Ltd.

Sonpate, H. L. (1977). *Hmar History*. Churachandpur: Private Circulation.

Soppitt, C. A. (1976 [1893]). *A Short Account of the Kuki-Lushai Tribes on the North-East Frontier* (Districts Cachar, Sylhet, Nága Hills, etc., and the North Cachar Hills). Aizawl: Firma-KLM on behalf of Tribal Research Institute.

Stevenson, H. N. C. (1943). *The Economics of the Central Chin Tribes*. Bombay: The Times of India Press.

The Telegraph (2012). "Trouble Ahead for Asean Rally." *Calcutta: The Telegraph*, December 12, www.telegraphindia.com/1121212/jsp/northeast/story_16303537.jsp (accessed November 10, 2017).

The Times of India (2013). "KSDC Threatens to Block BCIM Car Rally in Manipur's 'Kuki Areas'." *The Times of India*, February 13, http://timesofindia.indiatimes.com/city/guwahati/KSDCthreatens-to-block-BCIM-car-rally-in-Manipurs-Kuki-areas/articleshow/18635655.cms (accessed November 10, 2017).

Vandenhelsken, M. and G. K. Bengt (2016). "Fluid Attachments in Northeast India: Introduction." *Asian Ethnicity* 17 (3): 330–339.

van Schendel, W. (2002). "Geographies of Knowing, Geographies of Ignorance: Jumping Scale in Southeast Asia." *Environment and Planning D: Society and Space* 20: 647–668.

———. (2005). *The Bengal Borderland: Beyond State and Nation in South Asia*. London: Anthem.

Vumson (1986). *Zo History: With an Introduction to Zo Culture, Economy, Religion and Their Status as an Ethnic Minority in India, Burma, and Bangladesh*. Aizawl: Published by the Author.

Weiner, M. (1985). "Transborder Peoples." In *Mexican-Americans in Comparative Perspective*, edited by W. Connor. Washington, DC: The Urban Institute Press, pp. 130–158.

Zawla, K. (1964). *Mizo Pipute Ieh An Thlahte Chanchin*. Aizawl: Gosen Press.

PART II

Proximity to connectivity

India–Myanmar in perspective

6

INDIA–MYANMAR RELATIONS

A perspective from the border

Alana Golmei

India and Myanmar share a 1,640 km border running between India's Northeastern states of Arunachal Pradesh, Manipur, Mizoram, Nagaland, and Myanmar's Chin state, Kachin state and Sagaing division. Significantly, these border regions in India and Myanmar are underdeveloped areas and are inhabited by ethnic communities, with a history of continued unrest in both countries. From India's viewpoint, Myanmar as an immediate neighbor is of vital importance for defense and internal security needs, stability and development in the Northeastern Region, and expansion of its influence in the Bay of Bengal region and Southeast Asia. (Bhatia 2016, 162).

India's relations with Myanmar have gathered a new momentum ever since India embarked on what was called its 'Look East' policy (LEP) starting in the early 1990s, led by late former Prime Minister Narasimha Rao. The hope was to connect India better to the increasingly prosperous nations of the far east and find new markets and new friends (Myint-U 2011, 236). The LEP was not just an external economic policy blueprint or a journey of openness and global economic integration, it also marked a strategic shift in India's vision and its place in the comity of nations. This visionary policy created a new framework for deepening economic, political, cultural and people-to-people ties between India and Myanmar in particular. Today, Myanmar has emerged as an important strategic partner for India. It is, after all, a 'land-bridge' between India and Southeast Asia.

India sees Myanmar as a springboard for its engagement with Southeast and East Asia and it remains a vital link in its strategic partnership with ASEAN. India sees its partnership with Myanmar not merely as a reaffirmation of ties with neighboring countries or as an instrument of economic development, but also as an integral part of its vision of a stable, secure and prosperous Asia and its surrounding Indian Ocean and Pacific regions. There is a tendency in some quarters to think of the LEP as something that was essentially exclusive or tailor-made for the Northeast.

This is clearly not the case. The LEP was an exhortation for India as a whole to turn to Southeast Asia for its economic future, building on India's cultural footprint that went back for a millennia and driven by the geopolitical developments and realities of the late 1980s and 1990s: continued tensions with Pakistan, the Iranian revolution and the Soviet intervention in Afghanistan that more or less closed off the west; the rapid growth of the Tiger economies in East and Southeast Asia; India's balance of payments crisis and P.M. Narasimha Rao's economic reforms; and the turmoil in, and eventual collapse of, the Soviet Union. Nevertheless, it was recognized from the outset that the LEP could hugely benefit the Northeast by freeing it from barriers of geography, history and politics. (Mukhopadhaya 2017).

The Act East Policy was set in motion by Prime Minister Narendra Modi at the East Asia Summit in Myanmar in November 2014 with the objective to promote economic cooperation, cultural ties and develop strategic relationship with countries in the Asia-Pacific region and for continuous engagement at bilateral, regional and multilateral levels thereby providing enhanced connectivity to the States of Northeastern Region. India's Act East Policy is not a replacement of the LEP but it is the consolidation, extension, expansion and diversification of India's policy to accord a high degree of importance to Southeast Asia and East Asia (Bhatia 2015, 6). With India continuing to build ties with ASEAN under New Delhi's Act East Policy, External Affairs Minister Sushma Swaraj called for greater connectivity between the northeastern states of India and southeast Asia. At an interactive session with the Chief Ministers of the northeastern states on the Act East Policy, she said that state governments of the northeastern region were active stakeholders in the Policy (The Express News 2018, 5 May).

What implications would the bilateral relations between the two countries have on these refugees who traverse these borderlands? In the context of increasing subregional cooperation, India and Myanmar conceptualized and proposed several bilateral ventures in the areas of 'infrastructural development, communications, road and rail connectivity.' However, the main question that needs to be addressed is how these connectivity projects impact the lives of people living in the India–Myanmar borderlands. In a nutshell, the chapter argues that these mega projects would have implications on the cross-border communities and would perhaps work in the favor of cross-border communities only if the two countries are able to establish 'vigorous and meaningful people-to-people contacts in the India–Myanmar borderlands.' The chapter discusses in detail the prospects and concerns of opening India–Myanmar borders in the Naga areas, in the Manipur border areas and Mizoram.

The borderlands: linkages with border states

Geography and ethnic bonds are the oldest links between India and Myanmar. A shared border and familial/tribal ties ensure certain uniqueness to India–Myanmar relations if special attention is paid to Northeastern Region (Bhatia 2016, 162). Communities in India's border have strong historical and geographical link with ethnic groups on the other sides of the border. These relations are rooted in shared historical, ethnic, cultural and religious ties. Also the official policy of allowing the local people to cross the border has facilitated their contacts (Fernandes et al. 2015, 168). For example, the Chin and Mizo people share similar historical, cultural and religious backgrounds, which opened doors for most of the Chin economic migrants, who crossed the India–Myanmar border for a better livelihood and future in India. With an estimated population of 500,000, the Chin state is located in the western part of Myanmar, bordered by Bangladesh and India in the west, Rakhine state in the south, and Magwe and Sagaing Division in the east. According to the latest report from the staff of Chin Human Rights Organization, approximately 50,000 Chin refugees are living in Mizoram at present.

Similarly in the Manipur border, the Kuki-Chin family speaks the same language and practices the same religion, which enables them to integrate well in the community. They are concentrated mainly in the southern parts of the state, especially in Churachandpur district and in the town of Moreh in Tengnoupal district (before the recent creation of new districts, it was in Chandel district).

As such, the ethnological unit or origin and the relationships of the Chins of Burma and India have been conspicuously transmitted through their culture, social life, history, tradition, language, poetry and songs and customs as marked by their uniform celebrations of National Festivals, etc. And the chain of their relationship is circumscribed not only by geographical bounds but more often by racial unity (ZRO 2005, 142). Now widely distributed and found in Myanmar, India and Bangladesh, a Kuki-Chin and others who claim to have the same ethnic identity have conceived the notion since a century ago that they had been scrambled and scattered by the British by means of their imperialistic policy to the different directions in the regions, thus losing their independent entity with deeper agonies and separation (Sangkima 2009, 110).

Nagaland is another border state with Myanmar connecting through Mon district. Since there are more social connections between communities living across the border, instead of seeking help from central Myanmar, it is more convenient for those Nagas in Myanmar to seek support from Nagaland. One example is, during an outbreak of deadly measles in the Naga inhabited areas in Myanmar, Nagas in Myanmar sought help from the Indian side of the community. Not only Nagas but different communities living on the Indian side of the border rendered help mainly in the form of monetary support during that unfortunate outbreak in 2016. Similarly, Mizo support was rendered to their Chin brethren during the storms that affected Chin state in July 2015. According to informed sources, there is a US$ 25 million, 5-year Border Area Development program in the Naga and Chin areas of Myanmar that is intended to improve living conditions of Myanmar Naga and Chin that is an important initiative used mainly for construction of schools, bridges and roads.

Arunachal Pradesh is another state sharing a border with Myanmar, with 520 km. Unlike the border in Moreh in Manipur, which is very close and where most villagers travel on foot, in Arunachal Pradesh people from Therimkan take 2 to 4 hours to reach the border and it takes more than 12 hours from Injan, while it is only one hour from Khonsa and Chongkham (Walter Fernandes et al. 2015, 167). There is a fairly big group of young persons from across the border in the villages of Arunachal Pradesh; most statements about good quality schools and the possibility of earning a higher income than on the Myanmar side of the border came from them (Walter Fernandes et al. 2015, 174).

Several Northeastern Chief Ministers have taken the initiative to visit Myanmar and hosted Chief Ministers of the border states of Myanmar, organized trade events (Assam, Manipur, Meghalaya), and participated in each others' cultural festivals such as the Sangai festival of Manipur and the Hornbill festival of Nagaland (where Prime Minister Modi received the Chief Ministers of Sagaing Region and Kachin state in 2014). Musical troupes from Nagaland have performed in Southeast Asian capitals, and rock bands from Arunachal Pradesh and Meghalaya have performed in Yangon. Music festivals in Arunachal have also attracted rock bands from Myanmar (Mukhopadhaya 2017).

Implications and role of Northeastern region

India's growing engagement with Southeast Asia in general and Myanmar in particular has raised the stakes for the people of Northeast India. The region has the potential to become India's trade gateway to the ASEAN countries. India's Northeast is expected to act as the strategic catalyst and a game changer. The Modi Government's Act East Policy has formally recognized the strategic importance of the much-neglected Northeast. If this policy is implemented in right earnest, the Northeast region can realize its potential as India's strategic bridgehead and economic corridors to Southeast Asia.

Ajay Gondane, former Joint Secretary, Border Connectivity, Ministry of External Affairs said,

> India is making a conscious endeavour to strengthen connectivity in our eastern neighborhood. The Indo–Myanmar friendship road is an illustrating case in point. The Sittwe to Paletwa Inland Water Transport is almost complete, Imphal-Moreh Tamu road is in working condition, Land Customs Stations in Awangkhu (Nagaland) will be revived while the Land Customs Stations in Arunachal Pradesh have been identified though these are yet to be operational.
>
> *(Gondane 2014, 7)*

It is true that the policy has brought the Northeast of India in the forefront of regional diplomacy, but it is only now that the real interests on and importance of the region are being realized. As part of the policy, the region emerged as an important element in India's bilateral relations with Myanmar, Bangladesh and other Southeast Asian nations (Yhome 2015, 23).

Connectivity is of utmost interest as far as India's engagement with the Southeast Asian countries is concerned. Over the years several bilateral ventures between

India and Myanmar have been conceptualized, proposed and announced in the areas of infrastructural development, communications, road and rail connectivity and other long-term projects by both India and Myanmar.

Border trade, infrastructural development and a host of possibilities promise a bright future for the Northeast. However, connectivity projects will become connectivity corridors only when people-to-people engagements become vigorous and meaningful. People of Northeast India stand to benefit the most from the connectivity corridors and civil society engagements. This will be of equal benefit to the people of Myanmar, particularly those residing in the neighboring regions of India.

The Northeast region is expected to benefit from the multi-pronged Look East/Act East Policy. In fact, the road to development in India's Northeast passes through Myanmar. India has announced a target of increasing the share of manufacturing in its GDP from 15 percent to 25 percent by 2025. Myanmar would play a critical role if India hopes to fully integrate itself with Southeast Asia. It offers tremendous potential and scope for all-round development of the Northeastern region, given its proximity, historical ties and complementarities of varying nature with Myanmar and other neighboring countries. The development of physical connectivity between the North Eastern States and Myanmar therefore assumes paramount importance.

Connectivity: prospects and concerns

One of the landmark developments is the opening of the Indo–Myanmar international land border in August 2018. The opening of the land border marked the abolishing of special land entry permission which was previously required for visitors entering the country via land routes. The agreement on land border crossing was signed between the two countries at Nay Pyi Taw, Myanmar during the visit of External Affairs Minister Sushma Swaraj in May 2018. The opening ceremony was held at land border point at Tamu-Moreh Manipur, and also Rikhawadar (Chin state) and Zowkhawthar, Mizoram (The Indian Express 2018, 9 August).

Consequently, the Ministry of Labour, Immigration and Population and the Myanmar Embassy in India announced in September 2018 that checkpoints along the India–Myanmar border would begin using e-visas for travel between the two countries. According to an official announcement, the system will start in September at two checkpoints: the Tamu-Moreh checkpoint, along India's border with Sagaing Region; and the Rih Khaw Dar-Zokhawthar checkpoint, along India's border with Chin State (The Irrawaddy 2018, 18 September) The Tamu-Moreh checkpoint connects upper Sagaing Region with Manipur State of India. The Rih Khaw Dar-Zokhawthar checkpoint connects Chin State with India's Mizoram State. Both have been important trade corridors for Indian and Myanmar nationals travelling between the two countries for many years (ibid.).

The joint projects and initiatives including the transportation and infrastructure projects require good understanding among the countries. Similarly, issues like border trade, drug trafficking and transborder militancy require removal of restrictions

FIGURE 6.1 Passenger terminal at Moreh in Manipur–Myanmar border.

Source: Photograph by Mr. David (Moreh) in October 2018

of various kinds and streamlining border management. Past experience suggests that many of the well-intentioned policies failed to yield the desired effect in the absence of sustained engagements with the Northeastern stakeholders.

While many ambitious projects have been drawn up and a few have even been implemented, the Indian government has received much criticism for delays in the execution of two of its flagship projects – the Trilateral Highway project that would link India, Myanmar and Thailand and the Kaladan Multi-modal Transport project that would link Kolkata via Sittwe with Mizoram (Bhatia 2016, 166).

(i) Nagaland border

Nagaland shares a border stretch of 215 km with Myanmar. A local journalist observed during a visit to the border areas and shared the views with the author in a discussion in the following words,

> the economic development and stability in the north-eastern region and a better infrastructure along its borders, is crucial for India's Look East/Act East policy to see the light of the day. Despite the realisation that infrastructural development at the borders is a necessity if India is sincerely looking for stronger ties with Myanmar vis-a-vis the Look East/Act East Policy, the

development at the border is dismal. One can take the instance of Pangsha village under Tuensang district of Nagaland connecting Myanmar. Despite the existence of International Trade Centre (ITC) at Dan village along the border near Pangsha village, there is no definite road system. When there is no proper road connectivity, one cannot expect the people to carry on cross-border trade activities. Owing to lack of road infrastructure, trade between the two sides at the ITC is almost absent except for a short period only once in a year when vegetables from nearby Naga villages in Myanmar and Indian made goods from Nagaland side are sold/bought or bartered.

Even the very infrastructure of International Trade Center itself is a mere shed. Since there is no proper road, bikes mostly China made have become very popular for commuting and transporting goods even though they are less in quantity. Those who cannot afford bikes travel on foot all the way to Lahe or Khamti in Myanmar, which are the only two trading towns in the Naga areas of Myanmar (Sumi 2014, 55).

(ii) Manipur border

Manipur, which shares 398 km of international boundary with Myanmar, is one of the most important strategic border states. A scholar from Manipur during his interaction with the author when this research was conducted observed,

> to make the Northeast partner and stakeholder in the Act East Policy, overland transport system and institutions to allow investment, movement of people and goods across the borders are required. But it cannot replace significance of intra-Northeast transportation system. In other words, the central government should make sincere efforts to maintain the National Highways properly. A stretch of dirt track with the official designation National Highway does not change the realities on the ground.

Without connecting such missing links, talking about transnational connectivity projects would be like imagining connectivity. After the Indo–Myanmar Friendship Road, the trilateral highway project connecting Moreh (India) and Mae Sot (Thailand) via Myanmar is the second most important overland connectivity project. The first connects Tamu with Kaleywa on the Chindwin, while the latter upgrades the road from Kaleywa to Yargyi connecting onward to Mandalay to South Eastern Myanmar and Thailand (Puyam 2015, 15).

Unlike the Myanmar-China border and Myanmar-Thailand border, trade across the Indo–Myanmar border is negligible. The negligible trade and economic activities across the Indo–Myanmar border are to be traced to half-hearted efforts because of security concerns. The ongoing extension of the road and repairing of 69 old bridges [may] *should* bring some positive changes. The Imphal-Mandalay bus service is yet to be launched (Puyam 2015, 16).

A visit to Manipur in the Indo–Myanmar border to explore areas of cooperation and to identify the stakeholders has an underlying message. There are huge gaps between the government's policy pronouncements and intent and the reality on the ground. Given the background of neglect and indifference, the various stakeholders have serious misgivings about any new initiative or policy.

The construction of fencing going on near Moreh in Manipur-Myanmar border, supposed to be major outlet to Southeast Asia, is at cross purposes with the Act East Policy of the government. For a common man in the border, such a picture of security fencing gave the prospect of militarization. Besides disrupting the local cross-border markets it also divides border communities as the British colonialists did to them earlier (Gangmei 2014, 65). The process of boundary demarcation between Manipur and Burma began with the conclusion of the First Anglo-Burmese War by the treaty of Yandaboo in 1826 and the subsequent agreement

FIGURE 6.2 Border fencing in Manipur–Myanmar border.

Source: Photograph by author during her visit in 2015

in 1834 between the two parties (Piang 2008, 51). In this treaty the King of Ava recognized Manipur's independence, and in the agreement of 1834, Kabo Valley was ceded to Burma and the boundary between Manipur and Burma was drawn vaguely northward from the valley on the basis of the imaginary line of Pemberton (Piang 2008, 52).

Recently, there was also a public outcry in Manipur over the construction of a boundary pillar along the Indo–Myanmar border. According to local media reports, the residents of the border village of Kwatha Khunou alleged that the Indian government moved a border pillar about 3 km into Manipur, triggering opposition from several civil society organizations and political parties as it would mean 'giving away' the state's land to Myanmar (The Wire 2018, 9 July). The external affairs ministry has, however, denied the allegations.

(iii) Mizoram border

Like Manipur, Mizoram occupies an area of great strategic importance in the region that shares a 404 km international border with Myanmar. Gautam Mukhopadhaya (former Indian Ambassador to Myanmar) during a telephonic interview conducted by the author for the research observed,

> Mizoram has the potential to cater to the needs of Myanmar with regards to education, health, power, consumer goods, markets and other goods and services. Common ethnicity and languages among people of both sides of the border from Arunachal to Mizoram provide an excellent foundation for trade and economic and cultural cooperation that have not been tapped by border states of the Centre.

There is an opportunity for closer connection between peoples on both sides of the border. But there are also concerns as to whether the people will be able to connect freely within the policy of the governments of India and Myanmar. One of the factors is border fencing initiated by government of both the countries to control the movement of rebel groups and illegal migrants. However, ethnic groups and tribes in the borders feel that erecting this fence will have a negative outcome as it will divide many ethnic communities whose lands straddle the regions between the two countries (Lalremruata 2015, 22–23).

The first border trade in Mizoram at Zokhawthar was started in 2004, formally inaugurated after 11 years in 2015. However, there is a lack of infrastructural development like bank facilities, internet connection, post office, etc. There is also a major concern that the border trade may become a hub for smuggling drugs and arms as well as other illegal items. Human trafficking is also another concern as Southeast Asia continues to be a major hub for sex business and human trafficking. Improving connectivity with high unemployment rate in the area can further aggravate the situation as the Indo–Myanmar border is one of the prone areas for such forms of trafficking. While the government is giving priority to connectivity, they also need to focus on the health and welfare of the people. Communities and tribes living in both sides of the border still lack health care facilities (ibid.).

Conclusions and perspectives

With the government of India implementing the Act East Policy and New Delhi settling down to business, there is renewed hope for the people of Northeast India for possible openings and economic advantages, particularly in the states along the Indo–Myanmar borders. There is a great expectation that such an initiative will entail a major shift in India's economic and foreign policies viz. Asian countries to the east, and the indigenous people in the region will reap the benefits by connecting to them.

It is believed that local communities living on both sides of the border will receive increased infrastructure development such as good roads, waterways, electricity, communication etc., which will further integrate them for economic and cultural gains. There will be a great boost for border trade, which will become useful outlets for Indian manufactured goods and will create employment opportunities and better livelihood and will wean away the youths in the region from militancy. With links to Kunming via Stilwell road, Mandalay-Yangon via Moreh and Zawkathar, and to Sittwe via Zochachhua by road and Kaladan riverways, Northeast India will no more be landlocked. Thus the region will be set free from

FIGURE 6.3 Road construction Near Lawngtlai (Mizoram–Myanmar border) under KMTTP.

Source: Photograph by Terah, CHRO in September 2018

isolation and boosted to interconnectivity. This will also strengthen cultural integration and common mutual interests of the communities on both sides of the borders such as Lisu (Yobin), Naga, Kuki-Chin, Mizo/Zomi, Meitei and others (Gangmei 2014, 64, 66).

Said a local intellectual from Mizoram,

> At present there is no significant development in the border area except for the ongoing road construction in both Kaladan and Rih-Tiddim Falam road. The Government of India should speed up and complete the work. Since it will be connecting Kolkata and rest of Southeast Asia it will be very good for the people in the state of Mizoram and the people are looking forward to it.

Clearance of trees, forest and cultivation areas have started already for building roads and pavements from the Myanmar side under the Kaladan Multimodal Transit Project. Bungalows are also built and most of them have been completed for road construction workers to reside in. Conditions of Rih-Tedim-Falam roads are not good, though they have been expanded. Local people are facing difficulties travelling in those areas as the conditions are not good during the rainy season, and landslides on those newly built roads also often interrupt travel. The roads can be used only during the dry season (Thantluang 2018, 11 September). Therefore construction of roads and infrastructure development are yet to pick up momentum in the border regions.

But according to official reports, three projects – Paletwa-Zorinpui in India–Myanmar Border, 69 bridges along the Tamu-Kalewa stretch and a two-lane highway in the Kalewa-Yargyi section of the proposed India-Myanmar-Thailand (IMT) Trilateral Highway – have all been mobilized with a timeline to be finished in three years.

In spite of initiatives by the government, still most of the people along Indo–Myanmar border areas remain unaware and are not ready for the opportunity thrown up under the Look East/Act East Policy. The same is being felt by those residing on the Myanmar side of the border and although they agree that there has been some development in the Indo–Myanmar border area including the opening up of the border gate for a short-term visit, they are not aware of the exact initiatives of the government. 'If possible from India, it would be very good if the government follows the international standard just like the Free Prior and Informed Consent (FPIC) and have proper consultation with the local villagers so that they will understand better what is happening around them' as told to the author during telephonic interview with Thantluang, CHRO based in Mizoram-Myanmar border, displays this exact sentiment with regard to this situation.

A local from Moreh (Manipur-Myanmar border) observed,

> Most of the people or communities have very little economic sense. They are generally more wary of the demographical changes that will trigger than the economic benefits that can be taken advantage of. The people's sense of

identity and freedom is still strongly rooted in territory. So as long as they can access their land unhindered, they will not object. However, if it affects their access to their land and resources, as regulations from the state are bound to, they will not be happy. They expressed inability to visualize the future. In other words, there is a gap in their understanding of the project in terms of its long-term impact on their land, culture, language, politics, and society.

A plausible conclusion to be derived from a discussion based on these matters would be that development in all forms should be welcomed with speculative and innovative thought. However, besides that, it is the prerogative and the right of the people or citizens to [be investigative] *question?* of the proposed ideas and works while they push for opportunity and advancement on society. In other words, as much as development should come, stakeholders should always be taken into account. Hence it becomes very important for the government and the authorities to have transparency in their works and all ventures and to be in constant interaction with the people so that they are kept aware of all initiatives by the government. These steps in relationship building will further lead to trust and like-mindedness among those who all have equal roles to play in pushing the visions of a better tomorrow into a lived reality.

References

Bhatia, Rajiv (2015). Keynote Address in India–Myanmar Relations: Looking from the Border, Conference Report, Institute of Social Sciences, New Delhi, India, p. 6.
———. (2016). *India-Myanmar Relations Changing Contours*. New Delhi: Routledge.
The Express News (2018). "Northeastern States Active Stakeholders in India's Act East Policy, says Sushma Swaraj." May 5, https://indianexpress.com/article/north-east-india/ne-states-active-stakeholders-in-indias-act-east-policy-sushma-swaraj-5164003/ (accessed August 1, 2018).
Fernandes, Walter, et al. (2015). *Relations Across Borders: Communities Separated by the Indo-Myanmar Border.* Yangon and Guwahati: Northeastern Social Research Centre, Guwahati and Animation and Research Centre-Myanmar.
Gangmei, Kabi (2014). "India-Myanmar Border Areas: Connectivity, Prospects and Concerns- First Hand Account in in Look East Policy: India and Myanmar Pitching for Greater Connectivity." Conference Report, Institute of Social Sciences, New Delhi, India, August 4.
Gondane, Ajay (2014). Inaugural Speech in Look East Policy: India and Myanmar Pitching for Greater Connectivity, Conference Report, Institute of Social Sciences, New Delhi, India.
The Indian Express (2018). "Myanmar Officially Opens Indo-Myanmar Land Border, Special Land Entry Permissions Abolished." August 9, https://indianexpress.com/article/india/myanmar-officially-opens-indo-myanmar-land-border-special-land-entry-permissions-abolished/ (accessed September 10, 2018).
Interview with Terah Thantluang, Chin Human Rights Organisation (CHRO) (2018). Mizoram, September 11.
The Irrawaddy (2018). "India, Myanmar to Begin Using E-Visas Along Land Border." September 18, www.irrawaddy.com/news/burma/india-myanmar-begin-using-e-visas-along-land-border.html (accessed September 30, 2018).

Lalremruata, C. (2015). *India-Myanmar Relations: Looking from Mizoram Border in India-Myanmar Relations: Looking from the Border*. New Delhi, India: Institute of Social Sciences, pp. 22–23, October 28–29.

Mukhopadhaya, Gautam (2017). Lecture delivered at the India International Centre as part of Beyond Borders: India International Centre-National Foundation of India Lecture Series, New Delhi, January 31.

Myint-U, Thant (2011). *Where China Meets India*. London: Faber and Faber Limited.

Piang, Lam Khan (2008). *The Process of Ethnification of the Zo People*. Prism of the Zo People., Lamka, Manipur: 60th Zomi Nam Ni Celebration Committee.

Rakesh Singh, Puyam (2015). "Crossing the Indo-Myanmar Border: Fear, Cooperation and Mistrust in 'Act East' Policy." In *India-Myanmar Relations: Looking from the Border*. New Delhi, India: Institute of Social Sciences, October 28–29.

Sangkima (2009). "The Sources of the Development of the Word 'Zo'." In *Chin: History, Culture & Identity*, edited by K. Robin. New Delhi: Euro Burma Office Belgium, p. 110.

Sumi, K. Filip (2014). "India-Myanmar Border Development – Nagaland Perspective in Look East Policy: India and Myanmar Pitching for Greater Connectivity." Conference Report, Institute of Social Sciences, New Delhi, India, August 4.

The Wire (2018). "Public Outcry in Manipur Over Construction of Boundary Pillar Along Indo-Myanmar Border." July 9, https://thewire.in/diplomacy/public-outcry-in-manipur-over-construction-of-boundary-pillar-along-indo-myanmar-border (accessed September 20, 2018).

Yhome, Khriezo (2015). "From Look East to Act East: What It Means for India's Northeast." *Eastern Quarterly* 11 (I & II).

Zomi Re-Unification Organisation (ZRO) (2005). *The Indigenous Zomi*. New Delhi and Ciimnuai: ZRO.

7

INDIA–MYANMAR BORDERLAND

Pressing concerns in public health hazards

Anasua Basu Ray Chaudhury and Sreeparna Banerjee[1]

India shares a 1643 km long border with Myanmar in four northeastern states, namely Arunachal (520 km), Nagaland (215 km), Manipur (398 km) and Mizoram (510 km), with Myanmar's Sagaing Region and Chin State. Borders between India and Myanmar are not only porous but often cut across common cultural and linguistic communities. The situation in and around the border has become much more complex due to prolonged ethnic conflict coupled with poverty. The porous international boundary has resulted in easy flow of arms, drugs, illegal migrants and easy access of insurgents from bases established in the neighboring countries like China, Bhutan, Bangladesh and Myanmar. The Golden Triangle constituted by Myanmar, Laos and Thailand in the vicinity results in the drug trade spilling over into Northeast India, resulting in a high degree of drug addiction, especially among the youth of this region. More so, the bordering areas of both the countries face similar public health problems, especially in terms of the threat posed by infectious border diseases like malaria, human immunodeficiency virus infection and acquired immune deficiency syndrome (HIV AIDS) and tuberculosis (TB). While malaria on both sides could be triggered by similar climatic and ecological conditions, others like HIV and TB are more likely to be caused by free movement of people across the border and other factors such as unregulated drug-trafficking and involvement of refugee/migrant Chin/ Kuki women in the sex industry. Against this backdrop this chapter seeks to identify correlation between migration and the spread of diseases especially HIV-AIDS, HIV-hepatitis C and HIV-TB co-infection along the border areas, if any. It also evaluates existing status of the said diseases among the bordering states of Northeast India and Myanmar. Lastly, it attempts to address collaborative efforts between both the nations for an effective border health infrastructure, management and disease control strategy.

Divided communities: dynamics of borderland

In order to understand the dynamics of India–Myanmar border and borderlands it is important to take into account the divided communities and their social, cultural and economic interactions between the Chin and Kachin states and the Sagain region of Myanmar and the northeastern states of Arunachal Pradesh, Nagaland, Manipur and Mizoram. Like most of the boundaries that India shares with its neighbors, the India–Myanmar border is also an artificial line which is superimposed on the socio-cultural landscape of the borderland.

Myanmar was formed as a separate state from India in 1935. The decolonization of the subcontinent in 1947 divided ethnic communities living along the Indo–Myanmar border. These communities, or rather ethnic groups, felt a deep sense of reservation since they became relegated to the status of ethnic minorities on both side of the border. They also found the newly created boundary to be inconsistent with the traditional limits of the region they inhabited (Kent 2017).

Sagaing Region bordering with Nagaland and Manipur has Bamar, Chin, Shan and Naga population practicing Buddhism and Christianity. Chin State located in Western Myanmar shares boundaries with Manipur in north and Mizoram in the west. It is sparsely populated and remains one of the least developed areas of Myanmar with a high rate of unemployment. Chin is the major ethnic group and Christianity is the major religion. Chins and Manipuris have long ethnic linkages since feudal era as parts of Chin Hills were under the suzerainty of Manipur and vice versa. Hence, people on both sides of the border have ethnic, religious and cultural ties since centuries. Due to historic ethnic linkages, people in border villages own land/property and have socioeconomic interests across the borders. In some instances, the imaginary borderline cuts across houses, land and villages. People, especially those living on the Indian side, own land holdings including cultivated lands and forested areas across the border and are completely dependent on such areas for their livelihood. For instance, the Konyak tribal community chief's house is divided between Nagaland and Hukong valley of Myanmar. Most shops are on the Nagaland side of the border and people from Sagaing region travel there to buy goods (Fernandez 2014).

These tribes, however, refuse to accept the artificial line and continue to maintain strong linkages with their kith and kin across the border. For instance, constant movement as well as intermarriage exists across the border between the tribes living in Myanmar and Arunachal Pradesh, especially more in Changlang than in Tirup districts (ibid.).

To address their concerns and enable greater interaction among them, the Indian and Myanmarese governments established the Free Movement Regime (FMR), which allowed them to travel 16 km across the border on either side without any visa requirements. From the Myanmar side, a lot of villagers come to the Indian side to buy basic essentials. Even the border *haats* (rural markets) present play an important role in the economic and social life of these people.

Currently the region representing the conjunction of India, China and Myanmar is gaining more attention for a number of reasons. Violence has long been endemic in the region since communities and people were left divided by the imposition and policing of officially demarcated borders between India and Myanmar. The nature of the porous border is also leading to increasing severity of transnational challenges such as drug-trafficking, informal trade, insurgency, and the spread of diseases. Given the dynamics of the border areas in terms of the age-old ties within the two countries, this factor is being exploited by some of the ethnic militant groups in Northeast India to seek shelter in Chin State and Sagaing Region for their anti-India activities.

As a result, security as well as economic concerns linked to the insurgency, smuggling of arms and ammunition, illegal trade and other similar activities prompted the decision in 2003 by India to fence the porous border between the two counties. But the work got stalled due to the protests raised by the local Tangkhul, Kuki and Naga communities. According to them, a huge stretch of land would go to the Myanmar territory. This will also create conflict among the Lushei, Nagas, Chins and Kukis whose lands straddle the regions of both the countries. Thus to resolve the boundary issue a joint survey was supposed to be conducted before fencing is undertaken. The opposition to the fencing of the Indo–Myanmar border has continued ever since. The reality remains, despite the fact that the boundary between India and Myanmar had been demarcated in 1967, there has been no manifestation of the boundary line on the ground except for the presence of border pillars. According to MEA press release in 2013 there is no boundary dispute between India and Myanmar. Nevertheless, nine unresolved boundary pillars (BP) (MEA 2013) along the India–Myanmar Border in the Manipur sector does exist though no steps have been taken to resolve that part as yet. The two sides hold regular dialogue on issues related with boundary demarcation and border management, through institutionalized mechanisms, such as Foreign Office Consultations, National Level Meetings (NLM) and Sectoral Level Meetings (SLM). Meetings are also held at the level of the Heads of Survey Department and Director (Survey), where issues related to boundary demarcation, joint survey, inspection and maintenance of boundary pillars are, inter alia, discussed. As a result, the boundary line cuts across houses and villages, thus dividing several tribes such as the Singphos, Nagas, Kukis, Mizos, etc., and forcing them to reside as citizens of different countries.

However, it is to be noted that the much-awaited step of streamlining the free movement of people within 16 km along the border of Myanmar and India has been deferred by the former on March 4, 2018. Though India was keen to sign the agreement since 2017 but Myanmar citing "domestic compulsions" as reason has asked more time before the agreement is sealed. Though publicly stated that this MoU is aimed to enhance connectivity and increase interaction between the border populations but in reality both the propositions remain very much active by practice. This step is basically intended to secure the free movement of extremists and smugglers across the border (*The Hindu* 4 March 2018).

Though the FMR is in place however, not many avail of such facilitation and thus cross the border illegally. Some are unaware and others find it difficult to get a permit in order to cross the border. On the other hand, the insurgents also use this agreement to slip into Indian Territory for acquiring arms and planning attacks, and then conveniently heading back to the Myanmar side. Also, taking advantage of the FMR, a sizeable number of students living in these border lands in Myanmar also study in schools on the Indian side of the border. Mizoram and Manipur also face the problem of illegal and clandestine migration from Myanmar. Burmese people frequently cross over to the Indian side of the border in search of economic opportunities and work as labourers, coolies, street vendors and domestic workers (Levesque and Rahman 2008). These migrants also constitute the floating population, i.e. they come and go as they please without often intending to settle down in India. Thus the FMR coupled with the divided community ties has transformed migration into a continuous process.

Borderland, public health and migration

As per WHO, public health is defined as the science of protecting the safety and improving the health of communities through education, policy making and research for disease and injury prevention. Activities to strengthen public health capacities and service aim to provide conditions under which people can maintain to be healthy, improve their health and wellbeing, or prevent the deterioration of their health.

For almost a decade, the predominant trend in existing scholars has been to emphasize the link between health hazards and international migration. It is interesting to note that the economic question of facilitating mobility is subordinated by nation-states to the political issue of migrants as new citizens (Ahanthem 2010) or 'carriers of diseases.' The emergence of border towns and the opening of economic trading zones under the ambit of globalization have led to the increasing mobility of capital, goods and labour across political boundaries. Thus, increased population mobility and opening up of multiple channels of international trade and communication heighten the risk of the transmission of infectious and noninfectious diseases across borders (Gushulak and Douglas 2003).

A pioneering study conducted by UNESCO and UNAIDS in 2000 sought to demonstrate the impact of migrant population on the spread of HIV AIDS. The study pointed out that migrant population are exposed to greater risks of health hazards owing to the three factors namely economic transition and legal disabilities experienced by them; inability of the host or the destination country health services to respond to the practices of the migrant population and reduced access of the migrants to availability and accessibility of health and other social welfare services. Recent researches have reinforced this argument in a more nuanced manner. It is now being argued that migration in itself may not cause public health hazards but may contribute to the vulnerability of the migrants by exposing them to discrimination, gender inequality, sexual violence and exploitation, poor living conditions and lack of access to education, social services and healthcare facilities.

In this context it is interesting to note that the Chins who fled from Myanmar due to increasing violence of the Myanmar army (Human Watch 2009, 9–17) are currently living in the Indian state of Mizoram. The Mizos in Champai feel that the Chins control trade in their area and fix the price of goods daily traded across the border. While on the other hand the Chins who are known to be illegal migrants or "economic migrants" (Basavapatna 2010) perceive that they are exploited in host population and feel helpless. General perception of the locals is also noteworthy here. To the locals these Chins are the carriers of infectious diseases like HIV AIDS.

Attached to the threat of migration is the threat of HIV AIDS which is termed as a travelling mobile disease (Banerjee 2010). As the north eastern region of India seeks to build upon these existing linkages to facilitate greater integration with Myanmar it faces the complex challenges of unregulated drugs and arms trafficking, free movement of insurgent groups across the border and lastly, cross-border transmission of lethal communicable/infectious diseases like HIV AIDS, TB and Malaria. The FMR present increases the chances of migration and this makes it a cyclic process.

HIV AIDS

In India's Northeast

HIV AIDS constitutes one of the most potent non-traditional security threats claiming millions of lives worldwide. Northeast India is an isolated and mountainous area. It is a home to a wide range of different ethnic groups, each with its own distinct culture, traditions and language. Many of these ethnic groups are in conflict with the Indian government, demanding more autonomy or independence. Several ethnic movements are in armed struggle, pressing for their political demands. Conflict and underdevelopment in the region have propelled drug consumption and production which will be discussed in detail in our following section.

In India about 2.17 million people are living with HIV. As per India's National AIDS Control Organization (NACO 2017) report, the highest prevalence of the disease has been recorded in India's Northeastern states namely Nagaland (1.29%), Mizoram (0.81%) and Manipur (0.60%). Injecting Drug Use (IDU) remains the chief driver of HIV AIDS in these states (see Figure 7.1), thereby hinting at the deeper social and economic roots of the disease. It must be noted that the HIV prevalence among women who inject drugs was nearly twice or more than the figures for their male counterparts (UNAIDS 2014).

It was also interesting to note that the role of migrants or rather single male migrants (SMM) and long-distance truckers (LDT) is being acknowledged since 2006 to get an estimate of the epidemic among the bridge due to the clandestine nature and thus remains untouched in the NACO report. Thus, despite being an important driver of the HIV epidemic in India, data on migrant sexual behaviour remains limited due to its clandestine nature in the northeast India.

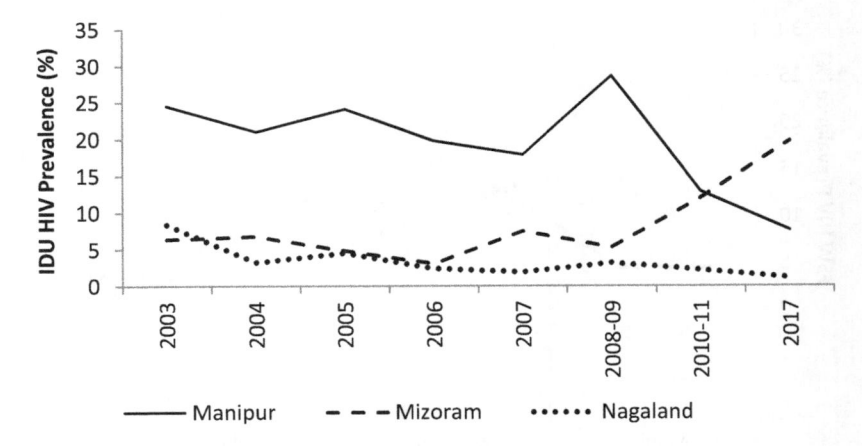

FIGURE 7.1   IDU HIV Prevalence in Northeast India.

Source: Figure prepared by researchers based on the HIV Sentinel Surveillance 2016–17, Technical Brief, National AIDS Control Organization (NACO), Government of India, New Delhi, December 2017

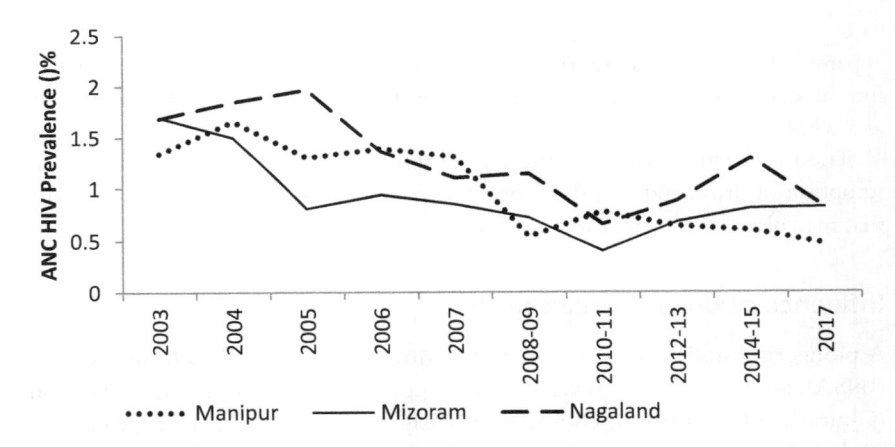

FIGURE 7.2   ANC HIV Prevalence in Northeast India.

Source: Figure prepared by researchers based on the HIV Sentinel Surveillance 2016–17, Technical Brief, National AIDS Control Organization (NACO), Government of India, New Delhi, December 2017

It is well known that both women and homosexuals are regarded as the carriers of this deadly disease. They are treated with suspicion and remain marginalized in the society (Banerjee 2010. However it is noteworthy that in the northeast as reflected in Figure 7.3 the current trend of HIV AIDS among female sex workers is decreasing. But it also must be kept in mind that in several places, sex work and drug use are interconnected. Many people who inject drugs either buy or sell sex and vice versa (Banerjee 2010). Therefore, categorizing each group in watertight compartments seems difficult and overlapping within each category becomes

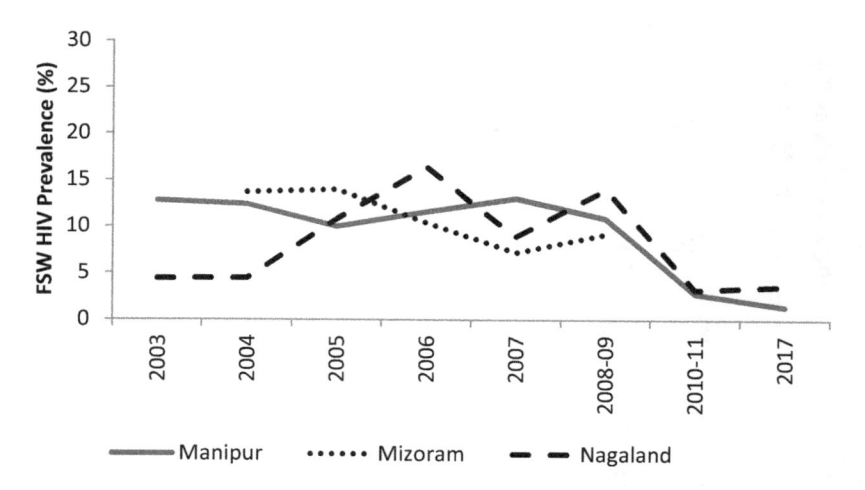

FIGURE 7.3   FSW HIV Prevalence in Northeast India.

Source: Figure prepared by researchers based on the HIV Sentinel Surveillance 2016–17, Technical Brief, National AIDS Control Organization (NACO), Government of India, New Delhi, December 2017

apparent. Though the systematic health checks and ART therapy seem to have increased; the blame game and stigmatization has helped less to curb the infection as a whole.

The next section will elaborate on the spread of HIV AIDS through the consumption of drugs and will focus on the dynamics of India–Myanmar borderland that may play an important role in this.

Influence of drugs: spread of HIV

A pioneering study conducted by the Institute of Narcotics Study and Analysis (INSA), an Indian NGO reveals illicit poppy to have been grown in Manipur (Churachandpur, Imphal, Ukhrul and Senapati districts), Nagaland (Mong and Mokokchung districts) and Arunachal Pradesh (Lohit, Anjaw, Tirap, Changlang and Yingkong districts) in Northeast India and Shan State, Kachin State and Kayah State in Myanmar, all of which are conflict-ridden areas. Moreover, these areas are inhabited by ethnic groups, mostly subsistence farmers, who resort to illicit poppy cultivation as a means to compensate for food shortages while also using it for both medicinal/ritualistic and consumption purposes (Kramer Tom et al. 2014). In terms of consumption, use of heroin, an opiate drug processed out of opium and known to generate euphoric effects, was prevalent till the 1990s after which the consumption of amphetamine type substances (ATS) became more popular. ATS contains ephedrine, also known as 'yellow cannabis' that causes psychotic disorders, leading to violent behaviour and the propensity to indulge in criminal activities. Manipur is the chief conduit through which large quantities of contraband ATS are trafficked from New Delhi into Burma (Goswami 2014).

The state of Manipur is closer to the drug circuits of Shan Hills and Tiddim Kachin. This provides an easy access and means of smuggling drugs to different part of the world, making Manipur the transit state. Manipur has the highest estimated adult HIV prevalence of 1.15 percent followed by Mizoram (0.80%) and Nagaland (0.78%) (NACO 201617). Mandalay, Tiddim Tahang, Homatin, Kheinam and Tamu are the main drug centers in Myanmar. It is from these centers that the heroin is smuggled to other parts of the world through Manipur via the towns of Manipur namely Behiang (Churchandpur District), New Samtal (Chandel District) and Kamjong (Ukhrul District) (Singh and Singh 2014). HIV related to IDU is high in Thoubal, Ukhrul, Churachandpur, Imphal West and Chandel districts. Some of these districts share border with Myanmar.

The unfenced border between Mizoram and Myanmar serves as a two-way route for cross-border drug trade based in Myanmar. There are two main routes through which drugs are trafficked from Western Burma to the Indian north eastern states of Manipur, Mizoram and Nagaland and vice versa. Of the two routes, the more traversed one begins in Mandalay and meanders through Monewa and Kalewa where it bifurcates in two directions: northward to the Tamu-Moreh border crossing and eventually through the National Highway (NH-39) into Manipur; southward through Rih-Champhai into Mizoram. The other route starts from Bhamo in Kachin state down to Homalin in the Sagaing region from where it enters Nagaland and further into Assam, Kolkata and rest of India (Chouvey 2013). According to the newspaper reports in January 2018 around 6.035 kg of heroin, 13,400 methamphetamine tablets and 159,471 tablets of pseudo-ephedrine were seized in 2017 in Mizoram which resulted in the death of 68 (*Business Standard* 15 January 2018). Heroin and other drugs are smuggled into Mizoram from Myanmar. While pseudo-ephedrine tablets are being smuggled into Myanmar from India in trucks to Guwahati from where they are taken to Manipur or Mizoram before entering Myanmar. Karimganj and Silchar act as transit points in this regard. In Myanmar they are manufactured into methamphetamine in clandestine laboratories mostly run by militants gaining seed money which is later used to procure weapons in the black market. This leaves a dark mark on the security system and check gates.

As the Government of India and Myanmar commit themselves to reviving the Tamu-Monewa-Kalewa road to use it as an economic corridor, steps must be taken to ensure stricter surveillance of the border by the narcotics department and the Border Security Forces (BSF) so that movement of goods and people does not go unmonitored. The same holds true for Rih-Tiddim road that is scheduled to be completed by the end of 2019. To prevent the evolving economic corridor from turning into a crime and trafficking corridor, it is incumbent upon both India and Myanmar to work out a two-pronged strategy to regulate drug-trafficking and HIV AIDS, with special focus on the border regions.

In Myanmar

Myanmar remains the hub of opium cultivation in Asia; the second largest producer and exporter of illicit opium in the world after Afghanistan. Myanmar is an integral part of the Golden Triangle that accounts for the highest percentage of opium cultivation in Asia. The Golden Triangle refers to the region between the borders of Myanmar, Laos and Thailand. Within Myanmar, cultivation of opium is highest in Kachin, North Shan, South Shan and East Shan. There are reports of new cultivation areas opening up in Sagaing region that borders with the Indian states of Manipur and Nagaland.

In 2017 it was estimated that there were 220,000 people living with HIV. The UNAIDS 2017 report estimates people who inject drugs (34.9%) to be the chief reason for this epidemic. Since age of infected population remained under 25, the findings have bolstered the argument that the risk associated with injecting drug use and HIV vulnerability should make the case for developing more youth-targeted programs. Although the burden of HIV prevalence is traditionally limited to urban towns and cities in Myanmar, injectable opium use is endemic with rates of high HIV prevalence evident in the more rural northern and north eastern areas of the country where the drug is produced. For example, in Waingmaw in Kachin State, HIV prevalence among people who inject drugs was particularly high at 47 percent during 2014.

Though migration did not feature as a separate category, but increasingly open borders make Myanmar more vulnerable to HIV incidence with an increase of migrants coming from bordering high prevalence countries. The 2014 census estimated that over 11 million residents have migrated internally or externally. As HIV testing is not a condition for entry, work or residence in Myanmar there is not much comprehensive information available on HIV prevalence or risk behaviours associated with the migrant population. Nevertheless, in 2014, the IOM data project did find that 18 percent of people identified as migrants in Mon and Kayin states were HIV positive – although it is difficult to assess if the point of infection happened within country (NSP on HIV and AIDS Myanmar 2016). However, it is broadly assumed that migrants might face residency and social restrictions that limit their access to HIV programming services, as well as other general forms of healthcare.

In 2016, the Government has pledged US$15 million for HIV treatment including ARVs and other commodities and US$1 million for the procurement of methadone. The Myanmar Health Sector Coordinating Committee (M-HSCC), established as a part of the Nay Pyi Taw Accord in 2013, has the broad mandate as the coordinating body for all public health sector issues (Ibid.). The current National Strategy Plan for HIV also proposes developing specific packages for people near transit points in addition to cross-border referral mechanisms and agreements to strengthen access to health services in destination countries.

Though a lot of efforts are being made in order to combat this deadly disease it cannot be ignored that Myanmar has one of the worst health indicators in the world. The public health care system in the country is severely under-resourced. The discrepancies in the access and coverage of healthcare facilities further accounts for the poor health indices in the country. Therefore, an effective border health management and disease control strategy is central to the Government of India's vision for greater connectivity and regional integration with her eastern neighbors.

Across-border women as HIV carriers

It is important to understand that women on either side of the border face the stigma of being carriers and cause for the spread of this 'deadly' disease. Women face the brunt of violence and borders encourage a regime of control, violence and counter violence. The position thus is extremely vulnerable and should be dealt with utmost care. According to Paula Banerjee (2010) the marginalized groups such as the migrants, homosexuals as well as female sex workers have been the soft targets in the anti HIV campaigns. Ironically though, women in Moreh who work as sex workers explain their circumstance as one out of a lack of choice, they are disapproving of women who come in from other districts or who cross over from the border to take up sex as work (Ahanthem 2010). In Nagaland, women sex workers are held in high risk groups. The transfer of HIV AIDS from husband to wife is high in Myanmar, thus in many cases after the husband's death the wife is shunned from her husband's as well as parents' home due to the ignorance and fear surrounding the HIV virus which causes AIDS (Strategic Information and M&E Working Group 2010). Thus, the crisis of living in perpetual poverty, conflict, poor infrastructure and development, compounded with a ready association for drug use and its associated HIV/AIDS companion has only served to marginalize and isolate the women further from the mainstream society. According to Chitra Ahanthem (2010), women drug users refrain from providing their accounts for the fear of being stigmatized in their community. Also, women who work at poppy plantation along the porous boundary refused to share their narratives and took affront that they 'would be involved in such activities.'

While access to ART is becoming easier on both sides of the border, there are still challenges in delivering treatment because of the shortage of staff, particularly doctors. It is a poor scenario since district doctors are mostly irregular in attendance at the district hospitals. Thus, the patients have to spend their money and sometimes have to travel to city to get a health check up (Ahanthem 2010). Some patients, especially widows, either take ART without informing doctors due to the fear of stigmatization or stop taking ART due to side effects such as rashes, swollen face, etc. (Kipgen 2012). Thus, it is important for health facilitators as well as government officials to be welcoming to their patients and deal with their situation with utmost empathy and care.

Increasing concerns in spread of HIV-Hepatitis C (HCV)

Hepatitis C or HCV is an emerging public health threat in Northeast India and Myanmar that has close associations with HIV AIDS. HCV is a liver disease caused by hepatitis C virus. According to WHO, HIV-affected IDUs are at high risk of contracting HCV if they share needles. There is no vaccine for hepatitis C. According to a survey conducted by the Indian Council of Medical Research, 98 percent of HIV positive people in Manipur's Churachandpur district were co-infected with hepatitis-C. Manipur is among the three northeastern states where hepatitis-C is silently killing people. Nagaland and Mizoram are the other two states where the prevalence rate of HIV and hepatitis-C co-infection is very high. Yaswant Rao Gaitonde Center for Aids Research Education (YRGCARE), a Chennai based NGO in collaboration with various NGOs based in Manipur like Social Awareness Service Organization (SASO), Care Foundation, Manipur Network of Positive People (MNP+) and also Manipur State AIDS Society are currently willingly to treat people with hepatitis C in Manipur free of cost (Nagaland Post 13 May 2017). Such initiative will enhance cooperation if it is extended to other states and also people living across the border.

HIV-TB co-infection

According to the World Health Organization's latest report on tuberculosis (TB), India and Myanmar fall under the category of high-burden countries along with Brazil, Cambodia, China, Ethiopia, the Philippine, Uganda and Vietnam.

The threat of TB looms large in India's northeastern states of Nagaland, Mizoram and Manipur. Nagaland has a high percentage of population suffering from TB. As per the government estimate, the detection rate of TB in the year 2014 was 81 percent as against the national target of 70 percent and the cure rate was 91 percent as against the national target of 85 percent. While all that points to the success of the Department of Health in meeting its target, recent researches present a dismal picture. The link between people who use/inject illicit drugs (PWID) and their chances of contracting TB is increasingly becoming visible, the reasons being poverty, unemployment, malnutrition, social stigma and limited access to health care.

In addressing the challenge posed by HIV-TB co-infection in India, the National AIDS Control Program (NACP) and the revised National TB Control Program (RNTCP) started collaborative HIV/TB control activities in the six high-burden states in 2001. Such joint efforts were further scaled up in 2007 within a National Framework for collaborative HIV-TB activities. By 2012 the intensified HIV-TB package achieved national coverage (TB India 2015).

A host of other actors such as medical associations, international NGOs and faith-based organizations (FBOs) are engaged in TB control efforts.

Notwithstanding such measures being adopted by both the governments in their respective domains, there have been little efforts toward building a systematic framework for cross-border health infrastructure. Except for few NGOs such as the Centre for Social Development (CSD) that has been working amongst border areas, there is little or no initiative toward developing cross-border disease surveillance mechanism. In the Myanmar side of the border, health organizations from Arakan, Chin, Kuki and Naga ethnic groups are engaged in providing preventive services and treatment for AIDS in the Sagaing region albeit on a limited basis. However, health workers on either side of the India-Burma border hardly coordinate with each other. The Assam Rifle that has a formidable presence in the northeast obstructs the activities of Burmese health workers by intimidating them or arresting them on slightest suspicion of their involvement in the insurgencies (JHSPH 2007).

The paramilitary forces whose task is to curb insurgencies and drug-trafficking in the border regions wrongly choose to assert their daunting presence in the region by rounding up well-meaning health workers and in the process, undermines prospects of meaningful cross-border exchanges.

Keeping these facts in consideration it is important to evaluate the government mechanisms on both sides of the border in order to understand and observe any negotiation to mitigate these issues.

Responses from the governments of India and Myanmar

In the wake of the political transition in Myanmar and the introduction of the multiparty democracy in 2011, former President U Thein Sein prioritized the upgradation of healthcare services. He emphasized the need to seek the cooperation of local population in implementing health reforms. Since 2013 the Myanmar Government has increased total expenditure on health from kyat 7,688 million in 2000–01 to kyat 652,745 million in 2014–15 (Ministry of Health 2014).

In implementing healthcare reforms, the former Myanmarese President U Thein Sein sought financial assistance from India. During President U Thein Sein's visit to India in October 2011, India signed a Memorandum of Understanding with Myanmar for the upgradation of the Yangon's Children Hospital and Sittwe General Hospital. India offered US$ 7 million for the upgradation project that was to be managed and overseen by Hospital Service Consultancy Corporation India ltd (HSCC). India also facilitated in the construction of Monywa General Hospital.

The most recent endeavours made in the direction of building up collaboration in the health sector has been the signing of a Memorandum of Understanding between the Ministry of AYUSH, Government of India and the Ministry of Health and Sports of the Government of Myanmar in the sphere of traditional medicine on 29 August 2016. It is indeed a significant step toward creating a common framework of knowledge and healing practices between the two neighbors.

In 2017, both sides have agreed to start consultations to establish and operate a state-of-the-art hospital in Nay Pyi Taw in association with one of the leading Indian hospital groups, based on modalities to be mutually decided (MEA 2017).

Thus, the above initiatives between both the nations remain generic and it is indeed noteworthy that there have been no specific steps or initiatives taken to mitigate the major concern related to HIVAIDS and HIV-TBco-Infection. As India is a cost-effective destination for well-developed medical facilities, state-of-the-art medical facilities should be established in bordering areas along the India–Myanmar border, which will benefit not only the people of the peripheries of India but also the people of the other side of the border. Moreover, Indian government may encourage the Northeastern states to tap potential of Healthcare tourism. There is need for synergy between local government agencies and civil society groups/ NGOs/ FBOs/ UN Agencies working in these disease-affected areas in India in preventing and controlling the spread of communicable diseases like HIV AIDS and HIV-TB co-infection on a sustained and long-term basis.

In this regard there are some steps which can be taken for cross-border health collaboration as well as cooperation.

- It is important to build a common framework of disease prevention and control strategy across the border with special reference to HIV AIDS, HCV, and HIV-TB co-infection.
- It is needed to ensure availability of healthcare to people living in the hard to reach areas. Well-equipped Primary Health Care Centers (PHCs) in the border towns and villages can not only cater to the needs of the rural population in remote areas but also address health problems of the poor Myanmarese nationals who often cross over to the Indian side of the border for treatment.
- Both India and Myanmar may take joint initiative to improve infrastructure of border hospitals on both sides.

Note

1 An earlier version of this article was presented at the ASEAN Studies Centre-sponsored seminar on "Border and Connectivity: North-East India and South-East Asia" and published as Anasua Basu Ray Chaudhury, "Connecting Lives on India – Myanmar Border: Issues in Migration and Public Health Hazards," in K. Vidya Sagar Reddy and C. Joshua Thomas (eds), *Border and Connectivity: North-East India and South-East Asia* (New Delhi: Pentagon Press, 2019).

References

Ahanthem, Chitra (2010). "Sanitized Societies and Dangerous Interlopers I: Women of a Border Town: Moreh." In *Endangered Lives on the Border: Women in the Northeast*. Mahanirban Calcutta Research Group, pp. 17–29.

Banerjee, Paula (2010). "Mobile Diseases and the Border." In *Borders, Histories, Existences: Gender and Beyond*. New Delhi: Sage Publications, pp. 160–192.

Basavapatna, Sahana (2010). "Sanitized Society and Dangerous Interlopers II: Law and the Chins in Mizoram." In *Endangered Lives on the Border: Women in the Northeast*. Mahanirban Calcutta Research Group, pp. 17–29.

Chouvey, Pierre Arnaud (2013). "Drug Trafficking in and Out of the Golden Triangle." In *An Atlas of Trafficking in South-East Asia*, edited by Pierre Arnaud Chouveyed. London and New York: IB Tauris.

"Drug Abuse Killed 65 in Mizoram in 2017." (2018). *Business Standard*, January 15, www.business-standard.com/article/news-ians/drug-abuse-killed-65-in-mizoram-in-2017-118011500365_1.html (accessed June 20, 2018).

Fernandez, Walter (2014). "Relations Between Divided Tribes: NE India and Western Myanmar." Conference Report on Look East Policy India and Myanmar Pitching for Greater Connectivity, Institute of Social Sciences, Burma Centre Delhi, New Delhi, August 4, https://in.boell.org/sites/default/files/report_-_look_east_policy_1.pdf (accessed June 14, 2018).

"Free Hepatitis C Treatment Facility in Mnp." (2017). *Nagaland Post*, May 13, www.nagalandpost.com/ChannelNews/Regional/RegionalNews.aspx?news=TkVXUzEwMDExNDQxMA%3D%3D (accessed June 20, 2018).

Goswami, Namrata (2014). "Drugs and the Golden Triangle: Renewed Concerns for Northeast India." *IDSA Comment*, February 10, http://idsa.in/idsacomments/Drugsandthe GoldenTriangle_ngoswami_100214 (accessed June 20, 2018).

Gushulak, Brian D. and Douglas W. Macpherson (2003). "Population Mobility and Infectious Diseases: The Diminishing Impact of Classical Infectious Diseases and New Approaches for the 21st Century." *Clinical Infectious Diseases* 31 (3) (September): 776–780.

Kent, George (2017). "When Burma and India Went Their Separate Ways." *Frontier Myanmar*, September 5, https://frontiermyanmar.net/en/when-burma-and-india-went-their-separate-ways (accessed May 18, 2018).

Kipgen, Jennifer (2012). "Utilization Patterns of Health Services by Widows Living with HIV/AIDS: A Study in Manipur." Unpublished PhD diss., School of Social Work, Tata Institute of Social Sciences.

Kramer, Tom, et al. (2014). "Bouncing Back: Relapse in the Golden Triangle." *Transnational Institute*, June, www.tni.org/files/download/tni-2014-bouncingback-web-klein.pdf.

Levesque, Julien and Rahman Mirza Zulfiqar (2008). "Tension in the Rolling Hills: Burmese Population and Border Trade in Mizoram." IPCS Research Papers, April.

Malhotra, Brigadier V. P. (Retd.). (2011). *Terrorism and Counter Terrorism in South Asia and India*. New Delhi: Vij Books India Pvt. Ltd., p. 90.

Ministry of External Affairs. Government of India (2017). (2013) "Q NO.2165 Indo-Myanmar Border Dispute." Unstarred Question No. 2165 Raised at Lok Sabha, Media Center, New Delhi, December 18, http://mea.gov.in/lok-sabha.htm?dtl/22666/Q+NO2165+I NDOMYANMAR+BORDER+DISPUTE (accessed 20 June 2018).

————. "India-Myanmar Joint Statement Issued on the Occasion of the State Visit of Prime Minister of India to Myanmar (September 5–7, 2017)." New Delhi, September 6, www.mea.gov.in/bilateral-documents.htm?dtl/28924/IndiaMyanmar+Joint+Statemen t+issued+on+the+occasion+of+the+State+Visit+of+Prime+Minister+of+India+to+ Myanmar+September+57 + 2017 (accessed June 20, 2018).

Myanmar Health Care System (2014). "Health in Myanmar." Ministry of Health and Sports. The Republic of the Union of Myanmar.

"Myanmar Puts Off Border Pact with India." (2018). *The Hindu*, March 4, www.thehindu. com/news/national/myanmar-puts-off-border-pact-with-india/article22925706.ece (accessed June 16, 2018).

National AIDS Control Organisation (NACO) (2017). "Annual Report (2016–17)." Chapter 24, Government of India, New Delhi, pp. 339–340, http://naco.gov.in/sites/default/ files/NACO%20ANNUAL%20REPORT%202016-17.pdf (accessed 15 May, 2018).

National Strategic Plan on HIV and AIDS, Myanmar 2016–2020 (2016). Department of Public Health, Ministry of Health and Sports, Myanmar, The Republic of the Union of Myanmar, www.aidsdatahub.org/sites/default/files/highlight-reference/document/Myanmar_ National_Strategic_Plan_on_HIV_and_AIDS_2016-2020.pdf (accessed June 20, 2018).

"Security Beefed Up Along Mizoram-Myanmar Border to Check Entry of Rohingya Muslims." (2017). *The Hindustan Times*, September 19, www.hindustantimes.com/india-news/security-beefed-up-along-mizoram-myanmar-border-to-check-entry-of-roh ingya-muslims/story-5Pho2YryZpDhsNsD4gP9AK.html (accessed June 20, 2018).

Singh, Moirangmayum Sanjeev and Singh Rajkumar Meiraba (2014). "Cross Border Crime and Its Impact in Manipur, India." *International Journal of Interdisciplinary and Multidisciplinary Studies (IJIMS)* 1 (5): 161–165. www.ijims.com/uploads/6123c4cd506070e2d8bazp pd_575.pdf (accessed June 20, 2018).

Stover, Eric, et al. (2007). "The Gathering Storm: Infectious Diseases and Human Rights in Burma." Human Rights Center. University of California, Berkeley and Center for Public

Health and Human Rights and Johns Hopkins Bloomberg School of Public Health, July, www.jhsph.edu/research/centers-and-institutes/center-for-public-health-and-human-rights/_pdf/GatheringStorm.pdf (accessed June 15, 2018).

Strategic Information and M&E Working Group (2010). "HIV Estimates and Projections, Asian Epidemiological Model, Myanmar 2010–2015." National AIDS Programme, Myanmar, www.aidsdatahub.org/sites/default/files/documents/Myanmar_HIV_Esti mates_2010-2015.pdf (accessed June 20, 2018).

"TB India 2015: Annual Status Report." Government of India, www.tbcindia.nic.in/show file.php?lid=3166 (accessed June 20, 2018).

UNAIDS (2014). "Gap Report." United Nations HIV/AIDS Work Across Borders, www. oxfam.org/sites/www.oxfam.org/files/manipur.pdf.

———. (2017). "HIV and AIDS Estimates, Country Factsheets, Myanmar 2017." www. unaids.org/en/regionscountries/countries/myanmar.

"'We Are Like Forgotten People' The Chin People of Burma: Unsafe in Burma, Unprotected in India." (2009). *Human Watch*, www.hrw.org/sites/default/files/reports/burma0 109webwcover_0.pdf (accessed June 20, 2018).

"4 Northeastern States Have Highest Death Rates Due to Malaria." (2017). *Fact Checker*, November 8, http://factchecker.in/4-northeastern-states-have-highest-death-rates-due-to-malaria/ (accessed June 20, 2018).

8

EMPLOYING PROXIMITY

Boosting bilateral ties between India and Myanmar

Pratnashree Basu

Regional connectivity can be viewed in terms of bridging domestic goals and geopolitical ambitions. Physical connectivity i.e. connectivity through pipelines, highways and sea routes is only one aspect of connectivity. Physical connectivity should be made to work to the advantage of all stakeholders so that it is predicated by policy connectivity, giving rise to a set of institutions with formal and informal norms that facilitate and harmonize the flow of labour, capital and goods as well as ensure the free movement of people.

Myanmar is India's gateway to the southeast and this fact is one of the fundamental drivers of the Look East Policy and the now refurbished Act East policy. Besides financial aid and cooperation in economic and energy sectors, India's ties with Myanmar leave a lot of room for development and cultivation. Ties between the two countries based on a foundation of shared ethnic, cultural, religious and historical ties date back centuries. Officially, bilateral relations got a start after the signing of the Treaty of Friendship in 1951 and a trade agreement in 1994. Despite high-level visits and agreements on several bilateral projects, the development of relations has remained a very gradual one due to political complexities, security issues, difficult physical terrain and deplorable road links. Nevertheless, India's policy of 'realpolitik' and preference for 'non-interference and active engagement' with Myanmar through the major part of bilateral history has stood it in good stead. In the absence of this approach, ties between the two may have become non-recoverable.

While the last couple of decades have seen a significant improvement in bilateral ties, there is much ground to be covered with respect to furthering bilateral cooperation. The most important of these areas include cross-border infrastructural development; trade and services; cooperation in technology and tourism. At the heart of these areas of enhancing bilateral ties is the building of Indian presence in Myanmar and vice versa.

This chapter will explore the possibilities of advancing bilateral engagement in the above mentioned areas with a focus on the implementation of short-term policy goals which would prove beneficial to the sustenance of long-term policy goals. The chapter will highlight how, being neighbors, sharing a common historical past and cultural similarities present a useful opportunity for both countries to employ their proximity to their advantage.

Geographical proximity

The significance of the geographical location of Myanmar is not lost among the Indian intelligentsia. For years it has been acknowledged that the unique location of Myanmar positions it as a bridge between the countries of South Asia and Southeast Asia. Myanmar shares borders with India, Bangladesh, Thailand, Laos and China and straddles South and Southeast Asia. The country's unique location has ensured its participation in regional and subregional blocks such as the ASEAN, BIMSTEC and the GMS (Greater Mekong Sub-region) Development Program (Yhome 2008). The strategic significance of Myanmar has also been highlighted by projects like the Asian Highway Network and the Trans-Asian Railway.

However, political turmoil and protracted periods of instability have made it difficult for the country to employ the benefits of its location not only to its own advantage but also that of the neighborhood. Nevertheless, since the political transition in Myanmar began, it has been regarded that the country will play a fundamental role in reorienting Asia's geography –

> Burma, long seen in Western policy circles as little more than an intractable human rights conundrum, may soon sit astride one of the world's newest and most strategically significant crossroads. Mammoth infrastructure projects are taming a once inhospitable landscape. More importantly, Burma and adjacent areas, which had long acted as a barrier between the two ancient civilizations, are reaching demographic and environmental as well as political watersheds. Ancient barriers are being broken, and the map of Asia is being redone.
>
> *(Myint-U 2011)*

In the Look East Policy of the Indian government, now refurbished as the Act East Initiative, Myanmar was to play a central role as a gateway to countries of Southeast Asia. And indeed, Myanmar's location makes it suitably poised to assume the role of a confluence between countries of South Asia and Southeast Asia.

Connectivity and security

Physical connectivity through multi-modal links is essential for boosting commercial ties as well as enhancing people to people relations. For functional and effective connectivity links, there is a requirement of both the 'hardware' and 'software' of connectivity (Osius 2013). The former refers to the physical links such as roads, railway networks, bridges and so on; while the latter refers to the systems, procedures, regulations and technology, which make the physical links serviceable. Both complement each other and are equally important in the promotion and strengthening of commercial, political and cultural ties.

There are about eight road connectivity projects between the two countries – the Kaladan Multi-Modal Transit Transport Project (KMTTP), the India-Myanmar-Thailand Trilateral Highway Project, the Mekong-India Economic Corridor, the Stilwell Road (the Ledo Road and the Burma Road), the Delhi-Hanoi Railway Link, the Rhi-Tiddim Road in Myanmar, the BCIM Economic Corridor and the Tamu-Kalewa-Kalemyo Friendship Road. Of these, only the Tamu-Kalewa-Kalemyo Friendship Road one has been completed. Of these, the India-Myanmar-Thailand Trilateral Highway is considered to be the most important one, which may in future also be extended up to Cambodia, Laos, and Vietnam. Once completed, the Highway will function as not just a connectivity link but also an economic and development corridor with special economic zones (Iyer 2017), which would have the potential to transform local aspirations.

Being a multi-modal link covering a sea route, river route and land links, the KMTTP is arguably the most prominent of these projects. However, it has faced countless shifting deadlines and only construction of a jetty at the Sittwe port (providing a maritime link with the Kolkata port) has been completed. Coastal shipping between the two countries has also been considered and a cargo ferry service began operations in 2014 from Chennai to Yangon.

Connectivity through rail links also need to be considered as they will reduce the duration of transport and would also be cost effective in comparison to transport via road. Feasibility studies for a rail link between Jiribam in Manipur to Mandalay in Myanmar have been conducted including studies on smaller sections along this route, which is part of the Trans-Asian Railway Network. In 2013, the Northeast Frontier Railway in India proposed a master plan to connect the northeastern states of the country with Myanmar and Bangladesh.

Many of these projects (especially road links) have faced difficulties such as land issues, apprehensions regarding possible displacement, environmental concerns, political repercussions and bureaucratic inertia. Hence, despite having been envisioned and agreed to on chapter, the implementation of these connectivity projects has languished. In addition, in places where work is ongoing, the delays have resulted in escalation of estimated costs of construction. Other problems such as the difficulty of using feeder roads connecting infrastructure projects around the year due to difficult terrain also contribute to extending the time allotted for completion of the projects.

Another vital mode of physical connectivity is the establishment of air links. An increase in the number of direct flights is required to avoid longer flight durations are longer for people travelling from either country. There is only one bi-weekly direct flight service from Kolkata to Yangon and another weekly flight service from New Delhi to Yangon via Gaya. Given that religious tourism (discussed later) can be of great potential for enhancing bilateral ties, increasing flight services will make it much easier for people to travel.

The issue of cross-border security is a two-pronged one. First, the northeastern states of India, which share the land boundary with Myanmar, have been beset with internal strife for decades and across the border, ethnic conflicts have also erupted from time to time. Militant outfits from both sides have found refuge along the border areas because of the difficult physical landscape, which makes it difficult for security forces to have enough and effective monitoring.

Second, the border areas are located close to the 'Golden Triangle,' which is notorious for the production and trade of drugs, illegal trade in small arms and human trafficking. The region is also very prone to sexually transmitted diseases (STDs). These have in turn resulted in a region that has lacked stability and the establishment of institutions and processes that would enable the betterment of education and enhancement of living conditions. Together with this, corruption among government officials has also hindered efforts and measures that could have been implemented to address these challenges.

Illegal migration and security along the border is arguably the most important, yet often, sensitive issue for the two countries. In this regard, the northeastern states of India and the bordering provinces in Myanmar need to engage closely to ensure that cross-border relations are boosted. Measures also need to be put in place by the two governments to enable security forces on both sides of the border to strengthen their efforts toward curbing illegal migration, smuggling, trafficking in small arms and informal trade. Effective procedures for these checks are necessary as well. Security concerns therefore need the concerted and sustained efforts of the two governments.

Leveraging the Free Movement Regime

The Free Movement Regime (FMR) permits people either side of the border to enter and move freely within a distance of 16 km. The FMR has its advantages and disadvantages. While it is susceptible to being misused by militants and smugglers who gain easy access to either side of the border, at the same time, it is extremely beneficial to people who inhabit these areas and share similar cultural histories, especially the Naga, Meitei and Kuki tribes. In the border town of Zokhawtar for instance, located in Mizoram is comprised of only a bridge diving two parts of what is actually one large settlement. Since there are English medium schools on the Indian side of the town, children from across the border are enrolled in these schools and cross the bridge everyday to come and attend classes on the Indian side. The FMR has made this possible.

In early 2017, reports surfaced that fencing along the Myanmarese side of the border had begun. Authorities in Myanmar claimed that this was being done to effectively manage the border areas. The Indian government however stated that there was no proposal to fence the border. Earlier in 2003, fencing along the

Manipur section of the India–Myanmar border had been attempted following bilateral discussion but construction was stopped following protests by locals.

Following this, a government panel was instituted by India to look into the gaps in border relations between the two countries and despite security concerns such as the influx of Rohingya refugees, it is expected that the FMR will remain in force (Tripathi 2017). This has been done considering the close ethnic and cultural ties that are shared by people living on either side of the border. The panel has proposed the use of Aadhar identification cards by Indian nationals to prevent misappropriation by refugees.

It is important to ensure that the FMR remains in place and supports the interests of the local inhabitants for whom it was instituted. Both countries should therefore put in place supporting mechanisms that would facilitate free movement as well as act as a check on the exploitation of the same for illegal purposes. Dialogue regarding the FMR should also involve local stakeholders so that policies are comprehensive and accommodative of local interests.

India and Myanmar signed the Land Border Crossing Agreement in May 2018 (The Telegraph 2018). The agreement permits people (with valid passports and visas) from either side of the border to cross to the other side for education, health, tourism and pilgrimage. Being regarded as a landmark deal, the border agreement, has been deferred several before being finally signed. It is an important step toward facilitating people-to-people movement and cross-border interactions.

Infrastructural facilities at the border

While there are efforts toward the formalization of trade, for India and Myanmar, non-tariff barriers including restrictions on tradable items have impeded such efforts. Moreh and Zokhawtar in the Indian states of Manipur and Mizoram have been functioning border *haats* with their Myanmarese counterparts across the border – Tamu and Rih, respectively. The Moreh-Tamu border point is the more active one of the two and the Zokhawtar-Rih border point is quite recent. In both these places however, there is need for infrastructural facilities such as banking, laboratory testing, warehousing, and screening, among others. The Indian government has undertaken the development of the land customs station at Moreh to an Integrated Check Post with contemporary facilities and regulatory measures for the prevention of smuggling and informal trade. Facilities at the Integrated Check Post will include sheds for Cargo inspection, passenger terminal building, warehouse/cold storage, currency exchange, banks, and so on (Das 2016).

The lack of proper testing facilities at Moreh of food items being traded creates delays as the items are sent to Imphal for testing and the process can take up to two weeks. Often, samples are opened on the way to Imphal by security personnel creating scope for contamination. Myanmar has requested India for technological and financial assistance for expanding the existing mini lab at Tamu and establishing another one at Rih (Das 2016).

Market access and economic connectivity

Although it is less than a decade that Myanmar has begun to undertake economic reforms that would facilitate the opening up of the economy, The Stabilization Program commenced by the government from the late 1980s paved the way for an investment-friendly atmosphere with a market-based economy by invigorating the local economy. Over the recent years, the GDP per capita has risen gradually. In 2011, the government permitted selected private banks to trade foreign currency and in 2012 a fresh Foreign Investment Law (FIL) was signed, which resulted in a greater role of investments, allowed tax breaks, eased procedural constraints and land leases of up to 50 years (Chaudhury, Basu and Basu 2015).

Enhancing market access and invigorating the economy is however a painstaking process in Myanmar as other countries are wary about the domestic political scenario which can very quickly turn unfavorable to the interests of the market. The reenactment of the new FIL was a welcome move but the right to evaluate investment offers is reserved by the Myanmar Investment Commission, which is not known for its transparency.

India and Myanmar set up a Joint Trade Committee in 2003 to take stock of bilateral trade between the two, which was followed by a Bilateral Investment Promotion Agreement (BIPA), and a Double Taxation Avoidance Agreement (DTAA) in 2008. India has entered the Myanmarese market through sectors like healthcare, pharmaceuticals, banking and infrastructure. India in turn offers a huge market for companies in Myanmar and imports sizeable quantities of agricultural commodities. Nevertheless, bilateral trade continues to remain shy of expectations. This can be attributed to lack of effective financial infrastructure, high currency exchange rates in Myanmar, and cumbersome financial regulations. Poor connectivity links between the two countries is another factor, which compounded the problem (Chaudhury, Basu and Basu 2015).

An area in which the two countries can expand bilateral cooperation is the banking sector, which in turn would facilitate investments and therefore boost bilateral economic ties. Many Indian banks have opened their business in Myanmar and despite there being operational challenges; it would in the long run be beneficial. Efficient banking facilities, especially at border areas are imperative for curbing informal trade.

Being a country rich in natural resources like wood, non-metallic minerals and precious stones, it would be beneficial for the country to leverage the potential offered by these resources which are high-end and therefore, lucrative. In addition, Myanmar has a young labour pool and is located in a region that is both dynamic and fast growing. Coupled with these, a stable political system and sound economic policy mixes would provide the much needed fillip to spur the economy and engage more constructively with the neighborhood (Anukoonwattaka and Mikic 2012). Robust trade relations and greater economic relations in turn help to ensure safe and secure borders (Ghosh 2016).

Low hanging fruits

While infrastructural connectivity projects, dialogue on security issues and boosting bilateral economic engagement are long-term goals, there also needs to be short-term instruments of bilateral engagement which would be able to sustain the drive toward the achievement of long the term goals. These are the in other words, the 'low hanging fruits' which facilitate regular interactions and streamline bilateral engagement. Having these facilitators in place ensures that in times of political uncertainty, bilateral ties are not pushed two steps behind.

For instance, even though India and Myanmar are next door neighbors, barring the population living along the border (who share cultural and ethnic affinities), there is a general lack of awareness and interest among the population in both these countries about each other. A direct impact of this falls on the tourism industry. Despite both countries possessing a huge potential for the development of bilateral tourism, much of what does take place is limited to religious tourism. Other areas in which bilateral cooperation can take place on a much more visible and regular basis include exchange in services; cooperation in vocational training and education; enhancing cross-border economic linkages and the establishment of digital connectivity.

Low hanging fruits enable the utilization of simpler goals that can help the two countries to strengthen mutual understanding and cooperation. While not all of these instruments may be easily achievable, it is imperative that the two countries recognize the benefits that would accrue from developing these areas of cooperation so that constructive dialogue and ensuing processes can be initiated.

Encouraging local interest and involvement

The creation of local stake is crucial for making the connectivity architecture a sustainable one. Therefore there needs to be enabling mechanisms, which would leverage the geographical advantages and thus in turn contribute to the successful running of connectivity links (Basu 2015). To create local stake, the involvement of state governments is very important. For instance, for the development of ties among people, trade and services along the Myanmar-Mizoram border, the state government of Mizoram needs to play an active role. Tourism, cross-border trade and cooperation in services can be areas that would be useful in this regard. The encouragement of local involvement and the establishment of processes that would benefit the immediate neighborhoods on either side of the border would also engage people meaningfully. In addition, this would also enable the border areas to become more than just transit points for third-country trade.

Border *haats*(rural markets) which are already functional in certain points along the Indo–Myanmar are a vital mode of engaging the local population. Set up within 5 km on either side of the international border these *haats* serve as markets for trading in local items and produce and also for trade in items from third countries such as China. Border *haats* help in the enhancement of local trade and people-to-people ties. Another significant purpose of these local markets is to reduce informal trade. However, this purpose is also always served due to the restriction of items on the list of goods that can be traded and due to challenges posed by non-tariff barriers.

The first such *haat* was set up in the Pangsau Pass in Arunachal Pradesh in India and Sangaing region across the border in Myanmar. In addition to this, the Moreh-Tamu and Zowkhatar-Rih border *haats* are also operational with the former being the busier one. The Myanmar government expressed interest in increasing the number of these *haats* to support the socioeconomic development of people in these areas (Business Standard 2017). In May 2017, a five-member team led by Myanmar's Ministry of Labour Affairs visited the Kasaba border *haat* in Tripura on the India-Bangladesh border to study its functioning. The team also visited the Akhaura Integrated Checkpost, which is second largest border trading zone on the India-Bangladesh border. Four more haats on the Indian side in the state of Mizoram – Hnahlan, Vaphai, Zote and Pangkhua and Darkhai, Leilet, Fartlang and Thau on the corresponding side in Myanmar are also being planned (Northeast Today 2017).

Spurring the growth of tourism

The northeastern states of India are well known for their scenic beauty and are also home to many religious and historical sites of interest. On the other side of the border, Myanmar too has beautiful destinations. Given that there are also pockets of cultural similarities, it should be conducive to encourage cross-border tourism among the two countries. For instance the RihDil lake, which is located just a few kilometers across the border from the border town of Champhai (in Mizoram) is a beautiful scenic and spiritual destination which can be developed as a tourist spot. The lake holds a lot of spiritual as well as mythological significance for Mizos on the Indian side of the border and would be a popular location for tourism. There are also lesser-known places of historical interest for the people of either country. These include, among others, the tomb of Bahadur Shah Zafar in Yangon and the palace of Thibaw, the last king of Burma, located in Ratnagiri, Maharashtra.

Despite the fact that the government only authorizes tourists to visit specific locations such as Bagan and Mandalay among others, Myanmar has a rapidly growing tourism market and this sector has the potential to contribute significantly to the country's economy. The tourism industry also promotes ecotourism and special tourist packages like Art Cities of Myanmar, which are catered for unique experiences. Myanmar has also been engaged in inter and intra-regional tourism development efforts. It is estimated that over a million tourists came to Myanmar after the country's political landscape began to transform from 2011, which increased to almost 5 million in 2015. These numbers are however deceptive (Janssen 2017) as the majority of tourists coming into Myanmar comprise of day trippers from the bordering areas of Thailand and China.

In 2017, the Indian government announced a visa-free policy for tourists from Myanmar, following which, the number of tourists from Myanmar to India increased by 10 percent from that of the previous year (Myanmar Times 2018). Religious tourism is an important component of bilateral engagement in this regard. Besides religious tourism, medical and adventure tourism also have a lot of scope. Nevertheless, the number of travelers from India to Myanmar is much less than those going to other countries of Southeast Asia because of the comparatively higher costs of hotels in the country. An increase in the number of direct flights from India to Myanmar can also help to boost bilateral tourism.

The rise of tourism declined in 2016 in the wake of conflicts between ethnic groups and the military. The political climate in the country has a big impact on the tourism industry and till such a time as the situation is quelled and there is enough confidence in the sustenance of stability, the tourism sector will fail to gather momentum. Additionally, enhancement of visibility and awareness about the country is also required for generating interest among potential travelers. It is an unfortunate predicament, as growth of this sector would have a direct impact on the creation of jobs. The sector reportedly created an estimated 1.5 million jobs in 2016.

Following the Land Border Crossing Agreement and the Cross-border Travel Allowance Agreement signed between the two countries earlier in 2018, caravan tour operators on both sides are positive about a rise in the number of tourists from across the border in India through the Tamu-Moreh gate and Rikhawdar-Zokhawthar gate. Caravan tour groups on either side take travelers on short trips to locations across the border. Both governments are also expected to work out security plans to be adhered to by these operators. According to the Ministry of Hotels and Tourism in Myanmar, over 1500 travelers from India came to the country via caravan tour groups and about 700 Myanmarese travelers went across the border to India (Thu 2018).

The development of education and soft skills

Education lies at the heart of connectivity drives. Education and vocational programs for people on both sides of the border would contribute greatly to the overall development of quality of life and usher new opportunities for the development of these areas which at the moment are often not just remote in terms of distance but also in terms of standards of living.

This is an important sector in which the Indian central and state governments need to collaborate as it is the state-level governments which will be implementing the policies. Besides student exchange programs, there can special short and long-term courses in which teachers and scholars from India can be sent to institutions in Myanmar. For instance, there are vocational training centers at Pakokku and Myingyan set in by Hindustan Machine Tools International Ltd (HMTI) and the Government of Myanmar, providing training on Machinist-Fitting, Machinist-Turning/Milling, Tools and Die Making, Industrial Electricity, Sheet Metal and Welding (Chaudhury, Basu and Basu 2015). Two other initiatives include the Language Laboratories and E-Resource Center project trained officials in the Ministry of Foreign Affairs (MOFA), Myanmar in foreign languages; and the establishment of the India–Myanmar Center for Enhancement of Information Technology Skills (IMCEITS) which provides short-term courses on Software and Application Programming for student in Myanmar.

India's northeastern states are home to a diverse range of educational institutions including central universities and vocational institutes which provide quality education and can be beneficial for students from Myanmar. There is a high demand of academic, technical and professional training in Myanmar and young professionals from India can find a lot of scope.

Digital connectivity

Cross-border fiber optic links providing high-speed broadband link for voice and data transmission have been set up between India and Myanmar. The first one, running for a distance of 500 km, was set up from Moreh (in Manipur) to Mandalay in 2009. The Information and Communications Technology (ICT) sector has grown rapidly in Myanmar after having remained underdeveloped for the major part of the country's history with sharp increases in growth since 2013 (Premawardhana 2017). The government rolled out a policy framework for the development of ICT industry and introduced competition between foreign and domestic competitors. Indeed, investors have been eyeing this sector in Myanmar as the country is among the last untapped markets in Asia (Nam, Cham and Halili 2015)

In 2016, the first terrestrial optical fiber link between India and Myanmar operated by Bharti Airtel (a leading global telecommunications company based in India) went live. This is expected to heighten the growth of digital services. In late 2017, India announced a credit line of USD 1 billion as part of the country's Work Plan 2018, for the development of digital connectivity infrastructure with CLMV (Cambodia, Laos Myanmar and Vietnam) countries. Enhanced broadband penetration efforts are already being undertaken with Myanmar with the help of India's Gigabit Passive Optical Network technology (The Financial Express 2018). The Plan also involves cooperation in big data, cyber-security, cloud computing and e-governance. The Myanmar government also formed a digital economy development committee in 2017 to work in tandem with the Indian government (Myanmar Times 2018).

Enhancement of digital infrastructure and establishment of processes that utilize the same are essential to catch up and be at par with developments across the world. While physical connectivity networks no doubt are the bedrock for the betterment of commercial and people to people ties, in an age when much of world functions and interacts through digital technology, it is imperative to develop and employ the same. It is also vital that these efforts be buoyed by complementary policy, procedural and regulatory regimes (Saran 2015).

Conclusion

Bilateral relations are also often impacted by what is often referred to as 'a new Great Game,' which refers to the collision of geostrategic interests in Myanmar between India and China (Gottschlich 2015). Myanmar is rich in energy resources, which assumes significance for both India and China who are keen to diversify their sources of energy as their economies expand. Yangon is also important for Beijing to stimulate the growth of the latter's landlocked western provinces which border Myanmar (Credo 2015). Myanmar's trade with China is much greater than that with India. China has significant investments in Myanmar and plays a dominant role in oil and gas, hydropower and infrastructure sectors in Myanmar. Beijing's presence in Myanmar, however, has not always been a welcome one as the country seeks to balance its engagement with both China and India. On India's part, there needs to be clarity regarding policy, elimination of ambivalence and a long-term understanding about the approach necessary to work with the reality of China's increasing presence in the country (Lall 2008).

In South and Southeast Asia, there is an invariable apprehension regarding the expansion and nature of Beijing influence. When it comes to infrastructure projects and financial assistance, the role of Japan must also be considered. While China attracts much of the international attention for its projects like the Belt and Road Initiative, it must be noted that Japan has been involved in the development of infrastructure and resources in the region for decades spearheaded by the Asian Development Bank (ADB), the Japan International Cooperation Agency (JICA), and the Japan Infrastructure Initiative (Shepard 2018). Besides geostrategic competition with China, it is also believed that the time has come for Japan to reap the benefits of its long involvement in Myanmar (Strefford 2016). Interestingly, an ADB report (2017) estimated that developments in the Asia-Pacific would require about \$1.7 trillion per year through 2030 noting that the demand for infrastructure will surpass the existing arrangements. In this sense, as Shepard (2018) notes, 'the Asian infrastructure investment game has only just begun.'

Proximity is effective only when the benefits that it offers are realized, or constructive attempts are made for the same to be realized. While India and Myanmar have undertaken several measures that seek to leverage the benefits that each has to offer, there remains much more to be done. It is important in this context to sustain the intent to strengthen bilateral ties and expand areas of cooperation. Political relations between countries are never constant and there will be issues that need ironing out. The long-term goals of enhancing physical connectivity links, boosting commercial ties and enhancing people to people interaction need to be kept free from being held hostage to temporary political circumstances.

As Myint-U (2011) writes,

> The generation now coming of age is the first to grow up in an Asia that is both postcolonial and (with a few small exceptions) postwar. New rivalries may yet fuel 21st-century nationalisms and lead to a new Great Game, but there is great optimism nearly everywhere, at least among the middle classes and the elites that drive policy: a sense that history is on Asia's side and a desire to focus on future wealth, not hark back to the dark times that have only recently been left behind.

References

Anukoonwattaka, Witada and Mia Mikic (2012). "Myanmar: Opening Up to Its Trade and Foreign Direct Investment Potential." Staff Working Paper 01/12, Trade and Investment Division, UNESCAP, September 20.

Credo, Jeremie P. (2015). "Myanmar and the Future of Asia's New Great Game." *The Diplomat*, July 24.

Basu, Pratnashree (2015). "Stepping Stones for Cross-Border Engagement: The Case of Zowkhathar-Rih." July 20. Report of Field Trip, The Jadavpur Association of International Relations (JAIR)-MaulanaAbulKalam Azad Institute of Asian Studies (MAKAIAS).

Das, Ram Upendra (2016). "Enhancing India-Myanmar Border Trade Policy and Implementation Measures." Department of Commerce, Ministry of Commerce and Industry, Government of India. Ghosh, Lipi (2016). "India-Myanmar Relations: Context of Contemporary Geographical Routes and Linkages." ISAS Insights, No. 327, National University of Singapore, April 20.

Gottschlich, Pierre (2015). "New Developments in India – Myanmar Bilateral Relations?" *Journal of Current Southeast Asian Affairs* 34 (2) (June).

India Helping ASEAN Develop Digital Connectivity (2017). *The Myanmar Times*, December 14.

"India to Start Pilot Digital Projects in These Countries – Check List Here." (2018). *The Financial Express*, January 27.

"Information and Communication Technology Sector Toward Inclusive Growth." (2015). ADB Economics Working Paper Series, November.

Iyer, Roshan (2017). "A Promising Trilateral: India-Myanmar-Thailand." *The Diplomat*, September 14.

Janssen, Peter (2017). "No Holiday for Myanmar's Conflict-Hit Tourism." *Asia Times*, September 23.

Ko Ko, Thiha (2018). "Myanmar Drafts Digital Economy Master Plan." *Myanmar Times*, January 19.

Lall, Marie (2008). "India-Myanmar Relations – Geopolitics and Energy in Light of the New Balance of Power in Asia." ISAS Working Paper, No. 29, January 2.

"Meeting Asia's Infrastructure Needs." (2017). Asian Development Bank, February.

"Myanmar Keen to Set Up Border 'Haat'." (2017). *Business Standard*, May 10.

Myint-U, Thant (2011). "Asia's New Great Game." *Foreign Policy*, September 12.

Nam, Kee-Yung, Maria Rowena Cham and Paulo Rodelio Halili (2015). "Developing Myanmar's Information and Communication Technology Sector Toward Inclusive Growth." ADB Economics Working Papers, No. 462, November.

Osius, Ted (2013). "Enhancing India-ASEAN Connectivity." Centre for Strategic and International Studies, June.

Premawardhana, Namali (2017). "Myanmar Forges Ahead in ICT." *Myanmar Times*, December 18.

Ray Chaudhury, Anasua Basu and Pratnashree Basu (2015). "India's Connectivity with Myanmar: Possibilities and Challenges." Observer Research Foundation.

"Recent Economic Development of Myanmar." (2014). *Ministry of National Planning and Economic Development*, Nay Pyi Taw, June.

Saran, Shyam (2015). "From Proximity to Prosperity: Connectivity as a Resource for Development in a Globalised Economy." In Focus Article, Public Diplomacy Division, Ministry of External Affairs, Government of India, January 27.

Shepard, Wade (2018). "China and Japan's 'New Great Game' Intensifies In Myanmar." *Forbes*, January 29.

Strefford, Patrick (2016). "Japan Set to Reap Returns on Investment in Myanmar." *East Asia Forum*, August 26.

Thu, El El (2018a). "India's Visa-Free Policy Lures Myanmar Tourists." *The Myanmar Times*, May 9.

Thu, El El (2018b). "Myanmar-India Border Crossing Pact Aims to Increase Caravan Tourism." *The Myanmar Times*, May 16.

Tripathi, Salil (2017). "Rohingya Muslins Have Nowhere to Go." *Mint*, September 7.

Yhome, K. (2008). *Myanmar: Can the Generals Resist Change?* Rupa and Co.

"4 Border Haats in Mizoram-Myanmar Border Soon." (2017). *Northeast Today*, March 17.

PART III

Changing political landscape and India–Myanmar cooperation

9

POLITICAL ECONOMY OF SUBREGIONAL COOPERATION

'Interests' in reframing the peripheries of India and Myanmar

Rakhee Bhattacharya

As the purpose and idea of a subregion in Asia has been augmented in the recent past for both economic and security reasons, there was noticeable transformation toward an engaging approach of the political economy of subregional cooperation in India. Though this transformation in India can be referred back to early 1990s, but the political vendetta on economic development since 2014 has started to push the country more aggressively for such subregional cooperation and engagements. This is to expand and integrate the economies across the borders through policy channels of market, infrastructure and corridor network. As India is currently in the group of fastest growing economies in the world, it has the challenge to sustain its momentum of economic growth, market accessibility and capital investment. In this context, the country in the last five years, has introduced a new set of pro-market policies like Make in India, Start-up ventures and Ease of Doing Business. This is to attract both local and global capital in various such economic activities, spreading across its geographical areas. The policy aggression is seen even at the trans-border level through an approach of cooperation and engagement for attaining marketable surplus. In this context, India's 'Neighborhood first policy' and 'Act East Policy' were aimed toward renewed constructive engagements with Eastern and Southeastern neighboring nations, and at multilateral levels, various subregional blocks like BIM-STECK, BCIM, BBIN, ASEAN and others have regained significance in India's international relation studies. With this policy focus, India looks for larger potential of market interplay and geo-economy at the subregional levels and in a process also aims to become a leading power. By creating larger scope for economic engagements within a subregion through the channels of transport network, labor mobility, higher trade, institutional capacity and other economic flows with closer networks of physical, business, financial and human capital, India clearly aims to gain larger share in regional power. In this regard, better and skilled regional diplomacy is increasingly seem to have the potential to improve both bilateral and multilateral relations. Various channels other than State diplomacy, like non-state diplomacy, corporate diplomacy, business diplomacy, NGO diplomacy and track two diplomacy are finding their places in the larger lexicon of regional and economic diplomacy in India's current outward-looking and liberal macro-economic framework for framing sustainable subregions and neighborhood spaces. With its regional diplomacy taking a new height, some of the neighbors like Myanmar and Bangladesh are gaining renewed attention. This is most obviously for India's Northeast, which shares long (1643 and 1879 km. respectively) borders with both the nations. Myanmar is more significant and strategic for its geographical location, as it can provide an easy (and sustainable) entry-exist and transit space to India via its Northeast for rest of Southeast Asia and beyond. Having world's most important sea lane, it can also provide a trans-Asian maritime economic and connectivity network and can bring together the Asian community on board for constructive engagements. Similarly, being the reservoir of rich natural resources of mineral, oil and gas, Myanmar is a fresh site for the capitalist economy, especially after its political transition and economic liberalization.

In the decolonization period, as Myanmar had faced several Western sanctions due to its military junta regime, the nation was largely supported, protected and subsequently exploited by China. In the passing time with its huge resource reserves like oil, gas and forest, it easily became a periphery of China's rising industrial capitalism, and subsequently became a 'dependent' economy on advanced China. With China in Myanmar, and making the later a peripheral site of the industrialization of the former with huge resource extraction, Myanmar was developed as an 'underdeveloped,' and became one of the world's poorest nations over time. The militarized political regime of Myanmar was also heavily aligned with China and protected its 'interests' by being a major supplier of resources, and subsequently creating economic and social peripheralization within Myanmar. The country was also exposed to vast illegal and crony economy in opium production and circulation with a nexus of State apparatus, military power heads and China's corporate houses. All these have produced a complete economic stagnation in the Myanmar, while Chinese economic growth became staggering. This over time has vastly affected the people of Myanmar with multiple challenges of economic and human security issues like high unemployment rate, low human development, high poverty, geographical isolation, loss of livelihood and injustice toward marginalized sections. Myanmar's formal economy in turn shared only about 0.10 percent of world economy, and ranked 158th out of 186 nations in the Economic Freedom Index till the recent decade. Currently with the beginning of the process of political transition toward democracy in the Myanmar since 2011, it has attracted worldwide attention. It is also because of its strategic location, which has the potential to evolve an inner and outer Asia for larger trade and circulation network.

These have pushed India to focus attention on the Myanmar within its larger agenda of building neighborhood relation and subregional cooperation. India's Myanmar policy has become visibly proactive with a set of faster and deeper engagements, mostly during the post-2014. Thus in the larger frame of regional diplomacy on economic, political, cultural and strategic affairs, India has emphasized specifically on trade and investment promotion, aid and other financial flow management, tourism and institution creation, and management of all kinds of regulatory issues for an impactful policy of engagement in Myanmar. In this context, the chapter aims to situate Myanmar in the evolving dynamics of India's political economy of subregional cooperation by exploring and understanding its current policy focus. It also studies how the internal dynamics in Myanmar is creating 'interest groups' of various stakeholders in such subregional cooperation, which is interestingly converging toward reframing the peripheries of both India and Myanmar in an interface of geopolitics and geo-economics.

Idea of a subregion and India's 'Myanmar policy'

Currently India has been seen as a proactive Asian partner with its engaging foreign policies. One of the agendas of such proactive policy is to create economic gain by the means of trade, investment and business through all subregional, regional and global markets; and the mechanism has been through 'cooperative and supportive' neighborly relation. This is being done by creating increasing and meaningful dialogues and negotiations at various levels. With such idea of emerging Asian subregion in the context of economic integration and security cooperation, various peripheral spaces are also being re-imagined accordingly. India's Northeastern periphery in this regard is repositioning not only as a 'new frontier' but also as a 'natural gateway' toward achieving such goals. Scope for creating transit, routes, connectivity through India's Northeast is transforming its narrative of 'isolation,' and this geographical space is now re-imagined as paramount to the idea of subregion and its integrated and connected development projects.

India's Act East Policy is providing space for such larger subregional diplomacy and creation of external markets for economic integration. Southeast Asia, East Asia, and Sub-Himalayan region are seen important spaces to remap such concept of subregion, and India's Northeast is seen more as a connecting space for many geo-economic projects than an isolated and geopolitical space. In this context Myanmar, the immediate neighbor of the Northeast has also gained manifold attention in India's foreign policy. With Myanmar's first political change in 2011, India started to become a supportive partner toward such political change; and in the following year in 2012, the country's former Prime Minister, Manmohan Singh visited Myanmar and signed several Memorandums of Understanding (MOUs) for various collaborative assignments. Finally with the power shifts in India in 2014 and in Myanmar in 2015, India reiterated its position to play a 'constructive role to consolidate the democracy' of Myanmar through various State level visits and to 'support at every step' toward political change in Myanmar. This objective is to formulate an India–Myanmar policy in a broader, inclusive and long-term frame and moving beyond sheer bilateral trade relation. Needless to say, economic and trade engagements between these two nations in the past have been significantly low, as the issues of security and cross-border violence amongst various ethnic groups have largely affected and destabilized India's Northeast for a prolonged period. Table 9.1

TABLE 9.1 India's trade trend with Myanmar and ASEAN (Rs crores)

	1997–98		2006–07		2010–11		2014–15	
	Mym	*ASEAN*	*Mym*	*ASEAN*	*Mym*	*ASEAN*	*Mym*	*ASEAN*
Export	138.26	9160.32	633.74	57076.46	1459.03	116657.85	4739.34	195736.75
Share	0.14	7.09	0.11	9.82	0.13	10.26	0.25	10.31
Growth	14.21	−11.10	29.31	23.82	48.17	35.80	−1.38	−2.22
Import	832.53	12622.80	3540.94	81918.77	4651.15	139439.32	7476.53	273431.55
Share	0.54	8.19	0.42	9.74	0.28	8.28	0.27	9.99
Growth	32.35	21.19	52.06	70.01	−23.68	14.09	−10.90	9.55
Total	1015.79	21783.13	4174.69	138995.24	6110.18	256097.17	12215.88	469168.30
Share	0.36	7.68	0.30	9.84	0.22	9.08	0.26	10.12
Growth	28.66	5.13	48.11	47.42	−13.85	23.05	−7.44	4.31

Source: Export-Import Data Bank, Directorate General of Foreign Trade, Ministry of Commerce and Industry, Government of India, at www.dgft.gov.in/

brings out such insignificant shares of trade between India and Myanmar during India's neoliberal period since 1990s.

India in the past mostly emphasized on regional security cooperation with Myanmar as part of its bilateral relation for a long period; and the historic surgical strikes like Operation Blue Bird in 1995 to the current one in 2015 show the consistency in such bilateralism. As the current initiative is moving toward deeper economic engagements, there are several areas where India has started to extend support. This is to address Myanmar's internal socioeconomic situation, specifically in the areas of health, capacity building and maritime security. India started to create physical, economic, social and educational infrastructures in Myanmar, which eventually is expected to strengthen its own position in the country compared to China. Thus for supporting Myanmar to develop an indigenous industrialization and entrepreneurship, India has created Industrial Training Centers in its Pakokku and Myingyan and proposed two more at Monywa and Thaton respectively. The Myanmar-India Entrepreneurship Development Center and the Center for English Language Training at Yangon have also been upgraded by India currently to share the knowledge and skill capacity. This knowledge and skill development is essential for Myanmar to go beyond China's network and connect to the global network. The step toward industrial development is similarly expected to reduce Myanmar's externalities and 'dependency' on China's economy in the long run. Correspondingly for a sustainable agrarian development, India has extended support and cooperation in agricultural research and education in Myanmar. It has promised to operationalize an Advanced Center for Agricultural Research and Education at the Yezin Agricultural University and a Rice Bio Park at the Department of Agricultural Research in Myanmar. A flood management policy has also been initiated by India in Myanmar's agricultural belt of Rakhine state. For other central economic areas like trade, India has extended willingness to share knowledge skills to Myanmar for achieving better negotiation mechanism in international trade relation by creating trade training institute in the country and by imparting training on complex understanding of the WTO trade negotiation. Similarly for technological advancement, India has opened Myanmar Institute of Information Technology and India–Myanmar Center for Enhancement of IT skills. India has also extended policy support to Myanmar's feeble social sector. For example, to overcome the challenges of the devastated health sector of Myanmar, India has completed an upgradation of Yangon Children's Hospital and Sittwe General Hospital and another Monywa General Hospital is under construction. It also aims to establish one state-of-the-art hospital in Nay Pyi Taw in association with one of the leading Indian hospital groups. Such large-scale Indian investment in both social and economic sectors of Myanmar and by creating number of institutions and initiating capacity building process is for making the country self-reliant and a competing player in the subregional dynamics in Asia. This in the long run is expected to reduce China's policy of aggressive and extractive capitalism in Myanmar, which had largely made it a peripheral site with huge economic impoverishment. Such ambitious economic expansionism of China, as argued by Bhattacharjee, generally cares very little for human wellbeing and rights including within its own bordering areas, and India's deep and evolving bilateralism with Myanmar is significant. China so far has gained trust and business in Myanmar mostly by supporting its authoritarian regime (Bhattacharjee 2018), and had deeply affected its socio-economic landscape. This needs transformation through a democratic approach, and India's evolving support is significant now for Myanmar. Unlike China, India's approach is to build up cooperation in the line of equitable benefits for long-term relation and trust. Such persistent political and economic engagements with diplomatic consensus to defend the idea of equitable benefit will help to change India's prolonged estranged policy to an engaged policy toward Myanmar. Here India's Northeastern periphery is seen as an important geographical space for various larger economic cooperation and agglomeration with the restoration of the 'natural relation' of both the nations across their borders. A distributive and dependency-reducing (Axline 1977) trade and economic relation in this perceived subregion can not only help Myanmar to unshackle from Chinese capitalism, but also can impart a region-wide benefit for fair distribution. By dispersing economic surplus through any number of measures like redistribution of benefits, pay-offs or compensation of losses in the peripheral spaces (like Myanmar and India's Northeast), which are some of the natural consequences of political fragility and weak bargaining power; such perceived subregional cooperation can potentially create a sustainable future for Asia. In the wave of current bilateralism between India and Myanmar, the nations are working to reaffirm their shared commitments to deepen such subregional cooperation for maximizing their 'mutuality of interests.' This is also to ensure equitable share of benefits in the areas of trade, transport and energy cooperation. Thus agreeing to such mutuality, the two nations not only aim for long-term bilateral relation, but also have underpinned the importance of the subregional cooperation, which will help to improve the lives and livelihoods of people in this contiguous space. Both the nations now aim to set an example of 'good neighborliness in the region' and to progress together with shared interests and in a mutually beneficial interdependent environment. They have taken a drive for 'common aspirations for peace, collective prosperity and development of the region and beyond.'

In a more nuanced context of India's Myanmar policy, a special attention always is given to its Northeast, be it security or economy for the very crucial reason of geographical proximity. For a long period of time the Northeast was imagined as a problematic frontier and was a geopolitical theater in the State affairs not only for India but for the entire subregion of China, Myanmar, Bangladesh, Bhutan and Nepal having cross-border support and connections to make the space ethnically charged and politically unstructured and fragile, and by creating threat to India's national security. These were suitable grounds to imagine the Northeast a security-sensitive, a 'sub-complex' space, and a 'geo-body' for militancy and violence. As the administrative boundary between India and Myanmar (Burma) was drawn by the British government, it had unfortunately divided the homelands of many ethnic groups in the region and subsequently their voices and demand were sub-merged in the larger national interests of territoriality and security. The security dilemma especially, as pointed out by Choudhuri, in the Northeast has many times forced India to negotiate with Myanmar's military junta regime. The strategy has worked to some extent, especially to 'batter Naga insurgents' by the joint actions of the armies of India and Myanmar (Choudhuri 2012). The prolonged conflicts in the region have extensively damaged various cross-border (official) economic engagements like trade and commerce, though various unofficial exchanges remained functional, mostly to sustain everyday life of the people across this fluid borders (Bhattacharya 2014). Currently Myanmar's political change and economic liberalization are seen as the opportunities for India's Northeast, which may help to transform such prolonged cross-border issues and illegalities to a defined and constructive engagements. Given the 'mutuality of interests' of the people and the States, it therefore goes without saying that the Indo–Myanmar relation is imperative to normalize the cross-border relations. This can also ensure human security to this subregion, especially to the people of about 240 border villages who have been living in persistent threats of conflicts and militarization for a long period of time. To create such cross-border relation, India commenced an official border trade with Myanmar way back in the 1995 during its first phase of the Look East Policy through the custom posts at Moreh in Manipur and Zowkhathar in Mizoram corresponding to Tamu and Rhi in Myanmar with 22 initially and extending up to 40 permissible items at 5 percent duty. This was expected to enhance official border trade (overland trade by exchange of commodities) between the nations. The official border trade figures of the Ministry of Development of North Eastern Region (MDoNER) however shows a decline in border trade till 2010–11 with merely Rs 4.16 crores. The amount became half from Rs 8.82 crores in 2006–07, which was about Rs 87 crores in 1997–98 immediately after the route was formalized (Report 2005). This figure has ranked India as the lowest border trade partner of Myanmar, and issues of insurgency, illegal extortion and infrastructure deficits have been cited as the factors for such declining trade, especially in Moreh border of Manipur.

The unofficial border trade figure between India–Myanmar however continues to be much higher as worth of Rs 22,00 crores (Indian Institute of Foreign Trade 1998). This figure, according to the study of Downie, now runs in tens of billions (Downie 2015). However the report of the Ministry of External Affairs, Government of India mentions that the border trade with Myanmar had made a quantum jump during the year 2014–15 touching US$ 56.89 million from US$ 15.4 million in 2010–11 (Report 2015b). The small town Moreh is the most significant space for such cross-border trade which shares about 99 percent of formal overland trade through Asian Highway 1, followed by Champai route through Mizoram and Longwa route through Nagaland. Another study of Ch. Priyoranjan Singh of Manipur University, shows some contrast scenario, as it points out that the number of traders in Moreh has gone down drastically over time, and presently only three traders are working in the border from about 40 traders who obtained licenses in 1995 at the beginning. Also in this border trade activity, the people of Manipur have a marginal role to play, while the most powerful traders are from Myanmar side mostly selling the Chinese and Southeast Asian goods at cheaper rates (see Downie 2015). China on the contrary is making maximum surplus trade with Myanmar across its Ruili border, followed by Thailand and Bangladesh. Myanmar's formal border trade with China in the year 2007 shows a staggering figure of US $ 977.49 million followed by Thailand with US $ 304.96, Bangladesh with US $ 32.43. India is at the bottom with US $ 15.11. After eight years in 2015, the figures still showed that China tops the list sharing 87 percent of total border trade with Myanmar, followed by Thailand with 12 percent, and India and Bangladesh with 0.8 percent and 0.2 percent respectively (Report 2015a). In the context of China's dominance in the border trade activity with Myanmar, India's challenge is huge to expand its scale and volume. It needs to open and operationalize more formal trade routes and create various commerce centers like border *haats* in several border areas like Avangkhu and Lungwa in Nagaland, Pangsau pass of Arunachal Pradesh and Behiang, Skip and Tusom in Manipur with a large number of products, preferably made within the region. More aggressive and sustained measures can improve the volume of the formal border trade between the two nations. In the 6th meeting of the Myanmar-India Joint Trade Committee held in New Delhi in June, 2017, both the countries have rightly agreed to have regular meetings and interactions of Border Trade Committee and Border *Haats* Committee to ensure actions on the ground. Both the nations also have agreed to facilitate cross border movements across the common land border with various modes of transportation to promote bilateral trade and tourism. This is also to improve market accessibility by removing various trade barriers. A coordinated bus service between the two countries from Imphal in India to Mandalay in Myanmar has commenced recently as part of their bilateralism and to make the Northeastern region most important geography for such renewed cross-border relation. The two more land border-crossing agreements were passed recently for the Moreh-Tamu and Zokhawthar-Rhikhawdar passages. Construction of a rail link between Tamu and Mandalay in Myanmar is also taken up, while air connectivity has been explored to enhance people-to-people contacts as well as promote greater tourism networks. Both the Department of Civil Aviation (DCA) of Myanmar and the Airport Authority of India are working together to develop Pakokku and Kalay Airports with financial and technical assistance from India. India eventually aims to extend customized training and capacity building programs to the Air Traffic Controllers of Myanmar.

Reframing the peripheries or change in geopolitical theater?

As many of these policy initiatives have centralized India's Northeast both for enhancing bilateralism and creating subregionalism, there is a renewed imagination of the Indian State to reframe its Northeast as a connected geography. Such an imagination is aiming to replace the stereotypical narrative of the Northeast as an 'isolated periphery' by reframing it as an economic 'core.' In this context, both connectivity and corridor making are essentialized with the huge circulation of capital from both the developmental State and the global agents. This is to create linkages at trans-border level, where the Northeastern borderland and its borders are expected to play a role for economic integration at subregional level. This is ushering a new dynamics for subregional economy across the borders by enhancing market linkages and creating trade surplus. India has proposed to create Special Economic Zone (SEZ) in the Sittwe area in the Rakhine state of Myanmar to facilitate cross-border trade with power and agricultural products. Both India and Myanmar have underlined the need for greater integration of power and energy supply networks across their peripheral spaces of the Northeast and the Rakhine state. Myanmar has agreed to India's exploration and production of surplus energy by engaging and operationalizing its petrochemicals and petroleum companies, which also will support creating infrastructure of the LPG terminals in Myanmar. In this regard, both the countries have agreed to have Numaligarh Oil Refinery of India and Parami Energy Group of Myanmar to supply diesel to Myanmar across the land border and to provide cheaper and more reliable access to petroleum products in the Northern part of Myanmar. The countries have also agreed to collaborate in storage and retail marketing of petroleum products in Myanmar. The first consignment of the high-speed diesel has already reached Myanmar in September 2017. Such interplay in energy sector is creating a deep nuance in the bilateralism between India and Myanmar. But on a cautious note, such bilateralism is also creating a scope for extractive capitalism in this subregion, and therefore needs a deeper understanding for long-term implications. Currently this bilateralism is seen important for the local economies of the Northeast and the Rakhine state and their integration process in the subregional economy.

In the context of the changing dynamics of the Northeast as a 'natural gateway' of the Southeast and East Asia, there is a push for perceiving a peaceful space. This is a prerequisite for any cross-border economic engagements. India is therefore currently negotiating with its age-old and much contested security measures like the Armed Forces Special Power Act (AFSPA). With a gradual repealing of the AFSPA from states of Northeast (Tripura, Mizoram, Meghalaya) and by 'observing closely' the law and order situations in other states of the region, India aims to send a signal of peace and stability in the Northeast to its neighboring nations. There is also larger consensus within the Northeast to address the crises of livelihood and economic security issues by creating indigenous capacity and capitalism. As developmental State is creating space for new normal for the investors with infrastructural network in the Northeast along with the intense role of regional diplomacy focusing on geography, resource and economy as major game-changers, this periphery of India is no longer fervently imagined a geopolitical theater.

The effort to transform the narrative of the Northeast from the domain of geopolitics to geo-economics raises the question as where can be the new geopolitical theater in this subregion now? The current situation of conflicts, instability and up-rises in Myanmar's Rakhine state, which is also a reservoir of huge natural resources and has a very strategic location have drawn the attention and debates from various corners. Being geographically the most strategic space, which can potentially connect both South Asia and Southeast Asia even through coastal belts of the India Ocean and the Bay of Bengal, this is perceived to be a new geopolitical theater of the subregion. In the backdrop of a weak and evolving democracy in the Myanmar's political discourse, the coercion of ultra-nationalist group and military regime in the Rakhine state in the recent times has made this a visibly volatile and conflict prone space. The ongoing critical war against the Rohingya community of this area therefore necessarily demands a fresh articulation and understanding at length. With such resource reserve and State's interests, Rakhine state of Myanmar has become a new 'sub-complex' in this entire subregion. It has attracted attention for both economic prospects and military operation. The issue of 'ethnic cleansing' by the State apparatus has put Myanmar at the epicenter of the global watch on human rights violation and has attracted worldwide debates. This has thrown a deep challenge to its ongoing democratization process and its political representatives. Global political pressure has built up through the condemnation and fresh sanctions in Myanmar. State sponsored violence and militarization over marginalized Rohingya community in the Rakhine state proves the role and voice of the dominant force in the Myanmar's political discourse. Why did such violence take place and what was the driving force of such episode of eviction of the Rohingya community? According to A. Khan, the State coercion in the Rakhine state was primarily for its 'resourcefulness and geostrategic location,' which has also attracted the attention of the neighboring nations China and India and their corporate capitalist groups. As significance of the Rakhine state is assessed with its vast surplus land, new investors are looking for grabbing such land. The eviction of the local community and destruction of their traditional agricultural practices therefore is essential for many big economic projects. Thus the collusive force of various interested agencies of State, multinational corporates and elite actors have aimed to evict such small Rohingya landholders. They are the most marginalized community in Myanmar now and State has already destroyed their 362 villages, evicted more than 7 lakh people, and gave clearance to about 48 new investment projects in this same area (Khan 2018). Both India and China are interested in various mega economic and infrastructural projects for creating a trade network, and establishing SEZs in this area. This is also expected to enhance economic growth in the Myanmar. In this context, displacement of Rohingya community is 'seem to be planned' action of the State (Khan 2018). Myanmar has already agreed to move ahead with the deep sea port and SEZ of 1737 hectare projects with China in Kyaukphyu region of Rakhine state, which was initiated in 2013. The first phase of Kyaukphyu Deep Sea Port Project expects total investment of US$ 1.3 billion, where China will share the maximum capital, and the rest by Myanmar. The projects of such scale also aim for China-Myanmar economic corridor through this Rakhine region. Similarly India also has plans to set up SEZ in Sittwe of Rakhine State, where it has already built a port. This SEZ is likely to be located about 37 miles upstream of Sittwe town in Ponnagyun Township. Such long-term plans for mega economic projects has been pushing Myanmar to create land bank in this strategic space Rakhine, and the mass eviction of Rohingya community was essentialised within a securitized frame. New threat perception has been created by the Myanmar State on 'Rohingya militancy group' called Arakan Rohingya Salvation Army and the militarization in the Rakhine state is toward creating a new 'geopolitical headquarter' of this subregion. India remained 'complicit' about this issue, though has been otherwise supportive to Myanmar's democratic transition process. This could be for its economic interests in the Rakhine state and for larger bilateral relation of constructing a subregion having Myanmar as a pivotal nation. At this hour, therefore, Rakhine state is seen as a new 'geopolitical theater,' which can facilitate various such connectivity and economic projects to flourish (Khan 2018).

Democracy-development debate in the subregion

Reframing of peripheral spaces of India's Northeast and Myanmar's Rakhine state with various subregional connectivity and economic projects are significant and seen as gateways for subregional cooperation. The impending Trilateral Highway of India to connect its Manipur with Myanmar and Thailand, and Kaladan Multi Modal Transport Transit project on the Sittwe Port to connect its Mizoram with Myanmar through the Bay of Bengal are crucial to make such subregional dream a reality. On the other side, the Paletwa Inland Water Transport Terminal project along with six more cargo barges, which were handed over to Myanmar Port Authority and Inland Water Transport are also significant connectivity infrastructural projects for such subregional cooperation. The two sides have agreed to enter into a MoU on appointing a port operator that may include both sides to be responsible for the operation and maintenance of the port in keeping with the practice that has been adopted at other international ports in Myanmar. This would enable the Port and International Water Transport infrastructure to be used commercially to promote not only trade but also to develop the surrounding areas of the projects, like the road from Paletwa to Zorinpui, which is under construction. The reconstruction of bridges on the Tamu-Kyigone-Kalewa Road and on the Kalewa-Yargyi sector of the Trilateral Highway on the other side is also on progress for such connectivity network. With such emerging idea of a connected geography, there is no denial of the fact that this spatial intersect is evolving with the potential of creating a subregion in this part of Asia. This is also to compete with China's interests in the Rakhine state, as it is investing heavily in the projects to improve the Sittwe–Kunming route. This planned and 'systemic project' of China which 'aims to promote connectivity of Asia' is a sign of its renewed economic diplomacy to control over the Myanmar periphery. To encounter such ambition of China, India's push for such subregional cooperation is justified, and involves a perceived opportunity cost of participation of the member nations in their different proposals and negotiations. If India can succeed in such subregional game with cooperation from neighboring nations, including Myanmar, there can be a consensus of some 'like-minded' (Lu, Eder and Kiri 1998) States in Asia for constructive engagements within a democratic frame. In the decolonization period this could never be imagined for any long-term cooperation with regional forces, as the neighbors remained mostly 'unfriendly' on various territorialities and ethno-centric issues. The idea of such subregional cooperation can therefore help to create an 'economic territory of different kind' (Ghosh 2012). This subregional forum needs to create multiple mechanisms other than connectivity infrastructure to make various peripheral spaces competitive. This is to prevent the threat of new core-periphery disequilibrium and any asymmetric power relation in both decision making processes and controlling capital flows, which tends to create various enclaves of capitalism within such peripheral spaces.

Having such nuanced peripheral issues in the subregional forum, this emerging democratic space needs to play a stronger role toward connected development. The approach toward building a long-term relation on various essential development agendas can be helpful for the partnering nations of the subregion to achieve such connected development. Democracy, which is synonymous with free human choice and voice, individual sovereignty and equality, has a causal relationship with progressive economic development. Many democratic institutes therefore can create such connected development projects with a net positive effect on progressive growth which is necessarily inclusive in nature. In many practicing democracies (mostly developing nations), economic elites manage to retain disproportionate wealth and influence, and preserve the profit-seeking anti-poor biases. This distorts the idea and spirit of democracy, denying its social justice, and depriving many by excluding their voices and rights. This is primarily because the practicing development model is mostly the conventional Postwar Western capitalist model and is premised on rational individual, capital formation and idea of inequality. Such economic development which necessarily influences political discourse tends to create chaos and denies egalitarian frame, and distorts democracy to function suboptimally. To attend a causal relationship between economic development and political democracy, the existing approaches to developmentalism need to be reexamined. Here one can cite the case of Myanmar, which is evolving with some intriguing situation, where the military junta regime has dominated the power structure of the country for about half a century, and is currently changing toward a 'flawed democracy.' The military regime has substantially destroyed the political structure with various intra-ethnic conflicts; and crippled country's formal, transparent and even rational structure of the economy for long period with multiple coercion and cronyism. The parallel shadow economy has resulted skewed distribution of national wealth and abject poverty. The political democracy in Myanmar now has begun with the challenge of restoring such long standing issues along with peace and stability in the country by containing its internal conflicts. In the year 2015, the country had called for a Nation-wise Ceasefire Agreement (NCA) between the representatives from 16 ethnic armed organizations, the Army and Myanmar State for a political settlement. Myanmar President Thein Sein mentioned at a draft signing ceremony of this agreement that 'the people need peace, they desire peace, and they expect peace,' and therefore signing a full agreement is essential for the country (Kipgen 2015). This was a significant step for Myanmar, which is deeply divided across ethnic lines and has been in turbulence for long time. With such significant political step in the domestic front, it has sent a positive signal to the world community for trans-border economic cooperation and engagement.

India has been proactive in Myanmar's journey toward democratic transition. It also supported the other neighbor Bangladesh, which apparently can be beneficial for its Northeast. With the political changes in these two neighbouring nations, a democratic trans-border space can be an emerging possibility. This entire region has about 257 million population with huge reserve of natural resources and multiple transit and connecting points and routes for trans-border economic opportunities. The whole region has been conflict prone for a very long time, and thus was affected severely with economic and human security issues. About 70 million people in this region are living below poverty line (27%) and about 160 million people are displaced with land and livelihood threats (Report 2015). This figure is expected to be manifold due to a Rohingya displacement in Myanmar. All poverty, hunger, malnutrition will now intensify human security issue in the region. The indices for Sustainable Development in India, Myanmar and Bangladesh are respectively 110, 117 and 118. This is out of 149 Nations in 2016, where issues of health, hunger and malnutrition already were on top. Myanmar's ultra-nationalist approach and discrimination against communities also have affected many Indians in Myanmar. About 4 lakhs Persons of Indian Origin (PIO) have faced similar State persecution, many of whom are stateless now, which include communities from Bihar, Bengal, Tamil Nadu, Uttar Pradesh and Punjab. As the situation demands a change, its democratization process is expected to play an important role to create a space for political dialogue. Unfortunately the country is failing to contain such issues, and its democratization process has so far not been able to deal with these issues. In this situation, India needs to be more persuasive and purposive in demonstrating the power of democracy and needs to push its relation with Myanmar through its various time-tested democratic institutional mechanism. If Myanmar fails to create a space of congeniality, the idea of subregional forum is going to remain in dystopia.

Concluding observations

The journey toward such endeavour on subregional cooperation needs to continue more vigorously amidst conflicts and uncertainty in the political discourses of the neighbouring nations of Asia. Economic engagement is certainly a powerful mechanism to end cross-border conflicts, illegal trade, trafficking, and border disputes with the neighboring nations. As pointed out by Kulkarni, the political boundaries curved out of geography of this region had always remained barriers to overcome the issues of socioeconomic underdevelopment caused by the historical discourse. The initiatives and engagements in trade, transport and technology can help the region's geography to become an ally to create a new history of shared prosperity, progress and peace, while reviving the age-old cultural and civilizational ties of this region (Kulkarni 2015). India has become proactive with its engaged economic diplomacy and with its Act East Policy frame since 2014 to outmanoeuvre China, resolve its Northeast's internal issue, and turn this entire security-sensitive region to a vibrant economic hub. India's economic diplomacy in this regard has undergone paradigm shifts from focusing on sheer trade diplomacy to expanding networks and promoting various constructive engagements (Rana and Chatterjee 2011). With such strategic shifts, the conduct of economic diplomacy within government also has become increasingly large in size with various departments interfacing with their foreign counterparts and seeking facilitation and support of country's missions. Such dispersal mechanism now needs to reach effectively to transform the narrative of India's Northeast. On the other hand, in the non-state space, multinational corporations has also been powerful pressure groups with profound penetration into systems of international economic policy formulation. Apart from this, research institutions, media, environmental groups and other non-governmental organizations are also currently influencing the shape of the international economic agenda. In this expanding space, the role of the diplomats are also challenging to facilitate and support such efforts of various non-state and business groups (Rao 2011). For larger subregional interests, India also needs to find synergies through diplomatic push with other countries that have a strong presence and interests in Myanmar at this hour including Japan and Thailand. Japan, in particular, has intensified its relations with India and also increased its presence in Myanmar, and its approach is similar to India in terms of the conditions for assistance it imposes. Faced with the assertiveness of China, as reported, both India and Japan therefore have started 2 + 2 dialogue mechanism in 2018 for peace, stability and prosperity in Indo-Pacific subregion. They are also aiming to work together on rule-based and inclusive approach in this subregion through enhancing communication and connectivity for flow of trade, people, technology and ideas for a 'shared prosperity.' This has great substance, purpose and meaning to India's Act East Policy (The Indian Express 2018). In the context of growing India-Japan relation, Japan also aims to provide connectivity assistance to India between its Northeast and Myanmar. Similar synergies can also be found with countries like Singapore that have a growing presence in Myanmar. These synergies can ensure that no single country will influence Myanmar. It also can ensure the prospect of equitable share of influence in the subregional cooperation and partnership and can promote the idea of complementarities with a bottom-up approach toward the idea of new subregionalism in this part of Asia. According to Dent and Huang (2002), the five driving forces which are important for any new (sub)regionalism are economic complementarities, geographical proximity, political and economic framework, infrastructural linkage and market accessibility of the countries. These driving forces help in attaining closer integration and cooperation to achieve prosperity. For example, the Asian subregion BIMSTECK is the home of 1.5 billion people and constitutes 21 percent of the global population, and has more than 2.5 trillion-dollar economy. This subregion is also a home of several million people who live in the darkness of poverty, victims of nature's fury, impoverished due to lack of human development. The challenge of the member nations of this subregion therefore is to transform such darkness through meaningful cooperation, and by sharing the prosperity across various weaker and peripheral spaces.

References

Axline, A. Andrew (1977). "Underdevelopment, Dependence and Integration: The Politics of Regionalism in the Third World." *International Organization* 31 (1): 83–103.

Bhattacharjee, Govind (2018). "Trap of the Century?" *The Statesman*, October 14.

Bhattacharya, Rakhee (2014). *Northeastern India and Its Neighbours: Negotiating Security and Development*. New Delhi: Routledge, p. 223.

Choudhuri, Pramit Pal (2012). "India's Equation with Generals." *Hindustan Times*, May 29.

Dent, C. M. and D. W. F. Huang (2002). *Northeast Asian Regionalism: Learning from the European Experience*. London: Routledge.

Downie, Edmund (2015). "Manipur and India's Act East Policy." *The Diplomat*, February 25.

Ghosh, Jayati (2012). "Emerging Left in Emerging World." *Economic and Political Weekly* 47 (24).

Khan, Ashrafuzzaman (2018). "Why Rakhine State is Important." *The Statesman*, September 4.

Kipgen, Nehginpao (2015). "Peace in Myanmar?" *The Hindu*, April 8.

Kulkarni, Sudeendra (2015). "Charting a New Asian History." *The Hindu*, September 1.

Lu, Ali Carko and Eder Kiri (1998). *The Political Economy of Regional Cooperation in the Middle East*. London: Routledge.

Rana, Kishan S. and Bipul Chatterjee (2011). "The Role of Embassies." *Economic Diplomat and India's Experience*, CUTS International, www.cuts-international.org/Book_Economic-Diplomacy.htm (accessed January 3, 2014).

Rao, Nirupama (2011). "Foreword." in *Economic Diplomacy and India's Experience*, CUTS International, www.cuts-international.org/Book_Economic-Diplomacy.htm (accessed January 2, 2014).

Report (1998). "Industrial Development and Export Potential of the North-Eastern Region", Vol I, Indian Institute of Foreign Trade, New Delhi.

———. (2005). "Border Trade." Ministry of Development of North East Region, Government of India, www.mdoner.gov.in/content/border-trade (accessed September 15, 2015).

———. (2015a). "Border Trade Tops 4 2.4 Billion: Official." *Myanmar Times*, September 15.

———. (2015b). "Indo-Myanmar Relation." Ministry of External affairs, Government of India.

Roy, Shubhajit (2018). "India, Japan Decide to Have 2 + 2 Talks Between Defence, Foreign Ministries." *The Indian Express*, October 30.

10

ACT EAST POLICY AND THE IMPORTANCE OF MYANMAR AND NORTHEAST INDIA REGION

Nehginpao Kipgen

It is important to understand the process of foreign policy making and how foreign policy is formulated and adopted by governments. It is equally intriguing to study why some issues are prioritized over the others. There is a general tendency that when a new political party comes to power or when a new coalition government is formed, the new leader or leaders would review foreign policy agendas of the previous government and formulate new policy priorities. Such policy can be the work of a strong leader or a collective effort of a group of leaders or experts. In international politics, heads of state and government usually pursue foreign policies on the basis of some dominant theories of International Relations, such as Realism, Liberalism, and Constructivism. But it is evident that these IR theories do not work equally and or efficiently for all states, especially in this 21st-century globalized world. Nevertheless, policy makers and practitioners have tried to adopt different theories or systems in their foreign policy-making process. One among them is actor-specific theory, which argues that all that happens between nations or across nations are grounded on human decision makers who are acting singly or in groups (Hudson 2005). These decision makers can be head of state or government and or a group of ministers or experts.

Hermann and Hermann in their work *Who Makes Foreign Policy Decisions and How: An Empirical Inquiry* suggest three types of ultimate decision-making units: a predominant leader, single group, and multiple autonomous actors. A predominant leader is an individual who has the power to make choice or decision as well as the ability to stifle the opposition, which requires strong leadership quality and personality. A single group would mean a group of individuals making decisions as a single unit in face-to-face interaction and have the power to obtain compliance. Multiple autonomous actors refer to different individuals, groups or coalitions in which if some or all agree that they can act together for the government but no one by itself has the power to decide and force compliance on others. Since they are autonomous to each other, there is no overarching unit among the members. For example, in the context of the American political system, the president may take a decision spontaneously when responding to an unexpected question during a press conference, which is the role of a prominent leader. And for a military issue, the Joint Chiefs of Staff may take a collective decision as a single group. But when it comes to issues such as treaty with a foreign government, the decision would involve the president, members of his executive branch, and the support of the Senate, which are multiple autonomous actors (Hermann and Hermann 1989).

The objective of this chapter is to examine the circumstances under which the Indian government adopted the Look East Policy (LEP) under the Congress government in the early 1990s, and why the Bharatiya Janata Party government changed or renamed it as Act East Policy (AEP) in 2014. While the historical development of AEP is studied, emphasis is given to understand the role of Myanmar and Northeast India, which shares direct border with Myanmar and serves as a connecting route to Southeast Asia. The chapter argues that Myanmar and Northeast India are crucial for the success of AEP.

LEP and ASEAN

The concept of India's LEP went back as far as the Sino-Indian war of 1962. China and India had competition in South and East Asia. China expanded its trade and economic ties with Asian nations. In doing so, China became the closest ally and supporter of the Myanmar military junta, which was isolated by the international community, particularly the Western democracies, in the aftermath of the 1988 pro-democracy uprising that believed to have killed thousands of people, mostly students, and the subsequent nullification of the 1990 general election results. China also established closer ties with India's neighbor and rival, Pakistan, and also competed for influence in Bangladesh and Nepal. The LEP officially started in 1991 during the Indian National Congress (INC) government under Prime Minister Pamulaparti Venkata (P.V.) Narasimha Rao (1991–1996), and it was subsequently pursued by successive governments – Bharatiya Janata Party (BJP)–led National Democratic Alliance (NDA) government under Prime Minister Atal Bihari Vajpayee (1998–2004), Congress Party–led United Progressive Alliance (UPA) government under Prime Minister Manmohan Singh (2004–2014), and BJP–led NDA government under Narendra Modi from 2014 onwards. One policy practitioner listed out six phases in India's outreach to the East: from ancient times to the medieval period; colonial phase; Nehru era; post-Nehru years; LEP of Narasimha Rao (1992–94 onwards); and AEP of the Modi government from November 2014 onwards (Bhatia 2018).

India became an Association of Southeast Asian Nations (ASEAN) sectoral dialogue partner in 1992 and a full dialogue partner in 1996. Since 2002, India has had annual summits with ASEAN. The ASEAN-India Free Trade Area (AIFTA) is a free trade area among the 10-member states of ASEAN and India. The initial framework agreement was signed on October 8, 2003 in Bali, Indonesia and the final agreement was signed on August 13, 2009, and came into effect on January 1, 2010. India hosted the ASEAN-India Commemorative Summit in New Delhi from December 20–21, 2012. As of 2011–2012, the two-way trade between ASEAN and India stood at US$79.86 billion surpassing the US$70 billion target.

During the 12th ASEAN-India Summit in Myanmar in November 2014, which was held on the sidelines of the 25th ASEAN Summit, Prime Minister Narendra Modi announced the change of LEP to AEP (Sasi 2014). The leaders reiterated their commitment to reach the ASEAN-India trade target of US$100 billion by 2015. The following year in 2013, the total trade between ASEAN and India reached US$67.9 billion. The 12th ASEAN-India Summit signed two milestone agreements: the agreement on trade in services and the agreement on investment of the framework agreement on comprehensive economic cooperation between ASEAN and India during the 46th ASEAN economic ministers meeting and related meetings held in Nay Pyi Taw from August 25–28, 2014. The leaders also underscored the importance of India's cooperation in implementing the ASEAN Agreement on Disaster Management and Emergency Response (AADMER) and the ASEAN Coordinating Center for Humanitarian Assistance on Disaster Management (Ministry of External Affairs, Government of India 2014). In January 2018, ASEAN and India celebrated 25 years of their relations. At the commemorative summit, the leaders reaffirmed their commitment to strengthen ties and called for enhancement in trade, investment and connectivity. Prime Minister Modi expressed his desire to deepen cooperation in the maritime domain, such as disaster relief efforts, security cooperation, freedom of navigation, rules-based order for the oceans and seas in accordance with international law (Toh 2018).

The philosophy behind LEP was a strategy to work with Asian partners to expand engagement with the rest of the world. The aim was that India's future economic and political interests would be better served by greater integration with East and Southeast Asian nations. Cooperation with ASEAN, formed in 1967, was India's recognition of the region's increasing importance strategically and economically. In other words, the LEP was not merely an economic policy, but was a strategic shift in India's vision of the world. It was a policy of economic liberalization, expansion of regional markets for trade, investments and industrial development. The LEP was aimed at setting a new course of action from the Cold War era, during which India was part of the nonaligned movement, while the world was literally divided into two super blocs led by the United States and the Soviet Union. The policy was also intended to check and or counterbalance China's growing strategic and military influence in the region (Kipgen 2016). Rajiv Bhatia,[1] observed that the main drivers behind Prime Minister Rao's LEP were the process of economic liberalization, challenges posed by insurgency, and the imperative to wean Myanmar away from exclusive dependence on China. He said the AEP was a shift from a primarily economic policy to a strategic one, complemented by an expansion of the geography covered from ASEAN to the Indo-Pacific region (Bhatia 2018).

During my interview with Gautam Mukhopadhaya[2] in Yangon, the ambassador said the concept of India's LEP was not in the context of Myanmar. Myanmar was a 'marginal player' and it was 'incidental' when the policy initially started. He said that the LEP is in the context of India's broader foreign policy. India saw that East and Southeast Asia were growing which coincided with India's 'economic opening' period. India was looking for 'economic opportunities, foreign investments, learning from each other, partnership trade, and market access.' The diplomat said the role of China and India's competition in Myanmar has been 'overemphasized by some scholars' (Personal Interview on February 27, 2014).

LEP and Myanmar

Traditionally, India supported the pro-democracy movement in Myanmar. Such support was evident especially in the aftermath of the 1988 pro-democracy uprising, during which tens of thousands of Myanmar democracy activists and the country's ethnic minorities fled the country. Not only do India and Myanmar have a shared border, but the two countries are home to millions of people from the same ethnic community, separated during the creation of India and Myanmar in 1947 and 1948 respectively. Examples are the Kachins, the Kukis, the Nagas and the Shans, who live side by side along the India–Myanmar border region. The nature of engagement between Myanmar and India has shifted significantly in the last three decades. During the 1988 pro-democracy uprising, when thousands of Myanmar people were killed and several tens of thousands fled the country, India was one of the first countries to welcome refugees into its own territory. India provided provisions and other logistical support for the Myanmar people in exile to continue their pro-democracy activities within India. New Delhi was also vocal about human rights and democratic reforms by openly criticizing the State Law and Order Restoration Council (SLORC), the then military government (Kipgen 2009). With the introduction of LEP, India's foreign policy toward Myanmar shifted from pro-democracy to pro-military regime, and the support for democracy movement gradually faded. The policy shift began during the Congress government and the BJP-led NDA government continued to pursue the same policy. This was an evidence of a broader support for LEP across the Indian political spectrum.

Myanmar's importance to LEP is defined by different factors, including its shared history, culture, ethnic relations and religious ties. The two countries share 1,643-kilometer border in four Northeast Indian states – Arunachal Pradesh (520 km), Manipur (398 km), Mizoram (510 km) and Nagaland (215 km) (Singh 2018). An estimate of about 2.5 million people of Indian origin live in Myanmar. The two countries also share the waters of Bay of Bengal, including the strategically important Andaman and Nicobar Islands. Myanmar serves as gateway to other ASEAN nations, and also provides a geographical contiguity to the Asia-Pacific region. Due to its geographical proximity, Myanmar also provides India a transit route to Southern China (Routray 2011). One scholar on Southeast Asian studies, G. Vijayachandra Naidu,[3] said, Myanmar is important for India in spreading its culture, trade, commerce, philosophy and other religious practices to the other Southeast Asian countries. There have been strong people-to-people relations between peoples of Northeast India and Myanmar since ancient times in which Buddhism has played an important role. The cultural similarities between them have significantly contributed to the development of economic cooperation apart from cultural relations. He also emphasized the importance of India's institutional linkages with ASEAN member states through track II diplomacy (Naidu 2018).

India was gradually fascinated by the rising trade and economic opportunities in Southeast Asia. The role of Myanmar in LEP became more significant when Myanmar took ASEAN membership in 1997. Subsequently, India instituted two institutional projects with Myanmar as its primary geographical node: the Bangladesh-India-Myanmar-Sri Lanka-Thailand Economic Cooperation (BIMSTEC) in 1997 and the Mekong-Ganga Cooperation (MGC) in 2000. On the other hand, China also launched the Kunming Initiative Bangladesh-China-India-Myanmar in 1999. The launch of such multilateral projects was welcomed by Myanmar since it provided an opportunity to revive regional diplomatic and commercial ties after years of isolation. The construction of infrastructure programs like the Trans-Asia Highway Project paved the way for regional cooperation (Egreteau 2008).

During Prime Minister Narendra Modi's visit to Myanmar in 2014, the two countries signed an agreement to construct 71 bridges along the road where the Indian buses will ply. The Myanmar government has started construction of two bridges, and the Indian government has sanctioned $55 million for constructing the remaining 69 bridges (Laithangbam 2016). Still, there is ample scope to develop India's relationship with Myanmar. A number of projects have commenced, of which the major ones are the Kaladan Multi-Modal Transport Project, which will connect Calcutta with Sittwe port in Rakhine state, and the India-Myanmar-Thailand Trilateral Highway. Infrastructure at border post like Moreh-Tamu is in dire need of repair. The first bus service between Imphal and Mandalay, a distance of 580 kilometers, started its first trial run on December 9, 2015, although the initial goal was to start in 2012–13 (Roy 2015). Apart from its strategic and economic importance, Myanmar is also important to India for the fact that it is a member of the Bay of Bengal Initiative for Multi-Sectoral Technical and Economic Cooperation (BIMSTEC), along with Bangladesh, India, Bhutan, Sri Lanka, Thailand and Nepal. Interestingly, both Myanmar and India are also part of the Bangladesh-China-India-Myanmar Forum for Regional Cooperation (BCIM).

Myanmar's response to the LEP

With the aim of improving bilateral ties with India, Myanmar President Thein Sein made a three-day visit to India from October 12–15 in 2011. Thein Sein's first visit as president of a nominal civilian government was significant for two reasons. First, the new government, although still dominated by former military generals, was seeking to improve Myanmar's international image by implementing democratic reforms. Second, the Myanmar government irked the Chinese government, India's traditional rival, by suspending a US$3.6 billion-worth hydroelectric project in Kachin state, which it announced on September 30, 2011. So, it was important for

Myanmar to have India as its important ally. India has invested in technology and transportation developmental projects, with a target of US$3 billion bilateral trade by 2015 (Kipgen 2011).

During Sein's visit, the two countries held discussion on a wide range of issues, including cooperation on tackling insurgency problems in Northeast India. Nay Pyi Taw sought New Delhi's recognition and support over its democratic reform process. The visit took place at a time when there was glimmers of hope for democratic change in Myanmar under the Union Solidarity and Development Party (USDP), a political party backed by former military generals. The visit was considered mutually beneficial and important for the two nations to strengthen their strategic partnership. Ahead of the high-level visit, the two countries had engaged in a series of low-level meetings. At the request of the Indian government, the Myanmar army, in the first week of September 2011, reportedly attacked the camps of Northeast Indian insurgents based in Sagaing region, Northwest Myanmar (Chakrabarty 2011). During those years, India was criticized by the Myanmar opposition and the Western democracies for not speaking out on human rights and democratic reforms. In order to strengthen bilateral relations, Prime Minister Manmohan Singh made a three-day visit to Myanmar in May 2012. As part of mending relations with the democratic forces, Congress President Sonia Gandhi, through Prime Minister Manmohan Singh, invited the Myanmar opposition leader Aung San Suu Kyi to visit India. Subsequently, Suu Kyi paid a week-long visit to India in November 2012 (Press Trust of India 2012).

During Prime Minister Manmohan Singh's visit to Myanmar in May 2012, the two countries signed a number of bilateral agreements: memorandum of understanding regarding US$500 million Line of Credit; air services agreement between India and Myanmar; memorandum of understanding on India–Myanmar border area development; memorandum of understanding on establishment of a joint trade and investment forum; memorandum of understanding on the establishment of Advance Center for Agriculture Research and Education (ACARE); memorandum of understanding on establishment of rice bio park at the Department of Agricultural Research in Nay Pyi Taw; memorandum of understanding toward setting up of Myanmar Institute of Information Technology; memorandum of understanding on cooperation between Dagon University and Calcutta University; memorandum of understanding on cooperation between Myanmar Institute of Strategic and International Studies and Indian Council of World Affairs; agreement on cooperation between the Myanmar Institute of Strategic and International Studies and the Institute for Defense Studies and Analyses; Cultural Exchange Program (2012–2015); and memorandum of understanding on establishing border haats across the border between the two countries (Singh 2012).

Still, there is ample scope to develop India's economic and other ties with Myanmar. While India has been helping Myanmar build institutional capacity and in the development of areas such as information technology, this often gets overshadowed by assistance from other countries – especially China, with cumulative foreign direct investment in Myanmar reaching US$14 billion in June 2014. On the other hand, some of the major projects initiated by China include the Myitsone dam, Tarpein hydroelectric project, Kyaukphyu-Kunming oil pipeline, Letpadaung-taung copper mine, and the Tagaung nickel mine. China's trade with Myanmar was US$6 billion in 2013, while India–Myanmar trade was US$2 billion. India's investment in Myanmar was more than US$270 million in August 2013, yet it was nowhere close to China's investment.

To further enhance bilateral ties, an 11-member team from Myanmar made a goodwill mission to Manipur state in April 2013. The Manipur state government from the Indian side and the Sagaing region government from Myanmar side reached certain bilateral agreements: Manipur to supply 2/3-megawatt power for use in Tamu township, with approval from the Indian central government; Manipur to set up coal-based thermal power plant at Moreh. The Myanmar government will provide the coal for the said thermal plant; Manipur government to install high tension power lines and transformers in Tamu township in Sagaing region. The two governments agreed to develop the Manipur-Myanmar connecting road into an all-weather road; and Myanmar to open a Consulate General office in Manipur at the earliest possible (*Sangai Express* 2013).

The Congress-led UPA's engagements with Myanmar was further strengthened by its successor BJP-led NDA government. In 2016, at the invitation of President Pranab Mukherjee, Myanmar President U Htin Kyaw visited India from August 23–30. Among others, the two sides agreed to promote trade and expand cooperation especially in agriculture, banking, power, energy sectors; an arrangement for supply of pulses from Myanmar to India that would be mutually beneficial to farmers of both countries; to encourage people-to-people contact and facilitate movement of people across land borders of the two countries by setting up immigration facilities at Tamu-Moreh and Rhi-Zowkhathar border crossing points at an early date. The two countries also signed a memorandum of understanding on cooperation in the field of traditional systems of medicine, renewable energy, the construction and upgradation of bridges and approach road in the Tamu-Kyigone-Kalewa section of the trilateral highway and the Kalewa-Yagyi section of the trilateral highway in Myanmar (Ministry of External Affairs, Government of India 2016).

Myanmar president's visit to India was reciprocated by the Indian prime minister's visit to Myanmar a year later. At the invitation of President Htin Kyaw, Prime Minister Narendra Modi visited Myanmar from September 5–7, 2017. Among others, the leaders of both countries emphasized the need to enhance air connectivity to boost people-to-people contacts as well as promote greater tourism, trade and investment flows; and agreed that a Detailed Project Report (DPR) would be prepared by the Airports Authority of India through close cooperation with the Department of Civil Aviation (DCA) of Myanmar for developing the Pakokku Airport or Kalay Airport with financial and technical assistance from India; and the centrality of culture in further deepening the close bonds of peoples of the two countries through the Cultural Exchange Program for the period of 2017–2020, which would promote cultural exchanges between the Northeastern states of India and the bordering states of Myanmar. The two countries also agreed to explore the feasibility of constructing a rail link between Tamu and Mandalay in Myanmar (Ministry of External Affairs, Government of India 2017).

A high-level visit was from May 10–11, 2018 when Sushma Swaraj, External Affairs Minister of India, called on Myanmar's President Win Myint, State Counselor Aung San Suu Kyi and Commander-in-Chief of the Defense Services, Senior General Min Aung Hlaing. During the meetings, the leaders discussed boundary and border related issues, peace and security matters, developments in the Rakhine state, including return of displaced persons, India's development assistance to Myanmar, ongoing projects, and other issues of mutual interest. The two countries also signed seven agreements and or memorandum of understanding: agreement on land border crossing, memorandum of understanding on restoration and preservation of earthquake-damaged pagodas in Bagan, memorandum of understanding on assistance to the joint ceasefire monitoring committee, memorandum of understanding on training of Myanmar foreign service officers, memorandum of understanding on setting up industrial training center (ITC) at Monywa, memorandum of understanding on ITC at Thaton, and exchange of letters on extending a maintenance contract for ITC Myingyan (Ministry of External Affairs, Government of India 2018).

Though India's engagement with Myanmar was part and partial of the broader LEP agenda, its fundamental objectives were: to seek Myanmar government's help in tackling insurgency problems in Northeast India; to limit or counter China's growing influence in the region; and to expand India's international market in Southeast Asia via Myanmar. By engaging Myanmar, the intent was to maximize India's security and its national interests. Myanmar serves as India's gateway to the other ten member states of ASEAN. Because of its strategic location and geographical proximity to China, it is crucial for India to befriend Myanmar, regardless of which group or party is in power. Myanmar is of immense strategic importance to India from the security perspective because it has a direct bearing on the security situation in the states of Arunachal Pradesh, Manipur, Mizoram, and Nagaland. Peace in these four Northeastern states is somehow dependent on Myanmar, albeit Nay Pyi Taw denies providing refuge to any anti-India elements from gaining ground within its territory.

Myanmar-India military cooperation

The military relation between India and Myanmar, especially between the Indian Army and the Myanmar Army, became significant since the early 1990s, with India as the supplier and Myanmar on the receiving end. With the inception of LEP, the Congress government began to supply weaponry and equipment including 105 mm guns, T-55 tanks, light helicopters, transport planes, artillery ammunition and some naval craft. Later, the BJP-led NDA government supplied infantry and artillery weapons to Myanmar, including imported weapons. This was evident when some of the weapons having batch numbers from the lot imported from Sweden fell into the hands of the Kachin Independence Army (KIA), which led to adverse international publicity and consequent embarrassment for India (Sen 2013).

In 2006, the Indian army provided special warfare training to the Myanmar army. The Indian army supplied a few light artillery guns and armored personal carriers. The Indian Air Force chief offered his Myanmar counterpart generous air force support in upgrading avionics of fighter aircraft in Myanmar's inventory. In August 2012 when Myanmar's Commander-in-Chief of Defense Services Senior General Min Aung Hlaing visited India, the Indian government again offered to train Myanmar army personnel (Sakhuja 2012). The increasing importance of military ties was further evidenced by the joint exercise of warships and the coordination of patrol in the Bay of Bengal for the first time in March 2013 (Pandit 2013). By providing military trainings and supplying weaponry and equipment, the Indian government anticipated the Myanmar army to take actions on the Northeast insurgents, which have bases inside Myanmar. New Delhi has been seeking Nay Pyi Taw's cooperation and assistance to neutralize the Indian insurgent groups. However, there has been little success on this front, as the armed groups continue to operate within Myanmar.

Taking military cooperation to a higher level, India and Myanmar conducted a joint military training exercise in November 2017. Calling it the India–Myanmar Bilateral Military Exercise 2017 (IMBAX-2017), the exercise aimed to train officers of the Myanmar Army in various United Nations peacekeeping roles and tasks (Parashar 2017). The military exercise was followed by a naval exercise by the two countries in March-April 2018, characterized as India–Myanmar Naval Exercise 2018 (IMNEX-18). The naval exercise included briefings, practical demonstrations, cross-deck visits, and sporting events, featuring fleet maneuvers, gun firings, and coordinated anti-submarine exercises (Parameswaran 2018). But because of the increased interactions between Myanmar and China, especially in the domain of economic assistance and developmental projects including China's Belt and Road Initiative, the ability of Myanmar to effectively protect India's interests against China has come into question.

Despite increased military-to-military cooperation, insurgency problems remain a challenge and a threat to the full realization of peace and prosperity in Northeast India. On many occasions and at different levels of bilateral meetings, the issue of insurgency problems has been raised. For example, the matter was raised during the Indian External Affairs Minister Sushma Swaraj's four-day visit to Myanmar in August 2014. During her meetings with Myanmar President Thein Sein and Foreign Minister Wunna Maung, Swaraj said India was gravely concerned with the Northeast India armed groups having bases inside Myanmar and asked the Myanmar government to take necessary action against them. The Myanmar leadership said it would not allow its territories to be used for terrorist activities (*Press Trust of India* 2014). The reported surgical attack on Northeast insurgents inside Myanmar territory in June 2015 by the Indian commandos was one such culmination of improved political and military ties between India and Myanmar.

LEP and Northeast India

The idea of the inclusion of 'Northeast Development Concern' as an important component of the LEP came up in 1997 following a report – Transforming the Northeast: High Level Commission Report – to the Prime Minister dated March 7, 1997. The Northeast India region provides a unique platform in terms of growth opportunities it offers by inter-locking the region with neighboring countries of South and Southeast Asia. There is also a potential to develop the region to become India's economic powerhouse considering its rich natural resources, such as energy, oil, natural gas, coal, limestone and other minerals, as well as the availability of water resources in the Brahmaputra river and its tributaries (Kalita 2018). The LEP was an integral part of 'NER Vision 2020,' which was a roadmap planned by the Indian government for the development of the Northeast region. The document of 'India's Vision of 2020' was aimed at making the Northeast a prosperous region which would help in contributing toward the growth of India's national economy and provide productive opportunities (Bhaumik 2009). The Northeast being a priority for the government of India today, this seems to be a justifiable reason for the inclusion of Northeast in the LEP. Clearly, this demonstrates a development concern for the Northeast. Integration aims to increase trading opportunities for the Northeast region with the promising markets of the East and Southeast Asia. International trade is expected to play the role of an engine of growth so as to transform the Northeast into a highly modernized industrial region.

But looking at the existing ground reality, the growth of border trade and tourism between the Northeastern region and neighboring countries has been considerably slow. One lingering problem that hinders development of the region is security concerns – both external and internal. For example, China even today does not openly accept Tawang district in Arunachal Pradesh as part of India. Insurgent outfits are internationally well connected. The porous borders are frequently used by the insurgents to escape from the Indian army. These outfits have their hideouts in the neighboring countries. LEP aims at the creation of an enabling environment so as to end the landlocked situation and isolation of the Northeastern region by opening up its borders and integrating the region's economy through improved trade and connectivity between Northeast India and Southeast Asian countries. But except the opening up of border trade between India and Myanmar at Moreh and Champhai and the much-hyped 165-km–long Indo–Myanmar friendship road connecting Tamu and Kalaymyo-Kalewa, no significant developments have materialized.

Discussing the importance of Northeast India for the success of AEP, Temjenmeren Ao[4] said that given its geographical proximity along with the shared and deep-rooted cultural linkages, the Northeast region is strategically significant for AEP, which in turn would help in the development and growth of the region. He said that there is persisting challenges of underdevelopment on account of poor connectivity, due to the difficult topography of the region, and the issue of land ownership that causes the prevailing poor coverage of surface roads, railway lines, and air connectivity in the region. He emphasized the need to acknowledge Northeast's vast potential of it becoming an export hub and providing employment opportunities in manufacturing, agro-based, and services related industries. Therefore, 'to look at the Northeast region as a mere transit route to ASEAN nations would grossly undermine its potential' and that 'development can charter the way forward for peace, stability, and growth in the region as India continues with its outreach into Southeast Asia and beyond' (Ao 2018).

While connectivity is important for the development of Northeast region as well as for the success of AEP, some put emphasis on the need to balance with the importance of productivity of the region. Gautam Mukhopadhaya[5] emphasized that productivity of the region is important, particularly agriculture and the allied sectors on which 70–80 percent of the population of the region depends. The necessary steps need to be taken so that the region becomes a net contributor to the economy. He suggested that India needs to invest in the agriculture and the allied sectors taking the entire region between Northeast India and Vietnam as one region taking advantage of existing and planner connectivity and regional trade arrangements, and cognizance of the development deficit between India and the CLMV countries – Cambodia, Laos, Myanmar and Vietnam. He even suggested that such investments extending from the Northeast India to Vietnam in partnership with countries of the region and India's strategic partners in Asia 'could conceivably be the only way India could respond to the Chinese challenge in infrastructure, manufacturing, exports, financial power and real estate development and thus have geopolitical significance' (Mukhopadhaya 2018).

Increased regional and international trade can shape the future destiny of the Northeast region by providing the scope for industrialization and growth. But mere facilitation of trade through the region with the neighboring countries will have only marginal impact on the economy unless the region can be converted into a production hub. For this the central government and the various state governments of the region must adopt proactive role. Instead of providing tax holidays for investment in the region, the governments should provide infrastructures including improved connectivity, political stability and good governance. The economic integration of states in the region is necessary to maximize the benefits from investment in various economic activities. Special export processing zones should be created in the region in such a way that investors find sufficient inducement to invest in locating production plans in the region.

Greater participation of the local people in production and distribution activities, and the education sector should be given prime importance. However, the vast rural masses have to be brought into the process of industrialization for political viability of the trade as a strategy of industrializing the region. For this utmost importance should be given to raise the agricultural productivity in the region with proper flood control measures and other steps. As it had happened in the past, without a parallel agricultural revolution in the region, trade alone will not be sufficient to transform the region into a sustainable development path. The growth in trading activities alone will largely benefit those people who are from outside the region and who are also economically more powerful to exploit the resources of the region.

Prioritizing a few projects in the Northeast region is not enough. The central government should also boost the local economy of these states by encouraging industrial growth and creating a strong service sector by promoting tourism in the region. The state and central governments should cooperate to promote tourism and investment, and consider hosting large-scale investor summits and trade fairs with a focus on attracting investors from Southeast Asia. The government should focus on developing its soft power regionally. For example, there should be greater investment in sports and sports infrastructure, and the Indian government should consider establishing sports tournaments between the Northeastern states and Myanmar, and at some stage even other countries in Southeast Asia. This would enhance people-to-people contact and has the potential to increase the influence and spread of India's soft power. The central government should also consider the views of state governments in the region in both economic and foreign policy matters. This is particularly important in the context of trade with Myanmar and Bangladesh, as well as infrastructure projects where any of the states of the Northeast is involved. A successful AEP will only be possible if New Delhi invests not just economically but also politically in India's Northeastern region.

Conclusions

A government official working on the issue said, there is an urgent need for India to develop stronger relations with its Eastern neighbors by introducing shorter and frequent flights between specific states in Northeast India and neighboring countries, such as Myanmar and Bangladesh. Due to its centrality in India's strategic interest, New Delhi should remain concerned with landmark developments in Myanmar's political structure, in its economy and in its socio-cultural environment. But the implementation of roadway projects is facing difficulty due to terrain and insurgency-related problems in the region. Moreover, there are also other problems, such as drugs, commercial smuggling and gun-running that hamper development (Doraiswami 2018)[6]

Regardless of which political party or coalition government comes to power in India, it is likely that AEP will remain an important front in India's foreign policy. Similarly, the Myanmar government (democratic or hybrid regime or military or any authoritarian regime) will continue to maintain bilateral ties with India largely because of economic and political reasons. A country's national and security interests primarily shape its foreign policy. The LEP was basically a goal change of the Indian government in the aftermath of the Cold War era. India shifted its policy from pro-democracy to pro-military junta as it best served the country's national and security interests. Myanmar diligently maneuvered India's political gesture by playing a balancing game between India and China. The LEP (now AEP) has been a mutually beneficial transaction for economic and political reasons between New Delhi and Nay Pyi Taw.

As much as Myanmar is India's gateway to its AEP, the Northeast region is a gateway for India to Myanmar. Therefore, the support and cooperation of the Northeastern states is essential in effectively linking India with the rest of Southeast Asian nations through Myanmar. Reliable road connectivity, such as regular bus and train service, introduction of visa on arrival facility at the border towns, frequent flight services from the region to Myanmar and other Southeast Asian nations, educational exchanges and enhancing people-to-people relation in different capacities are essential for the success of AEP. Moreover, the policy needs to focus on tangible results not only in economy but also on security and strategic domain, and investment in its extended neighborhood in light of China's increased assertiveness in the region, as well as greater cooperation and collaboration with Myanmar and Northeast India.

Acknowledgments

The author thanks the research contribution of Shagun Nayar, a student pursuing her master's degree in diplomacy, law and business, and Ankit Malhotra, a student pursuing his bachelor's degree in global affairs at Jindal School of International Affairs, O.P. Jindal Global University. Under the supervision of the author, the students worked as Research Assistant and Intern respectively at the Center for Southeast Asian Studies during the 2018 fall semester.

Notes

1 Rajiv Bhatia is Distinguished Fellow, Foreign Policy Studies Program at Gateway House, India and former Indian Ambassador to Myanmar (2002–2005).
2 The interview was conducted at the Ambassador's official residence in Yangon on February 27, 2014. The transcripts of all interviews used in this chapter are based on the author's conversations and do not necessarily ascribe official judgements or opinions in case of any disagreements.
3 G. Vijayachandra Naidu is Professor, Center for Indo-Pacific Studies, School of International Studies, Jawaharlal Nehru University, New Delhi, India.
4 Temjenmeren Ao is Research Fellow, Southeast Asia at the Indian Council of World Affairs, New Delhi, India and hails from Nagaland, a Northeastern state of India.
5 Gautam Mukhopadhaya is former Indian Ambassador to Myanmar (2013–2016).
6 Vikram Doraiswami is Joint Secretary (Ministry of External Affairs) for Myanmar and Bangladesh.

References

Ao, Temjenmeren (2018). Panel Discussion on Act East Policy and the Importance of Myanmar and Northeast India, O.P. Jindal Global University, September 27.
Bhatia, Rajiv (2018). Panel Discussion on Act East Policy and the Importance of Myanmar and Northeast India, O.P. Jindal Global University, September 27.
Bhaumik, Subi (2009). *Troubled Periphery: The Crisis of India's North East (SAGE Studies on India's North East)*. New Delhi: Sage Publications.

Chakrabarty, Rakhi (2011). "Baruah, Khaplang Escape Unhurt in Myanmar Army Attack on N-E Rebels' Camps." *The Times of India*, September 14, https://timesofindia.india times.com/india/Baruah-Khaplang-escape-unhurt-in-Myanmar-army-attack-on-N-E-rebels-camps/articleshow/9975034.cms (accessed July 28, 2018).

Doraiswami, Vikram (2018). Panel Discussion on Act East Policy and the Importance of Myanmar and Northeast India, O.P. Jindal Global University, September 27.

Egreteau, Renaud (2008). "India's Ambitions in Burma: More Frustration Than Success?" *Asian Survey* 48 (6): 936–957.

Hermann, Charles F. (1990). "Changing Course: When Governments Choose to Redirect Foreign Policy." *International Studies Quarterly* 34 (1): 3–21.

Hermann, Margaret G. and Charles F. Hermann (1989). "Who Makes Foreign Policy Decisions and How: An Empirical Inquiry." *International Studies Quarterly* 33 (4): 361–387.

Hudson, Valerie M. (2005). "Foreign Policy Analysis: Actor-Specific Theory and the Ground of International Relations." *Foreign Policy Analysis* 1: 1–30.

Kalita, Sanghamitra (2018). "India's Act East Policy and North-East: Prospects and Challenges." *International Journal of Advanced Research and Development* 3 (1): 268–270.

Kipgen, Nehginpao (2009). "India's Myanmar Policy Discouraging." *The Korea Times*, June 8, http://www.koreatimes.co.kr/www/news/opinon/2009/06/137_46374.html (accessed July 25, 2018).

——— (2011). "Myanmar's Balancing Acts with India, China." *The Korea Times*, October 17, www.koreatimes.co.kr/www/news/opinon/2011/10/137_96805.html (accessed July 20, 2018).

———. (2016). *Myanmar: A Political History*. New Delhi: Oxford University Press.

Laithangbam, Iboyaima (2016). "Imphal-Mandalay Bus Service Hits Infrastructure Roadblock." *The Morung Express*, January 8, http://morungexpress.com/imphal-mandalay-bus-service-hits-infrastructure-roadblock/ (accessed July 29, 2018).

Ministry of External Affairs, Government of India (2014). "Chairman's Statement of the 12th ASEAN-India Summit in Nay Pyi Taw, Myanmar." November 12, www.mea.gov. in/outoging-visit-detail.htm?24243/Chairmans+statement (accessed July 28, 2018).

———. (2016). "India-Myanmar Joint Statement During the visit of the President of Myanmar to India." August 29, www.mea.gov.in/bilateral-documents.htm?dtl/27343/ India+Myanmar+Joint+Statement+during+the+visit+of+the+President+of+Myanma r+to+India+29+August+2016 (accessed October 14, 2018).

———. (2017). "India-Myanmar Joint Statement Issued on the Occasion of the State Visit of Prime Minister of India to Myanmar (September 5–7, 2017)." September 6, www.mea. gov.in/bilateral-documents.htm?dtl/28924/IndiaMyanmar+Joint+Statement+issued+o n+the+occasion+of+the+State+Visit+of+Prime+Minister+of+India+to+Myanmar+S eptember+57+2017 (accessed October 14, 2018).

———. (2018). "Visit of External Affairs Minister to Myanmar (May 10–11, 2018)." May 11, www.mea.gov.in/press-releases.htm?dtl/29889/Visit+of+External+Affairs+Minister+t o+Myanmar+May+1011+2018 (accessed October 14, 2018).

Mukhopadhaya, Gautam (2014). Personal interview. Yangon, February 27.

———. (2018). Panel Discussion on Act East Policy and the Importance of Myanmar and Northeast India, O.P. Jindal Global University, September 27.

Naidu, G. Vijayachandra (2018). Panel Discussion on Act East Policy and the Importance of Myanmar and Northeast India, O.P. Jindal Global University, September 27.

Pandit, Rajat (2013). "India to Step Up Military Cooperation with Myanmar." *Times of India*, July 29, https://timesofindia.indiatimes.com/india/India-to-step-up-military-coopera tion-with-Myanmar/articleshow/21464912.cms (accessed July 25, 2018).

Parameswaran, Prashanth (2018). "What's Behind the New India-Myanmar Naval Exercise?" *The Diplomat*, March 29, https://thediplomat.com/2018/03/whats-behind-the-new-india-myanmar-naval-exercise/ (accessed October 11, 2018).

Parashar, Utpal (2017). "First Indo-Myanmar Joint Military Exercise Begins in Meghalaya." *Hindustan Times*, November 20, www.hindustantimes.com/india-news/first-indo-myanmar-joint-military-exercise-begins-in-meghalaya/story-uU6qctYcF5hbTa6UiOliDP.html (accessed October 11, 2018).

Press Trust of India (2012). "Suu Kyi on Week-Long Visit to India." *Business Standard*, November 14, www.business-standard.com/article/economy-policy/suu-kyi-on-week-long-visit-to-india-112111402002_1.html (accessed July 30, 2018).

———. (2014). "Sushma Swaraj Describes Myanmar Visit as 'Very Successful'." *Press Trust of India*, August 11, www.ndtv.com/india-news/sushma-swaraj-describes-myanmar-visit-as-very-successful-648259 (accessed July 17, 2018).

Routray, Bibhu Prasad (2011). "India-Myanmar Relations: Triumph of Pragmatism." *Jindal Journal of International Affairs* 1 (1): 299–321.

Roy, Esha (2015). "From Manipur to Myanmar by Bus, with Thailand Waiting to Be Next Stop." *The Indian Express*, December 25, https://indianexpress.com/article/india/india-news-india/manipur-to-myanmar-by-bus-with-thailand-waiting-to-be-next-stop/ (accessed July 26, 2018).

Sakhuja, Vijay (2012). "India and Myanmar: Choices for Military Cooperation." *Indian Council of World Affairs Issue Brief*, September 11, https://icwa.in/pdfs/IBindiamyanmar.pdf (accessed July 21, 2018).

Sangai Express (2013). "CM Assures Power Supply to Myanmar." *Sangai Express*, April 3, http://e-pao.net/GP.asp?src=1..040413.apr13 (accessed July 22, 2018).

Sasi, Anil (2014). "'Look East' Has Become 'Act East Policy', Says PM Modi at ASEAN Summit." *The Indian Express*, November 13, https://indianexpress.com/article/india/india-others/look-east-has-become-act-east-policy-pm-modi-at-asean/ (accessed July 26, 2018).

Sen, Gautam (2013). "Cooperation Between Indian and Myanmar Armed Forces: Need to Move Away from a Weapons & Equipment Supply-Based Relationship." *Institute for Defense Studies and Analyses*, January 15, https://idsa.in/idsacomments/CooperationBetweenIndianandMyanmarArmedForces_gsen_150113 (accessed July 25, 2018).

Singh, Udai Bhanu (2012). "An Assessment of Manmohan Singh's Visit to Myanmar." *Institute for Defense Studies and Analyses*, June 1, https://idsa.in/issuebrief/AnAssessmentofManmohanSinghsVisittoMyanmar (accessed July 26, 2018).

Singh, Vijaita (2018). "Myanmar Puts Off Border Pact with India." *The Hindu*, March 4, www.thehindu.com/news/national/myanmar-puts-off-border-pact-with-india/article22925706.ece (accessed October 14, 2018).

Toh, Elgin (2018). "Leaders Renew Commitment to Enhance Ties at Summit Co-Chaired by PM Lee and Modi." *The Straits Times*, January 26, www.straitstimes.com/asia/asean-india-celebrate-25-years-of-relations (accessed October 13, 2018).

11

INDIA–MYANMAR RELATIONS

Political transition and shared borderlands

K. Yhome

Since 2011, Myanmar has witnessed major changes in the country's internal political and socioeconomic landscapes as well as in its external relations with the outside world, having huge implications on the borderlands. Internally, the changes have brought about notional end to the over four-decade long military rule and set in motion a process of re-establishing a democratic system of government in the country. As the process unfolded, it created the historic victory of National League for Democracy (NLD) in 2015, but at the same time, it also unleashed new political forces in the form of ultra-nationalists that threatens to destabilise the fragile social fabric of the country. Externally, the process opened up more room in the country's foreign engagements that allowed multiple external players to re-enter and engage with the country. However, the continuing conflicts in the borderlands have not only hampered the democratization process but also economic development efforts. Under the circumstances, the future direction of Myanmar's internal politics and foreign policy is less clear than it was five years ago when the country initiated reforms as the international community finds itself divided.

It is within this changing context that India–Myanmar ties have been evolving with Myanmar's internal and external dynamics having direct and indirect implications on India's relations with Myanmar and on their shared borderlands. As political changes redefine Myanmar, the likely implications on India–Myanmar borderlands need re-assessment: How does Myanmar's democratic transition in the context of continuing conflicts and violence impact India–Myanmar borderlands? What are the opportunities and challenges for India and Myanmar in addressing the emerging issues in their shared borderlands? Importantly, the issues confronting Myanmar, internally and externally, are interrelated and the progress in one influences the other. In keeping with the theme of the book, this chapter takes up the three key issues –the ethno-religious question, security challenges and connectivity prospects to understand the emerging difficulties and potentials in India–Myanmar borderlands.

Myanmar's transition to democracy: an overview

After decades of military rule accompanied by violent suppression of democratic movements, Myanmar's military ruling elites began to take some concrete steps toward political reforms with the adoption of a new constitution in 2008. This new constitution enshrined a democratic system of polity, often described as a 'hybrid system' and/or a 'dual system' because of the power sharing arrangement it envisaged between the civilian and the military. (Diamond 2012; Blaževiè 2016). Under the new constitution, the country held its first general elections in 20 years in 2010, and again in 2015 that witnessed the victory of Aung San Suu Kyi and her party the NLD. Three issues have dominated the political discourse in the reforms period, namely diversification of foreign relations, finding a solution to the decade-old ethnic conflicts and economic development of the country that has fallen way behind under the military rule. As the country's reform unfolded, visible positive progress could be seen on many fronts, but the changes also created unintended consequences.

Internal political transformation has been accompanied by diversification of Myanmar's foreign policy. Guided by its desire to reduce dependence on China, a major recalibration of the country's external engagements has been geared toward re-engaging actors both within the region and beyond. The re-orientation of policy allowed several major powers to return to the country as the Western powers lifted economic sanctions, which also allowed international institutions such as the World Bank and the International Monetary Fund to return with financial and technical assistance in the country. Myanmar also began to play a more active role in regional affairs as it positioned itself to re-integrate with the region. In 2014, Myanmar was chair of the regional bloc Association of Southeast Asian Nations (ASEAN). It hosted the third summit of the subregional grouping, the Bay of Bengal Initiative for Multi-Sectoral Technical and Economic Cooperation (BIMSTEC) the same year.

One of the economic priorities of Myanmar in the reforms period been has to play catch-up with its neighbors. A major focus of the economic reforms was the need to develop and modernize the country's old infrastructure. In 2012, the country adopted a new investment law and created the Myanmar Investment Commission. A new Special Economic Zones (SEZs) law was also enacted with a focus on port-led development. As the country's diversifies economic engagements and with new foreign investment flowing in, growth rate recorded over 6 percent in the reform period with the Asian Development Bank projecting the country's growth rate to reach 7.2 percent in 2019 (*The Irrawaddy*, 11 April 2018). To be able to continue to expand and strengthen engagements with the outside world and to achieve rapid economic development, one of the pre-conditions has been to maintain peace and stability in the borderlands. Toward this end, a key focus has been to find a lasting solution to the decade-old ethnic conflicts in the country. The Thein Sein government initiated the ethnic peace process soon after assuming power and negotiated ceasefire with several ethnic armed groups. When the Aung San Suu Kyi government came to power it accorded the ethnic peace process a priority. Despite these efforts, finding peace in the troubled borderlands remain elusive. Adding to the troubled peace process, new conflicts involving the Rohingya Muslims in Rakhine state have raised several questions on the country's democratic future. It is against this backdrop that India's relations with Myanmar and the implications of these developments on the borderlands are examined here.

India welcomed the political transition in Myanmar and expressed its readiness to support and assist the country in its democratic transition process. Myanmar's democratization allowed Delhi to deepen engagement with Naypyidaw without the need to concern with the country's political divide between the military and the pro-democracy forces that had limited its engagements with the country in the past (Bhatia 2016). India–Myanmar relations also benefited from Naypyidaw's new foreign policy orientation in the reforms era that was marked by frequent exchanges of high-level visits to strengthen ties. Naypyidaw's strategic decision to minimize its dependence on China also found India a viable option in achieving that end. Like other countries, India also leveraged the opening up of Myanmar to deepen economic and security ties as well as to revitalize India's eastward drive in deepening relations with the ASEAN nations. It was not a coincidence that Prime Minister Narendra Modi launched the "Act East" policy in Naypyidaw during its visit to Myanmar to participate in the India-ASEAN summit in 2014. India has also been involved in infrastructure development in Myanmar under its development cooperation to assist in capacity building and development of infrastructure to meet the country's growing demands as well as to connect the country with the wider region.

The ethnic question: an elusive peace process and refugee issues

Myanmar's ethnic question is as old as the modern state of the country. Armed conflicts between the government forces and the ethnic armed groups have marked the country's politico-security landscape since the country's independence (Smith 1999). Much before the struggle for power between military and the pro-democracy forces that came to characterise the country's politics, the political history of Myanmar has revolved around the conflict between the Bamar Buddhist majority community and the various ethnic minorities, a saga that refuses to die. This has earned the country with the reputation of running 'the world's longest ethnic insurgency.' The country has been unable to find a system where the various ethnic groups can co-exist with each other. The problem lies in the ruling elites' inability to accept that the country is a multiracial, multilinguistic, multireligious nation. The 2008 Constitution guarantees a secular and federal nation, however, in practice, the ethno-religious question remains a challenge for the country with little headway made in finding a solution. On the contrary, the reforms opened up space for extremist forces along ethno-religious lines to express themselves violently with grave implications on the social fabric and security of the country and the region.

The military-backed Union Solidarity Development Party (USDP) that won the 2010 elections initiated the 'new peace process' with the hope of finding a solution to the decades old conflicts soon after assuming office in March 2011 under the leadership of Thein Sein (Oo Min 2014). Though regarded as an important part of the country's democratic transition, progress in the ethnic peace process met major setbacks with renewed fighting between the military forces and the Kachin Independence Organization (KIO) in 201, ending a 14-year ceasefire. To the credit of the Thein Sein government, after several rounds of peace talks, the Myanmar government signed bilateral ceasefire agreements with 14 major armed groups in 2013 (Oo Naing 2013). The government also institutionalised the peace process by creating two union-level peace committees – the Union Peace-Making Central Committee (UPCC) headed by the President and the Union Peace-Making Work Committee (UPWC) under the leadership of the first Vice-President (BNI 2014).

To consolidate the peace process, nationwide ceasefire talks were initiated in November 2013 between the government's UPWC and the ethnic armed groups' National Ceasefire Coordination Team (NCCT). After a yearlong negotiation between the two sides, a preliminary draft of the NCA was signed in March 2015. Subsequently, on October 15, 2015, the Myanmar government and the ethnic armed groups entered into the Nationwide Ceasefire Agreement (NCA) with the aim 'to secure an enduring peace based on the principles of dignity and justice, through an inclusive political dialogue process involving all relevant stakeholders' (Oo Naing 2013). Out of 21 major ethnic armed groups, eight signed the NCA, namely Kayin National Union (KNU), Kayin National Liberation Army (KNLA)-Peace Council, Pa-O Nationalities Liberation Organization (PNLO), All Burma Students' Democratic Front (ABSDF), Chin National Front (CNF), Arakan Liberation Party (ALP), Democratic Kayin Buddhist Army (DKBA) and Restoration Council of Shan State (RCSS)/Shan State Army-South (SSA-S). Describing the event as a major step in the road to future peace in Myanmar, President Thein Sein said '[r]eform would not succeed without peace' (Xinhua, 15 October 2015).

That left out seven major ethnic groups who expressed unreadiness to sign the NCA, namely, Kachin Independence Organization (KIO), Kayinni National Progressive Party (KNPP), National Democratic Alliance Army (NDAA), New Mon State Party (NMSP), National Socialist Council of Nagaland-Khaplang (NSCN-K), Palaung State Liberation Front (PSLF), Shan State Progressive Party/Shan State Army-North (SSPP/SSA-N) and United Wa State Army (UWSA). Apart from these, another six ethnic armed groups who were not invited to the NCA event, were involved in the peace talks –the government agreed to begin political dialogue with Lahu Democratic Union (LDU), Arakan National Council and Wa National Organization, while it decided to hold separate talks with Kokang's Myanmar National Democratic Alliance Army (MNDAA) and Arakan Army (AA). The Ta'ang National Liberation Army (TNLA) was already in talks with the government.

When the new NLD government came power in March 2016 after winning a landslide victory in the 2015 general elections, the new leadership relaunched the peace process under the '21st Century Panglong Conference' with the aim to revive the spirit of the 1947 Panglong Agreement that called for mutual respects and equality. The first 21st-Century Panglong conference was held on October 15, 2016 where the Myanmar government announced its 'Seven Steps Roadmap for National Reconciliation and Union Peace' (GNLM 2016). In a positive development, two more ethnic armed groups (the NMSP and the LDU) joined the NCA, taking the total signatories to ten by February 2018. Even as the peace process has continued with successive governments giving priority, several challenges remain in taking it to the next level of political dialogue. The complexity of the issue involves not just the problem of dealing with several stakeholders but to a large extent the reservations on the part of the ruling elites to redefine the national identity and sharing of resources. Sai Oo, Director of the Pyidaungsu Institute, sums up the status of peace process by comparing it under the USDP government and the NLD government as follows:

> The military is still very powerful in the negotiations. The election victory of the National League for Democracy (NLD) created a lot of expectations. After a while we all realised that the NLD still has many things to learn in order to fulfil its role as the government. It is still in a quite weak position. Under the [Thein Sein] government, the peace process had a slightly better position because there was a kind of informal dialogue. Under the NLD government, the military treats the peace process as a security issue. That is a significant change.
>
> *(Grein, February 2018)*

The formation of the Federal Political Negotiating and Consultative Committee (FPNCC), a coalition of seven armed groups including AA, KIO/KIA, MNDAA, TNLA, SSPP/SSA, NDAA and UWSA in April 2017 have further complicated the peace process as many members of the Committee have not signed the NCA as active conflict with the Myanmar army still continued. Recently, a couple of developments suggest that the Myanmar government has made some progress in involving the rebels that are still outside the peace process. In September 2018, the Myanmar government's peace negotiators met representatives of three ethnic armed groups – TNLA, AA and MDDAA in Kunming, China (The Myanmar Times, 6 September 2018). Earlier in July 2018, all the members of the Committee attended the third Panglong Conference as special guests (The Myanmar Times 16 July 2018). Both the events were facilitated by China (*The Myanmar Times* 21 May 2018).

As the government put in place mechanisms to take forward the peace process, the opening up of democratic space allowed long-suppressed voices to manifest themselves in violent conflicts. Failure to take forward the peace process and the rise of ultra-nationalists manifested in the form of renewed conflicts in different parts of the country. The worst affected as a result of this phenomenon has been the Rohingya Muslims community in Rakhine state in western Myanmar bordering Bangladesh. The rise of ultra-nationalism among the Bamar Buddhist forces coupled with historical animosities along ethno-religious lines that had long char-acterized relationship between the ethnic Rakhine Buddhists and the Rohingyas erupted into bloody communal violence in Rakhine state and spread to other parts of the country (Ibrahim 2017). In the aftermath of the military operation targeting the Rohingyas, triggered by Arakan Rohingya Salvation Army (ARSA) insurgent group's attacks on police and army outposts, pushed hundreds and thousands of Rohingyas to neighboring Bangladesh. By late 2017, the number of Rohingyas fleeing Myanmar reached over 700,000 in refugee camps in Bangladesh.

Myanmar's continued internal conflicts and efforts to find peace have attracted much attention and concern among the international community. Concerns over human rights violations turned into condemnation and threat of sanctions as the international community come down heavily on Myanmar. A UN-fact finding mission in its report strongly condemned the atrocities perpetrated against minor-ities and accused Myanmar of 'genocidal intent' against the Rohingyas (UNHRC. 18 Sept 2018). The UN Human Rights Council (UNHRC)–appointed Inde-pendent International Fact-Finding Mission on Myanmar in its report called for the UN Security Council (UNSC) to set up an ad hoc tribunal to try suspects or refer them to the International Criminal Court (ICC) in the Hague, impose an arms embargo on Myanmar and subject its officials to targeted sanctions and travel bans. Even as the UN report has yet again brought into focus the gravity of the issue before the international community, the veto-wielding members have often found themselves divided on Myanmar with China and Russia protecting it from any harsh action. The UN mission hinges its recommendations largely on the threat of legal action raising the question if international pressure on Myan-mar would be effective in finding a lasting resolution in a divided UNSC. On the other hand, the wider societal challenge in Myanmar needs urgent attention. Punishing the guilty needs to go hand-in-hand with finding ways in resolving the deep-rooted ethnic and religious animosities in the country. As the international community takes measures to punish the perpetrators of violence, it is equally important to help build social coexistence as a long-term guarantee to avoid renewed conflicts.

In the past, blanket economic sanctions by the Western countries on Myanmar had little impact in inducing a behavioural change among Myanmar military ruling elites. Last year, the US reimposed targeted sanctions on Myanmar, the effectiveness of which remains to be seen. The UN report recommends travel bans and targeted sanctions against Myanmar's military generals. Such measures may have symbolic significance, particularly if they come from the UN. The UN report has charged Myanmar's top military brass of the "gravest crimes" and blamed the country's de facto leader Aung San Suu Kyi for failing to use her "moral authority" to protect civilians. With the top military and civilian leadership under the scanner, both may work in unison to minimise the impact of the report. Thus, the country's internal politics has not been adversely affected by the report. Even as Myanmar rejected the UN report, the ICC has initiated a preliminary investigation into the Rohingya refugee crisis to determine whether a full investigation could be initiated based on the available evidences (*The Guardian* 19 Sept. 2018). The outcome of which remains to be seen.

India's role and interests

India supports the country's ethnic peace process as part of the wider political change. India has two direct interests in Myanmar's ethnic peace process. First, any political settlement involving the ethnic groups in Myanmar through the ongoing peace process would have immense impact on its side of the shared border where cross-border insurgency movements remain a challenge owing to ethnic groups inhabiting both sides of the border. Moreover, Myanmar's ethnic insurgent groups play a crucial role in providing safe havens for Indian ethnic insurgents from where they receive trainings and arms. India's strengthening border security cooperation with Myanmar aims at tackling cross-border insurgency (this aspect is taken up in detail in a later section on security). Second, India's position has been that a stable and strong Myanmar is in its long-term interests. The prolonged ethnic conflicts in Myanmar provide room for external players to play a role in the country, a factor that is not in Myanmar and India's long-term interests. China has and continues to have strong ties with the ethnic armed groups of Myanmar. These considerations have shaped India's approach toward the current ethnic peace process in Myanmar. New Delhi's approach comprises both political and socioeconomic elements.

At the political level, India has extended support to Myanmar's ethnic peace process in terms of sharing experiences both officially as well as from behind the scene. While New Delhi has refrained from imposing its views on Myanmar, it has shared its experiences at the request of Naypyidaw. India's role has been in creating a conducive environment for the peace talks between the Myanmar government and the ethnic armed groups. To this end, Zoramthanga, former rebel leader and chief minister of Mizoram, has played a role in mediating between the Myanmar government and the ethnic armed groups. No official title was designated such as 'special envoy' or 'emissary' by the government of India, but his involvement has been viewed in that capacity in Myanmar (BNI January 2017). In January 2015, Zoramthanga travelled to Thailand and Myanmar and met both sides including Myanmar government's chief negotiator Aung Min and N'ban La, chairman of the United Nationalities Federation Council (UNFC) (*The Indian Express* 9 March 2015).

The Indian government was aware of the visit but considered it an involvement at the personal capacity as New Delhi did not want to be seen playing a role in Myanmar's internal affairs. One of the reasons for the Indian government's hesitation was because no official invitation had come from the Myanmar government to take part in the peace talks then. Zoramthanga's involvement have been a result of invitation from Myanmar's ethnic armed groups. In fact, Zoramthanga had earlier received invitation to play the role of a peace broker in 2011 from Kachin leaders. However, his active involvement began only in 2015. Earlier, Dessislava Roussanova, one of the team members of former British Prime Minister Tony Blair on brokering peace in Myanmar had approached Zoramthanga to play a role in Myanmar's peace process in October 2014. India's involvement in Myanmar's peace process received the official sanction from Myanmar when Aung Ming wrote to India's National Security Advisor Ajit Doval for help in the peace process on February 26, 2015. The Indian government soon assigned a senior government official to travel with Zoramthanga to Bangkok to meet ethnic rebel leaders and later travelled to Naypyidaw to meet Aung Min and other government officials (*The Indian Express* 9 March 2015). Assessing the role of Mr. Zoramthanga, a document prepared by *Burma News International* observes:

> Another possible contribution [in] breaking the deadlock between the two sides was the invitation of the Mizo National Front leader Mr Zoramthanga to serve as an interlocutor to [build] trust between the [two] sides in early 2015. Although [he] was not directly involved in [actual] talks, he may have been instrumental in boosting confidence in the peace process
> *(BNI January 2017).*

India sent representatives to attend the signing ceremony of the NCA in October 2015 as one of the 'international witnesses' along with together with China, Japan, Thailand, UN and EU. NSA Doval and R N Ravi, the Indian government's interlocutor for the Naga peace talks in India represented the Indian government along with Zoramthanga at the ceremony (*The Indian Express* 15 October 2015). The joint statement issued during Prime Minister Narendra Modi's visit to Myanmar in September 2017 stated:

> The Prime Minister of India appreciated the measures taken by the Government of Myanmar towards peace and national reconciliation and commended the on-going peace process of the Government of Myanmar. He noted that peace and stability in Myanmar are of the highest priority to India and reiterated India's continued support to the Government of Myanmar in consolidating democratic institutions in Myanmar and for the emergence of a democratic Federal Republic.
> *(MEA, GoI. 6 September 2017)*

Taking India's interest and involvement in Myanmar's peace process to a higher level, a Memorandum of Understanding (MoU) on assistance to the Joint Ceasefire Monitoring Committee was signed when Indian External Affairs Minister Sushma Swaraj visited Myanmar in May 2018 (MEA, GoI. 11 May 2018). India also welcomed the joining of two more ethnic armed groups in the NCA in February 2018 (Mint. 14 February 2018), this further demonstrates India's 'continued support to the peace process in Myanmar' (MEA, GoI. 13 February 2018). Delhi has long opposed unilateral actions against Myanmar, although it has supported UN initiatives. India was part of a UNSC delegation that visited Myanmar in May 2018 along with three other neighbors – China, Laos, and Thailand. When the UNHRC passed the resolution extending the mandate of the fact-finding mission on Myanmar in September 2017, India did not openly disassociate itself from the resolution, even as it argued for 'constructive engagement' as a preferred approach to protect and promote human rights. The UN report has not changed India's official position on Myanmar and Delhi is likely to continue its constructive engagement with the country. Even so, given the magnitude of the allegations made by the UN report, external pressures on India in its bilateral dealings with Myanmar when the issue comes up in UN bodies cannot be ruled out.

At the socioeconomic front, India's involvement in the ethnic peace process and refugee issue has been aimed at assisting Myanmar in improving the socioeconomic conditions that would have a long-term positive impact. Toward this end, In December 2012, the then Indian External Affairs Minister Salman Khurshid visited Rakhine State and announced a US$ 1-million package of relief assistance to Myanmar. On December 20, 2017, Foreign Secretary S. Jaishankhar visited Myanmar and signed an MoU on Rakhine State Development Program with Myanmar's Ministry of Social Welfare, Relief and Resettlement aimed at 'socio-economic development and livelihood initiatives in Rakhine State' that included 'a project to build prefabricated housing in Rakhine State to meet the immediate needs of returning people' (Reuters 21 December 2017). Under the MoU, India pledged US$25 million for a five-year development project in Rakhine State. The MoU was operationalized during the visit of External Affairs Minister Sushma Swaraj's visit to Myanmar in May 2018. Myanmar's ethnic peace process and the emergence of renewed conflicts have presented both opportunities and challenges for India in transforming the shared borderlands. However, the efforts to find political settlement to the complex ethno-religious issues in Myanmar are still far from achieving the desired goals. India would continue to strengthen the mechanisms created to support the peace process and continue to nudge the Myanmar regime for speedy and safe repatriation of Rohingyas.

Connectivity: crossroads of Asia and India's gateway to the East

Located at the crossroads of Asia linking South, Southeast and East Asia, Myanmar is the gateway for exchanges of ideas, people and goods throughout history. It had served as a conduit for trade and cultures between civilizations and the country emerged as a global trading hub during the British colonial rule (Myint-U 2011). After a decade since independence of the country in 1948, the country increasingly turned inward overwhelmed by internal challenges and the military coup of 1962 further isolated the country from the outside world. The current efforts to reconnect with the region and the world is thus an effort to rediscover the past routes that once linked the country to the world. Some initiatives to connect with the neighbors began with limited opening up of the economy in the 1990s under the military regime. However, it was only in the reforms period that major policy measures were initiated to modernize and develop connectivity infrastructure of the country.

As part of the country's plan to rebuild the economy, the significance of developing connectivity infrastructure emerged as a key priority. As part of the economic reforms in the 1990s, Myanmar adopted a new port development policy. The process of privatization and decentralization of the management and operation of ports was initiated to attract the private sector in port development (Elly, Ganbat and Nam June 2015). In the period since the country began transitioning to democracy, new laws on Special Economic Zones (SEZ) and foreign investment have been enacted to support the development of the port industry. Myanmar has created three SEZs, namely, the Dawei SEZ in southern Tanintharyi region; the Kyaukphyu Economic and Technological Zone in western Rakhine state (a Chinese-led project that plans to build an industrial park and a deep-water port, the starting point of pipeline linking the coastal area with China's inland cities); and the Thilawa SEZ near Yangon, a Japan-driven project. The SEZs have been created near the ports with the intention to develop these ports. Myanmar actively participates in the various regional and subregional connectivity projects and plans as a member of ASEAN; the Bay of Bengal Initiative for Multi-Modal Technical and Economic Cooperation (BIMSTEC); the South Asian Subregional Economic Cooperation (SASEC); the member of the Greater Mekong Subregion (GMS); the Lancang-Mekong Cooperation (LMC) as well as the Mekong-Ganga Cooperation (MGC).

In a significant development, on September 9, 2018, Myanmar signed a MoU with China agreeing to establish the China-Myanmar Economic Corridor (CMEC) as part of China's Belt and Road Initiative (BRI) (*The Irrawaddy* 13 September 2018). The estimated 1,700-km–long corridor will connect Kunming, the capital city of China's Yunnan Province, to Myanmar's major economic centers – first to Mandalay in central Myanmar, and then east to Yangon and west to the Kyaukphyu Special Economic Zone (SEZ). Myanmar joined the Chinese BRI when State Counselor Suu Kyi attended the Belt and Road Forum for International Cooperation in Beijing in May 2017. A MoU on 'Cooperation within the Framework of the Silk Road Economic Belt and 21st Century Maritime Silk Road Initiative' was signed during the visit. Under the BRI scheme, two economic corridors – the Bangladesh-China-India-Myanmar-Economic Corridor (BCIM-EC) and the China-Indochina-Peninsula Economic Corridor (CIPEC) involve Myanmar, owing to its geographic location. Both Beijing and Naypyidaw recognize Myanmar's critical role in pushing forward these BRI projects. Beijing proposed the China-Myanmar-Economic Economic (CMEC) as part of the BRI at a time when Myanmar was increasingly under international pressure owing to its conduct on the Rohingya crisis. Beijing is aware that Myanmar needs its political and diplomatic support to fend off mounting international scrutiny.

Concerns remain about the implications of the troubled China-Myanmar borderlands on the mega-infrastructure projects under the BRI scheme. Ahead of the third round of peace talks under the government's 21st-Century Panglong Conference scheduled for June 11 to 16, 2018, Beijing has reassured Naypyidaw that it would continue to "keep helping and supporting" the country's peace process (*Radio Free Asia* 5 July 2018). The deal to establish the CMEC has raised concerns in Myanmar over financing issues (*The Irrawaddy* 17 September 2018). Naypyidaw may seek alternative options to reduce dependence on Chinese investment. However, with its internal conflicts in the borderlands and the need to ward off international pressures, Naypyidaw is currently going along with Beijing's initiatives. This would be accompanied by growing concerns and more questions on whether Naypyidaw's only option is to accept Chinese initiatives without having any initiative of its own.

India's role and interests

India has been playing its part in the development of connectivity infrastructure in Myanmar both to help the country's efforts to improve domestic connectivity as well as to link itself with Myanmar and beyond (Seshadri 2014; Yhome 2015). Sharing long land and maritime boundaries, several interconnected economic and strategic factors drive India's cross-border connectivity initiatives with Myanmar. Cross-border connectivity with Myanmar allows India to link itself by creating alternative routes to access its landlocked region. Moreover, alternative routes to India's underdeveloped border regions ease the pressure on the strategic Siliguri corridor, the narrow land of strip that connects the Northeast region with the rest of the country. For some time now, there is a recognition that economic development of border areas requires transnational cooperation. Security interests also motivate improvement of border connectivity, as better infrastructure enhances effective border management.

A key cross-border connectivity project is the India-Myanmar-Thailand Trilateral Highway, jointly being developed by the three countries to connect Moreh in India's bordering state of Manipur to Mae Sot in Thailand through Myanmar. Reconstruction work of 69 bridges on the Tamu-Kalewa-Kyigone sector and the 120-km–long Kalewa-Yargi sector currently being undertaken by India are expected to be completed by 2020–21. India along with the Mekong nations plan to extend the highway to Laos, Cambodia, and Vietnam in the second phase. The Kaladan Multi Modal Transit Transport Project is another major cross-border connectivity project that India has been developing jointly with Myanmar. The sea-river-land project will connect Kolkata to Sittwe in Rakhine state by sea; through the Kaladan river to Paletwa in Chin state of Myanmar; and from there to Zorinpui in India's bordering state of Mizoram. The project will facilitate the emergence of a development corridor in Myanmar and promote movement of cargo from one part of India to another. Expected to be completed by 2020, the project's key components, including the port in Sittwe, the Inland Water Terminal in Paletwa and the river channel, are all completed. Work is currently underway on the 109 km road from Zorinpui to Paletwa. Myanmar has proposed the Sittwe Economic Zone in Rakhine state where India has developed the port and from where the Kaladan multi-modal connectivity project plans to connect the Indian Northeast region with the bay. The SEZ plan in Sittwe is yet to take off (*The Myanmar Times*, 30 June 2014).

India has extended financial support for micro development assistance that includes construction of roads and bridges in Myanmar's Chin State and Naga self-administered zone such as the assistance of US$ 5 million each year for five years under India's Border Area Development Scheme for infrastructure development in the border areas. India has been involved in developing other road projects, such as the 80 km road connecting Tedim in Chin state to Rihkhawdar (Rih) in Myanmar-India border with the intention to spur development in remote border regions of Myanmar and facilitate border trade and commerce between the two countries. Two cross-border railway lines to connect the two countries are been considered. Surveys have been conducted between Imphal, the capital city of Manipur, and Moreh on the India–Myanmar border with the aim of ultimately extending the line to the towns of Tamu and Kalay in Myanmar. Another route, recently proposed, is from Tripura via Mizoram to Myanmar. The first optical fiber link between Imphal and Mandalay city in central Myanmar was operationalized in 2009. This Indian-funded project was executed by India's public sector Telecommunications Consultants India Limited (TCIL). In 2017 India began supplying cross-border electricity of 2–3 MW from Moreh to Tamu through a 11 kV transmission line. In September the same year, India also started exporting petroleum products to Myanmar using the land route at Moreh. The public sector Numaligarh Refinery Ltd in the Northeastern state of Assam started exporting of high-speed diesel (HSD) after it signed a sale-purchase agreement with a Myanmar company. There are plans to export 5,000 MT of HSD per month to Myanmar by road, and at a later stage to explore the possibility of laying a pipeline to export diesel to Myanmar.

The completion of the Rs. 13.60 billion Integrated Check Post (ICP) at Moreh and the recent agreement on land border crossing between India and Myanmar for international entry and exit is likely to boost movement of people and goods across the border. There are plans to now open a second ICP at Kawripuichhuah in Mizoram. The Moreh land border crossing point may help expedite the much-anticipated bus service between Imphal and Mandalay, a project that has been in the pipeline since 2003. One of the issues for the delay in operationalizing the service has been the lack of proper border immigration facilities.

According to official figures, India's current commitment for connectivity projects in Myanmar stands at US$ 844 million (Embassy of India 2017). India has also been tapping loans from multilateral institutions and key partners for financing various cross-border connectivity projects including from the World Bank, the Asian Development Bank and Japan. India has its own share of problems in connecting itself with Myanmar. Poor infrastructure in India's eastern seaboard, the Northeast region and the Andaman and Nicobar Islands has contributed to delay in the development of cross-border infrastructure with Myanmar. Lack of financial support and bureaucratic delays, further delay completion of projects. The India-funded Kalewa-Yargi sector took two years from the date of inviting tenders to actual work on the ground. With no serious complexities seemingly present in terms of land acquisition and availability of labour or construction materials, the lengthy processes of decision making involving different ministries delays the process. External factors, such as political instability and delays in decision making on the part of Myanmar, have also affected effective implementation of projects. For instance, Myanmar is yet give its final approval for the Rih-Tedim road project.

Apart from these challenges, there are a few inexplicable questions about actions taken – and indeed not taken – by New Delhi. A case in point is India's lack of interest in Myanmar's Dawei deep sea port project. The Dawei port could emerge as the hub for the Mekong-India Economic Corridor, a project that finds mention only in official joint statements, much like the Delhi-Hanoi Railway Link project. Also, it seems that in Delhi's official circles, the issue of re-opening the historic Stilwell Road (that connects Assam with northern Myanmar through Arunachal Pradesh) continues to remain trapped in the past with little movement beyond the same old security argument. Even so, Myanmar's opening up has boosted the prospects of creating cross-border connectivity and India has benefited as it provided enormous opportunities for India to connect with the country and through Myanmar to the wider region. The growing connectivity interests through Myanmar have also generated concerns within the country, as discussed above. Myanmar's growing wariness toward China's investments in infrastructure development is an opportunity for India to leverage with its approach to developing sustainable infrastructure projects as an alternative option.

Security: old and new issues

For decades, the Myanmar government's main security challenge has been internal driven, owing to the existence of several ethnic armed groups fighting the central government for greater autonomy. Myanmar's security threat perceptions have been rapidly evolving in the past three decades. From an internally oriented security posture that focused largely on counterinsurgency, it transformed to an externally driven maritime security posture, both real and perceived (Yhome March 2018). Even so, renewed conflicts in the borderlands remain a major challenge for Myanmar as new dimensions of ethnic armed groups re-emerged in the form of remobilization of ethnic armed groups pose serious security challenges not only to Myanmar but to the wider region. A new security threat that has been added to the increased security challenges is the emergence of the Rohingya insurgent group, ARSA, with reports of global terror groups based in Saudi Arabia and Pakistan (Singh 2016). The October 2017 attacks on border police posts along Myanmar-Bangladesh border by the Rohingya insurgent have heightened the security challenge emanating across the border using the maritime route.

The sources of border security challenges in the reform period continue to come from ethnic armed groups who still are outside the peace process and many of the related border security problems including narcotics production and smuggling in the borderlands continue unabated. Drugs production and smuggling have long been associated several ethnic armed groups of Myanmar. In recent years, according to the UN Office on Drugs and Crimes (UNODC), Myanmar appears to have successfully reduced poppy cultivation by 25 percent between 2015 and

2017 (UNODC 2017). However, the production of synthetic drugs, such as meth-amphetamine, has increased (*Frontier Myanmar* 21 May 2018). As noted earlier, renewed conflicts broke out between the Tatmadaw and the KIA in Kachin state the year the peace initiative was launched in 2011.

Since then, rebel groups in northern Myanmar has been engaged in military conflicts with the government troops which further intensified in 2015 when the Kokang (an ethnic Chinese) rebel group, MNDAA attacked the Myanmar mili-tary in northern Shan State. Conflicts further escalated in 2016 when four armed groups – the MNDAA, the TNLA, the AA and the KIA – formed the Northern Alliance-Burma (NAB) organized several coordinated attacks on the Myanmar army causing heavy casualties on both sides and forced several thousand civilians flee to China to take refuge, while another hundred thousand internally displaced in bordering Shan Stata (*Aljazeera* 20 December 2016). According to an observer, the reasons behind the renewed conflicts relates 'to direct military operations, pro-tection or interdiction of economic interests, protection of civilians, or retribution attacks' and, in addition to this, it may also have been triggered by 'military pres-sure to force the EAOs to sign the ceasefire accord' (Mathieson, September 2017). Although the Myanmar military has long fought insurgency, analysts see the for-mation of the NAB as 'Myanmar's first effective battlefield coalition of insurgents' and this may have long-term implications on the Myanmar military's counterin-surgency strategy as it 'threatens to up-end the strategy of divide and rule' (Davis 6 April 2017).

India's role and interests

India's security interests in Myanmar are primarily concerned with maintaining security and stability along the long-shared land and maritime boundaries in the Bay of Bengal. Ensuring that Myanmar's territory is not used by insurgents and criminals against India and to create a stable environment for socioeconomic development in the shared borderlands. These factors drive India's security and defense cooperation with Myanmar and a sector that has witnessed a growing trajectory in the reforms period. One of the high points of the border security cooperation between India and Myanmar during the reform period was the 'Spe-cial Operation' undertaken by the India army along India–Myanmar borderlands in June 2015 against camps of Indian militants. The operation generated some diplomatic goof-up when high-level officials in the government claimed that the attack was inside Myanmar's territory, it was later clarified by the Indian govern-ment that the Indian army did not enter Myanmar's territory and the opera-tion was carried out after the Myanmar authorities were taken into confidence (*Mint* 28 September 2017). The Special Operation was in retaliation to an ambush by the Northeast insurgents on a convoy of Indian army that killed 15 soldiers and injured several others in Chandel District of Manipur. The United Libera-tion Front of Western Southeast Asia (UNLFW), a newly floated group claimed responsivity (TOI, 5 June 2015).

The UNLFW is a conglomerate of Khaplang faction of the National Socialist Council of Nagaland (NSCN) that abrogated the ceasefire with the Government of India and along with the United Liberation Front of Asom (Independent) which is also known as anti-talk ULFA, Songbijit faction of the National Democratic Front of Boroland (NDFB) and the Kamatapur Liberation Organization with its headquarters in Taga in Maynmar's Sagiang State. The Front was formed in June 2015 (*The First Post*, 5 June 2015), according to ULFA leader Paresh Baruah, "to bring all revolutionary groups of the region fighting against India on a common platform" (Bhattacharyya 2014, 213). Baruah also claimed that the Front enjoys support from other 'fourteen organizations' but the Front did 'not to bring groups from Nepal, Sri Lanka and other countries because our struggle is not against those governments,' Baruah claimed (Bhattacharyya 2014, 213). NSCN leader SS Khaplang was the founder chairman of the Front and continued till his death in June 2017. Khango Konak, who had taken over as chairman of the NSCN(K) after SS Khaplang was made the new chairman of the Front in October 2017.

The Front's activities have been on the rise in recent years with ambush on Indian army vehicles as its main target that included the ambush in Tinsukia district of Assam that killed three jawans and injured four others (The Hindu, 19 November 2016). Though formation of umbrella organizations among Northeastern insurgent groups is not new, the emergence of the Front is seen as the immediate security threat at a time when the process of peace talks with other ethnic armed groups have been institutionalized. According to media reports citing Indian security and intelligence agencies, the idea of establishing the Front was first mooted in Ruili in China's Yunnan Province bordering Myanmar in 2011 (TOI, 5 June 2015. There is a strong view in India that China's growing strategic interests in the wider region would keep Beijing to have 'direct and indirect dealings with Indian insurgents . . . as part of its overall policy toward India'(*The Wire*. 13 June 2015). An analyst points out that '[i]t is evident that Chinese security services, at the very least, turn a blind eye to the presence and gun-running activities of Indian rebels in Yunnan' as a 'certain degree of turmoil in India's northeast serves China's interests in the region' (Linter, 8 July 2018).

In another significant development with huge political and security implications was the NSCN-K 'impeachment' of its chairman Khango Konyak, who was them replaced by Yung Aung, who is a Burmese Naga and nephew of SS Khaplang in August 2018 (TNIE, 8 August 2018). Khango Konyak is a Naga from the Indian side, while Yung Aung is a Naga from Myanmar. While the reasons for the split is not immediately clear, there has been speculation in the Indian media about the possible role played by India and Myanmar in splitting the two groups along nationality line citing the examples of the ULFA split between 'pro-talks' faction and 'anti-talks' faction (TOI, 3 October 2018). The NSCN-K (Khango) faction alleges that Yung Aung entered into a 'treacherous deal' with the Myanmar military, (TOI, 3 October 2018), though details of such supposed deal is not available. Whatever be the reason for the spilt, with both countries pushing for settlement with their respective ethnic armed groups, these developments are generally viewed as paving the way to take the process forward as this allows both countries to deal with the two factions under their respective sovereign jurisdiction.

It is within this evolving cross-border security and stability context that India and Myanmar have scale-up their border security cooperation in the reform period. Border security has long posed a challenge along the over 1600 km shared borderlands as it is often used by ethnic armed groups to carry out militant activities. Along the porous border, cross-border ethnic linkages are a day-to-day affair by taking advantage of mechanism such as the 'Free Movement Regime' that allows ethnic communities living on either side of the border to travel 16 km into the other side without a visa. Military-to-military cooperation between India and Myanmar have been strengthened in recent years with the establishment of various mechanisms including regular exchange of high-level military officials, coordinated operations, capacity building, border management, border fencing, etc. In 2014, the two countries agreed to step up cooperation in border security and signed an MoU that provides:

> a framework for security cooperation and exchange of information between Indian and Myanmar security agencies. A key provision is that of conduct of coordinated patrols on their respective sides of the international border and the maritime boundary by the Armed Forces of the two countries. Both sides have agreed to exchange information in the fight against insurgency, arms smuggling and drug, human and wildlife trafficking.
>
> *(MEA, GoI. 10 May, 2014)*

The MoU also spelled out 'the level and frequency of meetings between the Armed Forces, Drug Control Agencies and Wildlife Crime Control agencies' (MEA, GoI. 10 May, 2014).

Conclusion

The preceding discussion demonstrates how the three issues –the ethnic question, connectivity and security play a key role in maintaining peace, stability and the prospects of prosperity in the India–Myanmar borderlands. It also explicates how internal developments in Myanmar pertaining to these issues have direct and indirect implications on India's ties with Myanmar and on their shared borderlands. Myanmar's opening up has provided opportunities for India to strengthen ties with the country that is visible in the steady progress in political, economic and security cooperation. Deepening cooperation would open up new avenues for cooperation between the two countries to strengthen ties, but Myanmar's continued internal conflicts present challenges as well. One the one hand, India's role in assisting Myanmar's domestic transformation strengthens ties with the country, while on the other hand, the same internal difficulties cast a shadow over the potentials of deepening ties between the two countries. That said, India's options are limited and the most practical approach is a sustained engagement with and assistance to

Myanmar as the transformation unfolding inside the country, particularly in the borderlands. This is not only for the interests of its neighbor but also for India's interests. A peaceful and prosperous Myanmar is in India's long-term interests.

References

"ADB Sees More Growth for Myanmar Economy, Pushes for Reforms." (2018). *The Irrawaddy*, April 11, www.irrawaddy.com/news/adb-sees-growth-myanmar-economy-pushes-reforms.html.

Azeem, Ibrahim (2017). *The Rohingyas: Inside Myanmar's Hidden Genocide*. New Delhi: Speaking Tiger.

"Beyond Panglong: Myanmar's National Peace and Reform Dilemma." (2017). The Transitional Institute (TNI), September 21.

Bhatia, Rajiv (2016). *India – Myanmar Relations – Changing Contours*. New York: Routledge, ISEAS.

Bhattacharyya, Rajeev (2014). *Rendezvous with Rebels: Journey to Meet India's Most Wanted Men*. New Delhi: HarperCollins.

Blaževiè, Igor (2016). "Burma Votes for Change: The Challenges Ahead." *Journal of Democracy* 27 (2) (April): 101–115.

Burma News International (BNI) (2014). "Deciphering Myanmar's Peace Process – A Reference Guide 2014." Burma News International, March.

———. (2017). "Deciphering Myanmar's Peace Process – A Reference Guide 2016." Burma News International, January.

"Chief Impeached, NSCN-K Divided in Nagaland on Lines of Nationality." (2018). *The New Indian Express* (TNIE), August 8, www.newindianexpress.com/nation/2018/aug/18/chief-impeached-nscn-k-divided-in-nagaland-on-lines-of-nationality-1859417.html.

"China Urges Northern Alliance to Attend Panglong Conference." (2018). *The Myanmar Times*, May 21, www.mmtimes.com/news/china-urges-northern-alliance-attend-panglong-conference.html.

Davis, Anthony (2017). "Myanmar's Army Struggles Against a Strong New Rebel Alliance." *Nikkei Asian Review*, April 6, https://asia.nikkei.com/Politics/Myanmar-s-army-struggles-against-a-strong-new-rebel-alliance.

"Debt Trap' Alert Rises in Myanmar as More Belt and Road Projects Scrapped." (2018). *The Irrawaddy*, September 17, www.irrawaddy.com/news/burma/analysis-debt-trap-alert-rises-myanmar-belt-road-projects-scrapped.html/amp.

Diamond, Larry (2012). "The Opening in Burma: The Need for a Political Pact." *Journal of Democracy* 23 (4) (October): 138–149.

Draft of the Nationwide Ceasefire Agreement (NCA) Between the Government of the Republic of the Union of Myanmar and the Ethnic Armed Organisations (2015). October 15, https://peacemaker.un.org/sites/peacemaker.un.org/files/MM_151510_NCAAgreement.pdf.

Elly, Win, Enkhtsetseg Ganbat and Kichan Nam (2015). "Port Governance Structure: The Port of Yangon." *KMI International Journal of Maritime Affairs and Fisheries* 7 (1) (June): 1–15.

Embassy of India (2017). "Development Cooperation Projects Undertaken by Government of India." August 3.

"Government Meets with Northern Alliance Groups for First Time." (2018). *The Myanmar Times*, September 6, www.mmtimes.com/news/government-meets-northern-alliance-groups-first-time.html.

"The Government's Roadmap for National Reconciliation and Union Peace." (2016). *The Global New Light of Myanmar*, October 16, www.globalnewlightofmyanmar.com/the-governments-roadmap-for-national-reconciliation-and-union-peace/.

"Gov't Signs MoU with Beijing to Build China-Myanmar Economic Corridor." (2018). *The Irrawaddy*, September 13, www.irrawaddy.com/news/burma/govt-signs-mou-beijing-build-china-myanmar-economic-corridor.html.

Grein, Christina (2018). "Time to Renew Outdated Strategies: Current State of the Peace Process in Myanmar." Blickwechsel, Burma-Initiative der Stiftung Asienhaus, February, www.asienhaus.de/uploads/tx_news/2018_FEB___Myanmar___GB_02.pdf.

"Here's a Guide to Newly-Formed Insurgent Group UNLFW That Killed 20 Jawans in Manipur." (2015). *The First Post*, June 5. www.firstpost.com/india/heres-a-guide-to-newly-formed-insurgent-group-unlfw-that-killed-20-jawans-in-manipur-2280744.html.

"India Begins to Play Official Role in Myanmar Peace Process: Zoramthanga." (2015). *The Indian Express*, March 9, https://indianexpress.com/article/world/neighbours/india-begins-to-play-official-role-in-myanmar-peace-process-zoramthanga/.

"India, Myanmar Pull Off NSCN(K) Spilt." (2018). *The Times of India (TOI)*, October 3, https://timesofindia.indiatimes.com/india/india-myanmar-successfully-engineer-nscnk-split/articleshow/66043121.cms.

Litner, Bertil (2017). "Peace Process Descends into Farce." *Asia Times*, April 5, www.atimes.com/article/myanmars-peace-process-descends-farce/.

———. (2018). "The Rebels Who Keep India and Myanmar Apart." *Asia Times*, July 8, www.atimes.com/article/the-rebels-who-keep-india-and-myanmar-apart/.

Mathieson, David Scott (2017). "Burma's Northern Shan State and Prospects for Peace." Peace Brief 234, United States Institute of Peace, September.

"Mekong Rethinks Drug Policy as Syndicates Pump Meth from Myanmar." (2018). *Frontier Myanmar*, May 21, https://frontiermyanmar.net/en/mekong-rethinks-drug-policy-as-syndicates-pump-meth-from-myanmar.

Ministry of External Affairs (MEA), Government of India (GoI), (2014). "India and Myanmar Sign Memorandum of Understanding on Border Cooperation." May 10, www.mea.gov.in/press-releases.htm?dtl/23315/India+and+Myanmar+sign+Memorandum+of+Understanding+on+Border+Cooperation.

———. (2017). "India-Myanmar Joint Statement Issued on the Occasion of the State Visit of Prime Minister of India to Myanmar (September 5–7, 2017)." September 6, www.mea.gov.in/bilateral-documents.htm?dtl/28924/IndiaMyanmar+Joint+Statement+issued+on+the+occasion+of+the+State+Visit+of+Prime+Minister+of+India+to+Myanmar+September+57 + 2017.

———. (2018a). "Visit of External Affairs Minister to Myanmar (May 10–11, 2018)." May 11, www.mea.gov.in/press-releases.htm?dtl/29889/Visit+of+External+Affairs+Minister+to+Myanmar+May+1011 + 2018.

———. (2018b). "Official Spokesperson's Response to a Query on India's Presence at the Signing of National Ceasefire Agreement in Myanmar." February 13, https://mea.gov.in/media-briefings.htm?dtl/29482/official+spokespersons+response+to+a+query+on+indias+presence+at+the+signing+of+national+ceasefire+agreement+in+myanmar.

Mint (2017). "Indian Army Strikes Naga Insurgents Along India-Myanmar Border." September 28, www.livemint.com/Politics/qMqvAspdOyOOz1Rw5EPo5K/Surgical-strike-against-Naga-insurgents-along-India-Myanmar.html.

———. (2018). "India Welcomes Militant Groups Joining Myanmar Peace Process." February 14, www.livemint.com/Politics/68Hh1jf4qIstWGLEa1D9FJ/India-welcomes-militant-groups-joining-Myanmar-peace-process.html.

Misri, Vikram (2018). "India's Cooperation Efforts in Myanmar." *Development Cooperation Review* 1 (4) (July): 38–39.

"Myanmar Rohingya Crisis: ICC Begins Inquiry into Atrocities." (2018). *The Guardian*, September 19, www.theguardian.com/world/2018/sep/19/myanmar-rohingya-crisis-icc-begins-investigation-into-atrocities.

"Myanmar's Peace Process Makes Major Step Towards Ending Civil Conflict." (2015). *Xinhua*, October 15, www.xinhuanet.com/english/2015-10/15/c_134717277.htm.

Myint-U, Thant (2011). *Where China Meets India: Burma and the New Crossroads of Asia*. New York: Farrar, Straus and Groux.

"Northern Alliance, Government Agree to Continue Talks After Panglong Conference." (2018). *The Myanmar Times*, July 16, www.mmtimes.com/news/northern-alliance-government-agree-continue-talks-after-panglong-conference.html.

"NSA Ajit Doval, Ravi Watch Signing of Truce Between Myanmar Insurgents." (2015). *The Indian Express*, October 15, https://indianexpress.com/article/india/india-others/nsa-ajit-doval-ravi-watch-signing-of-truce-between-myanmar-insurgents/.

Oo, Min Zaw (2014). "Understanding Myanmar's Peace Process: Ceasefire Agreements." *Catalysing Reflection*, Swiss Peace 2.

Oo Naing, Aung (2013). "Nationwide Ceasefire Agreement: Myanmar's Road to Peace." *The Myanmar Times*, October 31, www.mmtimes.com/national-news/8643-nationwide-ceasefire-agreement-myanmar-s-road-to-peace.html.

"Publicity Doesn't Help: Interview with Former Indian Ambassador to Myanmar." (2015). *The Wire*, June 13, https://thewire.in/diplomacy/in-conversation-with-preet-malik-former-ambassador-to-myanmar.

Radio Free Asia (2018). "China Envoy Links Signature Beijing Infrastructure Plan to Myanmar Peace Process." July 5, www.rfa.org/english/news/myanmar/china-envoy-links-signature-beijing-infrastructure-plan-to-myanmar-peace-process-07052018170211.html.

"Report of the Detailed Findings of the Independent International Fact-Finding Mission on Myanmar." (2018). A/HRC/39/CRP.2, UN Human Rights Council (UNHRC), September 18, www.ohchr.org/Documents/HRBodies/HRCouncil/FFM-Myanmar/A_HRC_39_CRP.2.pdf.

Reuters (2017). "India Pledges $25 Million for Myanmar's Rakhine to Help Refugees Return." December 21, www.reuters.com/article/uk-myanmar-rohingya-india/india-pledges-25-million-for-myanmars-rakhine-to-help-refugees-return-idUKKBN1E F1RB.

Seshadri, V. S. (2014). "Transforming Connectivity Corridors Between India and Myanmar into Development Corridors." Research and Information System for Developing Countries.

Singh, Jasminder (2016). "The Rohingya Crisis: Regional Security Implications." RSIS Commentary. No. 293, December 2, www.rsis.edu.sg/wp-content/uploads/2016/12/CO16293.pdf.

"Sittwe Economic Zone in Limbo as Foreign Investors Get Cold Feet." (2014). *The Myanmar Times*, June 30, www.mmtimes.com/business/10835-sittwe-economic-zone-in-limbo-as-international-investors-get-cold-feet.html.

Smith, Martin (ed.). (1999). *Burma: Insurgency and the Politics of Ethnicity*. New York: Zed Books.

"Three Jawans Killed, Four Injured in Ambush in Assam." (2016). *The Hindu*, November 19, www.thehindubusinessline.com/news/national/three-jawans-killed-four-injured-in-ambush-in-assam/article9365070.ece.

"Thousands May Have Fled to China' Due to Fighting." (2016). *Aljazeera*, December 20, www.aljazeera.com/news/2016/12/fled-china-due-fighting-16122007520 4586.html.

"UNLFW: The New Name for Terror in NE." (2015). *The Times of India (TOI)*, June 5, https://timesofindia.indiatimes.com/india/UNLFW-The-new-name-for-terror-in-NE/articleshow/47547899.cms.

UN Office on Drugs and Crime (UNODC) (2017). *Myanmar Opium Survey*, December, www.unodc.org/documents/southeastasiaandpacific/Publications/2017/Myanmar_Opium_Survey_2017_web.pdf.

Yhome, K. (2011). "Myanmar's Changing Political Landscape: Key Players and Recent Trends." *ORF Strategic Trends* 1 (1) (September).

———. (2015). "The Burma Roads: India's Search for Connectivity Through Myanmar." *Asian Survey* 55 (6): 1217–1240.

———. (2017). "The Road to Mekong: The India-Myanmar-Thailand Trilateral Highway Project." *ORF Issue Brief* 171 (February).

———. (2018a). "Examining India's Stance on the Rohingya Crisis." *ORF Issue Brief* 247 (July 11).

———. (2018b). "The BRI and Myanmar's China Debate." *The China Chronicles*, July 11, www.orfonline.org/expert-speak/bri-myanmar-china-debate/.

———. (2018c). "Why UN's Report and Sanctions Are Unlikely to Change Myanmar." *Moneycontrol*, August 29, www.moneycontrol.com/news/world/opinion-why-uns-report-and-sanctions-are-unlikely-to-change-myanmar-2892011.html.

———. (2018d). "Can India Edify Myanmar to Keep the Peace?" *East Asia Forum*, January 4, www.eastasiaforum.org/2018/01/04/can-india-edify-myanmar-to-keep-the-peace/.

———. (2018e). "Myanmar's Response to Shifting Economic and Security Dynamics." *Seminar Magazine* 703 (March): 34–38.

INDEX